Caste, Knowledge, and Power

Caste, Knowledge, and Power explores the emergence of knowledge as a measure of the human in the colonial and casteist contexts in twentieth-century Malabar, India. It undertakes a comparative study of two caste communities in Malabar—Asharis (carpenter caste) and Nampoothiris (Brahmins)—for their varied interactions with and intervention in the emerging colonial forms of knowledge production. The author argues that caste location determined not only the presence or absence in the system of knowledge production, but also the cognitive process of knowing and hence the very idea of what is considered as knowledge. In other words, the marginalization of oppressed castes in the modern institutions of knowledge production, which has already been discussed widely in the scholarship, is not the primary focus here. Rather, the author focuses more on how the modern colonial–brahminical concept of knowledge invalidated many other forms of knowing practices and how historically caste domination transformed from the claims of superiority in *acharam* (ritual practices) to the claims of superiority in possession of knowledge.

K. N. Sunandan is Assistant Professor in the School of Arts and Sciences at Azim Premji University (APU), Bengaluru. Prior to joining APU, he was a postdoctoral fellow at the Centre for the Study of Developing Societies, New Delhi, as part of the Transnational Research Group project funded by the Max Weber Foundation, Germany. He has also taught at Tata Institute of Social Sciences, Tuljapur, Maharashtra. Besides his academic pursuits, he writes in Malayalam and has authored several articles and short stories.

Caste, Knowledge, and Power

Ways of Knowing in Twentieth-Century Malabar

K. N. Sunandan

CAMBRIDGE
UNIVERSITY PRESS

CAMBRIDGE
UNIVERSITY PRESS

University Printing House, Cambridge CB2 8BS, United Kingdom

One Liberty Plaza, 20th Floor, New York, NY 10006, USA

477 Williamstown Road, Port Melbourne, vic 3207, Australia

314 to 321, 3rd Floor, Plot No.3, Splendor Forum, Jasola District Centre, New Delhi 110025, India

103 Penang Road, #05–06/07, Visioncrest Commercial, Singapore 238467

Cambridge University Press is part of the University of Cambridge.

It furthers the University's mission by disseminating knowledge in the pursuit of education, learning and research at the highest international levels of excellence.

www.cambridge.org

Information on this title: www.cambridge.org/9781009273121

First published 2022

Printed in India by Thomson Press India Ltd.

A catalogue record for this publication is available from the British Library

ISBN 978-1-009-27312-1 Hardback

Contents

Acknowledgements

Finally, I have arrived at this station. It was a long journey that started many years ago. Or, perhaps, I was just wandering around without any particular destination in mind and accidentally reached here. There were numerous co-travellers with whom I shared the scenery: thoughts, feelings, drinks, dreams, and disappointments; then there were many onlookers who were wondering where I was going and still waved their hands to cheer me up. Some others sponsored food and shelter in different places and rejuvenated me, sometimes as part of their job and sometimes because of mere kindness and camaraderie. And there are those who were just there with me all the time, not always in the physical form, encouraging, criticizing, and sometimes silently appreciating. At the outset, thank you all.

Most of the ideas about Ashari practices in this book belong to the Ashari community, and I am grateful to each and every one of them who taught me, helped me unlearn and shift my paradigms of thinking, and allowed me to interpret their thoughts. My special thanks to K. Gopalan, Katampazhipuram; Shanmukhan Ashari, Mundoor; Manikantan Ashari, Kozhikode; and Kunjan Ashari, Keralasseri. I am sad that I cannot name numerous others (in Palakkad, Malappuram, Kozhikode, and Kannur districts) for reasons of privacy, but conversations with them were always moments of revelations, fun, and wisdom. This work would not be possible without them generously sharing the moments of knowing and directing me towards unknown geographies.

Formally, this journey began in 2003, at Jawaharlal Nehru University (JNU), New Delhi, with my research for MPhil degree. It is in JNU that I got the opportunity to meet wonderful comrades and brilliant thinkers who opened the doors for me to an all-new world of politics and knowledge. Thank you, Ponni Arasu, Mario Da Penha, Partha Pratim Shil, Shipra Nigam, and Udayakumar Manoharan. I was fortunate to have had Rohan Dsouza as my MPhil supervisor and Professor Nazir Tyabji as my teacher at the Centre for Studies in Science Policy in JNU, both of whom made my transition to history smoother. In Delhi, Nivedita Menon, Mary John, Charu Gupta, Dilip Menon, and M. S. S. Pandian encouraged and motivated me in their own different ways with their intellectual practices, activism, and friendship. I arrived in Atlanta, USA, in 2006 for my PhD at Emory University and was soon surrounded by the warmth of friendship and collegiality. Ajit Chittambalam, Anna Kurian, Moyukh Chatterjee, Durba Mitra, Aditya Pratap Deo, Debjani Bhattacharya, Shailaja Paik, Navyug Gill, Guirdex, and many others made my days in Atlanta intellectually stimulating and personally enchanting. I benefited most from the visits of Sanal Mohan and Premesh Lalu at Emory, and from my conversations with Nishaant Choksy at New York, New Delhi, and Ahmedabad. My sincere thanks to them for their intellectual interventions and friendship.

Dr Clifton Crais, my PhD supervisor, took the extra effort to guide me through the process of writing and made sure that I finished my thesis in time. He was strict and demanding in his thesis-supervising role, and warm, kind, and encouraging at a personal level. Thank you, Clifton, for your patient suggestions and thoughtful criticisms and for being with me in those difficult times. I extend my gratitude to my PhD committee members, Dr Pamela Scully and Dr Jeffrey Lesser, for their effort in improving my arguments. At Emory, I have benefited from interactions with several faculty members. I am grateful to Professors Bruce Knoft, Laurie Patton, Velcheru Narayana Rao, Gyanendra Pandey, Mark Ravina, and Tonio Andrade.

The journey from the PhD thesis to this book was slow and difficult for my own misconceptions, doubts, and inertia. However, I was lucky enough to have people around me who encouraged me to write and provided sufficient time to ruminate on themes and concepts. I am grateful to the German Historical Institute London (GHIL) for the postdoctoral fellowship at the Transnational Research Group, which gave me the opportunity to meet warm and intelligent colleagues, conversations with whom sharpened my thoughts and writing. Thank you, Andreas Gestrich and Indra Sengupta at GHIL for building such a vibrant community of scholars. It was a wonderful experience to be part of the research project led by Sarada Balagopalan, Janaki Nair, Neeladri Bhattacharya, and Geetha Nambissan, and to work along with Arun Kumar, Kaustubh Sengupta, Debarati Bagchi, Preeti, Sumeet Mhaskar, and Divya Kannan.

Archivists, librarians, and staff at different archives and libraries were critically involved in my research. My sincere thanks to all the staff at the Kerala State Archives at Kozhikode and Thiruvananthapuram, the Kerala Sahithya Academy Library and the Appan Thampuran Library at Thrissur, the Ulloor Smaraka Library and the Centre for Development Studies library at Thiruvananthapuram, the Deshaposhini Library at Kozhikode, the Nehru Memorial Museum and Library and the National Archives of India at New Delhi, the Centre for the

Study of Developing Societies library at New Delhi, the India Office of Records at the British Library, London, and the Tamil Nadu State Archives and Roja Muthayya Memorial Library at Chennai.

I conducted further research, revised my chapters, and wrote new ones at Azim Premji University (APU), Bangalore. I am grateful to the Research Centre at Azim Premji University for research support and grants. The intellectually invigorating, peaceful, and accommodative atmosphere (a rare condition in the academy under the current political scenario) at the School of Arts and Science (SAS, formerly School of Liberal Studies) provided the important space to finish my writing. I am grateful to Venu Narayan, the former director of SAS, for creating such a space, and Arjun Jaydev, the current director, and S. V. Srinivas, who leads the Humanities group, for continuing the support. It is hard to express in words my gratitude to my wonderful colleagues and friends for their unconditional support. I am indebted to Alex Thomas, Amit Basole, Amit Kumar, Asim Siddique, Karuna Dietrich, Kripa Gowrishanker, Sharmadip Basu, Subir Dey, Tarangini Sriraman, Usha Rajaram, Uthara Suvrathan, and Varuni Bhatia. My students at APU have been a great source of inspiration, and I continue learning from them.

Abhigna Arigala did the difficult job of editing and proofreading the whole manuscript in the most efficient and timely manner, and my sincere thanks to her for the work and her invaluable friendship. I am grateful to Sohini Ghosh at Cambridge University Press who patiently coordinated all the processes of publishing, from the very beginning to its end smoothly, and I extend my thanks to all the staff members at the Press, especially Priyanka Das in the production editorial team.

Ajit accompanied me all through the journey since our Emory days as we laughed together at the attempts of theorizing an apocalyptic world and shared the grief of personal losses and miseries. With Anna, I share the frustration of being in an unjust world and the hope of doing something about it. With Moyukh, I share the cynicism about this world and create many alternative worlds. From Raghu, one of the kindest and most humane individuals I have ever met, I learned how to be constantly disappointed about the world and remain deeply passionate about fellow human beings. With Toy, with his erudition and lucid encyclopaedic grasp of theory, I continue to experiment crazy ideas and ideologies and enjoy the spirited moments of friendship. I cherish the conversations, arguments, and debates with Tarangini, and I have learned much from her. Varuni always provided very unique perspectives and continues to share a warm collegiality and friendship. Alex with his calm, quiet but sharp questions and criticism warned me about complacencies and compromises. Asim as a friend and colleague shares many of my concerns and I enjoy working with him in many activities in and outside the University. In a friendship that spans over the last two decades and across continents, Ravindran Sreeramachandran enthusiastically engaged with my stories, shared his own, and inspired me to write this book. In Chennai, Mangai and Arasu hosted me at their home during my archival work, and I cherish the conversations we had at that time. I have had supportive friends in Ajith Antony, Deepa Chandran, Sajitha Madathil, and Sajitha Rajan. Friends in Thrissur—Sasi and Sunita—and in Sreekrishnapuram—Manikantan and Suresh—have always filled me with stories and warmth during my trips home, field visits, and archival journeys. Dileep Raj and friends at Samoohya Padhashala and Madhyamam Weekly generously provided me space for conversations with a larger community of scholars and activists in Kerala.

Suresh and Bindu K. C.—friends, colleagues, and my social family—have always been a delightful presence in our lives for the last three decades. J. Devika has always been a good friend who inspires me with her brilliance, scholarship, and passionate public engagement. P. Sanal Mohan's commitment to scholarship and his warm friendship is always a source of inspiration. Life in Suburban Bangalore—Sarjapur—would have been much different, dull, and difficult without the community of kind friends in Karen, Asim, Meghana, Sandeep, Vasvi, and Arvind. Thank you all for badminton, fitness classes, food, drinks, and mirth.

I am fortunate to have received great support and unconditional love from my family throughout these years, even when they were worried about my unpredictable departures and journeys. Thank you, Achan, Ushoppol, Beena, Varun, Deepak, Devna, Usha Mema, Kuttan, Vinitha, Appu, Subha, Diya, Megha, Adityan, and Richu. Over the last many decades, my cousin Hari has been a continuing presence of great friendship and solidarity. My uncle P. M. Aryan and aunt Prasanna Aryan believed in my quest and offered support in more ways than one at crucial times. Sudevan's (my brother and friend) untimely departure has left a deep hole in my heart that may never heal completely. His absence continues to be felt. It is my loss and sorrow that the people who would have been the happiest to see this book—my *amma*, Shantakumari, and my loving in-laws, Indira Devi and Aravindakshan—are no longer in this world.

In our journey together, Bindu and I have shared the great pleasures and pains of life. As my partner and my closest friend, she is the first and the most generous reader of everything I do and offers the most valuable critique. It is her immense love and inexhaustible care that enabled me to survive the most difficult of times. Her indomitable spirit and passion for life is what enlivens me and provides me with the energy to live and act in meaningful ways. This work is hers as much as it is mine.

Notes on Transliteration

The Malayalam words transliterated in the book are spelled to match both the Malayalam pronunciation and the way they are usually spelled in the Malayalam-speaking region. The words transliterated differently are given as follows along with the diacritic equivalents.

acharam	ācāram	kutiyan	kuṭiyān
adharam	ādhāram	mannan	maṇṇān
aynkammalar	aynkammālar	marumakkathayam	marumakkatāyam
ampalavasi	ampalavāsi	matam	maṭham
anacharam	anācāram	moothashari	mūtāṣāri
antharjanam	antarjanam	muzhakkol	muḻakkōl
arivu	aṟivu	nampoothiri	nampūtiri
ashari	āṣāri	nedikkal	nēdikkal
asharippani	āṣārippaṇi	pani	paṇi
avarna	avarṇa	parayar	paṟayar
ayurveda	āyurvēda	parishkaram	pariṣkāram
bhrashtu	bhraṣṭ	pazhaya	paḻaya
charatu	caraṭ	pooja	pūja
desham	dēsam	samajam	sāmājam
ezhava	īḻava	samudayam	samudāyam
gramam	grāmam	sathanam	sādhanam
illam	illam	savarna	savarṇa
janmi	janmi	sayip	sāyip
kalam	kālam	shasthram	śāstram
karanavar	kāraṇavar	shraddha	śraddha
karivan	karivān	smarthavicharam	smārtavicāram
karmabhoomi	karmabhūmi	sthree	strī
karyasthan	kāryastan	thampuran	tampurān

thattan	taṭṭān	veeram	vīram
thiru	tiru	veethuli	vītuḷi
othikkan	ōtikkan	vidyalayam	vidyālayam
vadhyar	vādhyār	vishwakarma	viśwakarma
varna	varṇa		

The general rule followed for the diacritics is as follows.

അ	ആ	ഇ	ഈ	ഉ	ഊ	ഋ	എ	ഏ	ഐ	ഒ	ഓ	ഔ
a	ā	i	ī	u	ū	r̥	e	ē	ai	o	ō	au

അം	അഃ
am	ah

ക	ഖ	ഗ	ഘ	ങ	ച	ഛ	ജ	ഝ	ഞ
ka	kha	ga	gha	ña	ca	cha	ja	jha	ña

സ	ഠ	ഡ	ഢ	ണ	ത	ഥ	ദ	ധ	ന
ṭa	ṭha	ḍa	ḍha	ṇa	ta	tha	da	dha	na

പ	ഫ	ബ	ഭ	മ	യ	ര	ല	വ	ശ	ഷ	സ	ഹ
pa	pha	ba	bha	ma	ya	ra	la	va	śa	ṣa	sa	ha

ള	ഴ	റ	ജ്ഞ	റ്റ	ൻ	ൺ	ൽ	ൾ	ർ
ḷa	ḻa	ṟa	jña	ṭṭa	n	ṇ	l	ḷ	r

കു	ചു	ടു	തു	പു	യു	രു	ലു	വു	ശു	ഷു	സു	ഹു
ku	cu	ṭu	tu	pu	yu	ru	lu	vu	śu	ṣu	su	hu

ളു	ഴു
ḷu	ḻu

Introduction
Caste, Knowledge, and Power

I am not your data, nor am I your vote bank,
I am not your project, or any exotic museum object,
I am not the soul waiting to be harvested,
Nor am I the lab where your theories are tested,
I am not your cannon fodder, or the invisible worker,
or your entertainment at India [H]abitat [C]entre,
I am not your field, your crowd, your history,
your help, your guilt, medallions of your victory,
I refuse, reject, resist your labels,
your judgments, documents, definitions,
your models, leaders and patrons,
because they deny me my existence, my vision, my space,
your words, maps, figures, indicators,
they all create illusions and put you on pedestal,
from where you look down upon me,
So I draw my own picture, and invent my own grammar,
I make my own tools to fight my own battle,
For me, my people, my world, and my Adivasi self!

—Abhay Xaxa[1]

The poem by Abhay Xaxa is the inspiration and provocation for this book, and the book is an exploration of the historical contexts in which the oppressive system of domination through knowledge, as explained in the poem, emerged. In the long history of human societies, the entanglement of power–knowledge[2] is rather a recent one. Emperors, kings, popes, witches, priests, landlords, shamans, poets, and even philosophers wielded power through other means: religion, ritual, military, art, rhetoric, or magic. Although knowledge sometimes helped sustain, grab, or increase power, it was not a necessary ingredient for the deployment of power. Only in the era of European imperialisms and colonialisms, knowledge became a measure of civilization and then an integral part of the exercise of power. Thereafter, knowledge experts built their own temples of power, from where power flowed out through various channels of knowledge. Universities, research institutes, and schools, aligning with the State, participated in ordering, categorizing, and controlling the population. Although this process emerged in the eighteenth and nineteenth centuries, historians, retrospectively, concluded that the connection between power and knowledge is eternal and integral to all human societies. It is reasonable to assume that the concepts of knowledge and power existed in most societies, but what they meant in different times and how they were used by different sections of a society within a period are not very clear. The major concern that underlies this book is the emergence of different notions of knowledge and power–knowledge in British colonial India and the varied engagement of different *jati*s with this entanglement.

Exploring the stories of Asharis (the carpenter jati in Malabar) and Nampoothiris (the Brahmin jati in the Malayalam-speaking region), I make two larger claims: the first being that while the caste system was always oppressive, exploitative, and hierarchical, caste hierarchy and oppression are sustained by different claims of superiority at different points of time and space; there is no single logic—such as purity and pollution, hierarchy and difference, possession of knowledge, and so on—that determines the caste discrimination and exploitation for all times and all spaces. There is no doubt that from the beginning of the caste system, different Brahmin jatis were dominant and oppressive groups; however, until the colonial period, neither did they have monopoly in knowledge production nor did they claim as such. If knowledge was not a measure of superiority, how did Brahmins justify their claims of domination? In the following chapters, we examine the nature of Nampoothiri claims of domination in comparison with the Ashari practice of knowing.

In nineteenth-century Malabar, Nampoothiris claimed that they were superior because they were the practitioners and protectors of *acharam* (customary ritual practice). After the emergence and spread of colonial institutions of knowledge production in this region, knowledge became the central organizing principle in the Nampoothiri claims of caste superiority. This shift in the claims of superiority towards knowledge changed the modalities and nature of caste oppression. Similarly, from the beginning of the twentieth century up to the 1970s, Asharis understood their jati by defining it based on *asharippani* (carpentry). It implies that asharippani as a practice of knowing was central to their jati identity. An important distinction is that while Nampoothiris considered acharam as the central organizing category of *every* jati, Asharis considered asharippani as the main organizing category of *only* their jati; in other words, the Nampoothiri claims were those of superiority and the Ashari claims were those of self-identity and difference. Further, by the last quarter of the twentieth century, Asharis entered the world of knowledge production through a different route than did Nampoothiris. This book juxtaposes the journey and the entry of Asharis and Nampoothiris into the order of knowledge from two different starting points in the early decades of the twentieth century and maps the corresponding changes in their understanding of their respective jatis.

The second claim that the book makes is that since the period of colonial domination in the Indian subcontinent, the dominant form of knowledge production has been not just colonial, as categorized by many scholars, but also colonial–brahmanical. Here, the category 'brahmanical' refers not just to the practices of Brahmins as a jati, but also to the brahmanical jati system in India, in the nineteenth and twentieth centuries. This means that the attribute 'modern' (which also is a claim rather than an actual condition) for certain forms of knowledge needs to be understood as incorporating the power relation of both the colonial and the brahmanical dominations in the region. I suggest that the ideas of objectivity, the depiction of theoretical knowledge as the ultimate form of knowledge, the exclusion of artisanal practices from the domain of knowledge production, and so on, which are generally considered as features of 'Western' knowledge, drew equally from the colonial and the brahmanical practices of power. Hence, as many scholars have pointed out, we cannot understand the modern forms of knowledge production in the Indian subcontinent without understanding the jati practices and vice-versa. Like power–knowledge, the caste–power–knowledge entanglement originated in the colonial period and became the central feature of the emerging institutions of production of knowledge and the new forms of caste oppressions. The following chapters engage, on the one hand, with the transformation of the respective practices of knowledge of various jatis in relation to the emerging institutions of knowledge production and, on the other hand, with the transformation of the self-definitions of various jatis through everyday life practices.

In the rest of the introduction, I explore two debates that are relevant to the questions asked in this book. The first one is regarding the nature of modern forms of knowledge and knowledge production, which have been categorized variously as universal, objective knowledge, modern knowledge, colonial knowledge, Western knowledge, and so on. The second debate that I engage with is regarding the relation between caste and knowledge production. This subject has been debated from varied perspectives, such as the critique of Western knowledge from an indigenous perspective, or the critique of traditional brahmanical knowledge from the perspective of modern scientific knowledge or from a subaltern perspective. In engaging with these debates, I have selected certain works that serve the purpose of introducing the debate and have mentioned some others in the note(s). These cited texts are not necessarily representatives of the various sides in the extensive body of research, and there is no attempt to refer to all the supposedly foundational or key texts. Also, the points of the discussion are not a summary of the debates but act as signposts that signal to the questions discussed in the other chapters.

Historians of science have pointed out that, from the sixteenth century onwards, the 'discoveries of new worlds' produced a need for new understandings of the world and a need for a cosmology that could incorporate the newly discovered spaces, beings, and things.[3] Missionaries, colonial officers, merchants, and travellers collected, explored, mapped, and invaded the new world, which later resulted in the emergence of various disciplines of modern knowledge. The radical developments in natural philosophy, astronomy, geography and map making, geology, navigational sciences, medicinal practices, history, and anthropology were a direct result and part of the colonization project.[4] In general, these historians have tried to develop a continuous narrative of colonialism along with the development of modern sciences from the sixteenth century to the twentieth century. Claude Alvares argued that the fundamental philosophy of modern science, which he considers to have emerged in the fifteenth century in Europe, remains the same throughout its history, from Galileo's theory of motions to the theory of space shuttles. According to him, the scientific worldview that emerged in Europe became a global perspective through colonialism and imperialism.[5] Alvares and several other critics of science viewed science as a Western colonial project, which expanded from the centre to the peripheries through European colonial invasions.[6]

Recently, scholars have criticized the aforementioned perspective by underscoring the contribution of colonized people in the production of modern knowledge. Analysing the development of botanical and cartographic knowledges in the eighteenth and nineteenth centuries, Kapil Raj demonstrated that science developed through intellectual interaction and encounters in which both the West and the non-West contributed significantly.[7] While Raj relocated the development of modern science from its Western location to a global space of circulation and encounters, he did not focus on the transformation of the idea of science itself in this circulation. For example, the history and the transformation of the concept of 'objectivity' or 'practical knowledge' is not part of this exploration. In other words, Raj did not historicize the very idea of knowledge.

For the seventeenth- and eighteenth-century colonialists, the difference between the Europeans and the colonized, or between 'us' and 'them', was irreducible and natural. The dichotomous difference was applicable not only to human culture but also to nature itself. The colonialists at this period considered the weather, the flora and fauna, and the diseases of the colonies as directly opposite to that of Europe. This led to a whole set of inventions of ideas of tropical weather, tropical forests, and tropical diseases.[8] The knowledge produced from these explanations constituted a separate register, different from the one in which they marked European weather or diseases. Until the second half of the nineteenth century, objectivity was not a central characteristic of colonial knowledge. The eighteenth-century investigators considered the belief pattern of the scholar and his proximity to the object of inquiry as important factors in producing facts and truthful knowledge about the material world.[9] By the middle of the nineteenth century, the process of colonial production of knowledge transformed significantly in its formative elements, methods, and self-description. Instead of dichotomies, *series* became the form in which objects were arranged and categorized, which created graded hierarchies rather than dichotomous oppositions. Objectivity became a measure in the production of knowledge and subjectivity was no more considered as a preferable element in this process.[10] Once the subjective elements were removed from the concept of knowledge, it could be produced 'from a distance'. All 'proximate' senses were excluded from the process, and visuality as a 'distant sense' was considered the most authentic sensation.[11] Knowledge became an exchangeable object and writing became the ultimate form of knowledge.[12] Among these features of production of knowledge, the most important one in the colonial encounter was the concept of series, which replaced the concept of an irreducible dichotomy.

Note that, the project of governing the population in colonies was not possible by a clear demarcation between 'us' and 'them'. While this difference was still important, for all practical purposes of governing, it was necessary to create a series of objects that would connect the colonizer to the colonized. The colonial investigators defined, described, and ordered objects in different hierarchical series, the two endpoints of which were the earlier binaries, or dichotomies. For example, the human became a hierarchical series, with the European white man on the top and the aboriginal tribal woman at the bottom.[13] Knowledge itself became a series, with knowledge and ignorance serving at the top and bottom ends, respectively, within which different kinds of knowledges were arranged according to their universality and objectivity. Not only was the construction of a series as part of creating an order of knowledge a discursive activity but the material practices of governing also followed the same process of creating hierarchical series. A new array of institutions, actions, and people was formed by creating a time–space between the 'government' and the 'people' and simultaneously connecting them through various middle objects. Educational institutions, public exhibitions, and museums were some of the important sites that were part of this process.[14]

The British orientalist scholarship, which was an integral part of colonial governing practices, incorporated the existing caste hierarchy in India into the hierarchical series of knowledge. On the one hand, colonialists launched strong criticisms of caste practices, describing it as the tyranny of Brahmins, Eastern despotism, and an archaic uncivilized tradition. On the other hand, as more and more European scholars started studying the so-called Hindu texts, they found a new ally in their project of producing knowledge about the colony.[15] This partnership—though it was never an equal partnership, as modern knowledge was considered superior to traditional knowledge—constructed a relation between traditional knowledge in India and the Brahmin caste. This is because the colonizers considered writing as one of the most important measures of knowledge, and they arranged bodily practices of knowing at the lower level of the knowledge series. Therefore, in India, in the process of creating the middle objects of the series, colonialists regarded Brahmins as the authority on traditional knowledge, as they were assumed to be the authors of written or orally transferred Sanskrit texts. And hence, the colonial concept of knowledge as text was crucial in inventing the traditional wisdom of the East.

Within the colonialist imagination, caste was the essential stratification criterion of Indian society, and hence, colonial activities in the domain of knowledge were reflected through the prism of caste. There was much confusion regarding the nature of the educational institutions that would be appropriate for the dominant-caste native elites. It was not clear until the 1850s whether this education should be that of European knowledges or 'traditional Indian knowledges' and whether the medium of education should be in English or vernacular. Whichever was the case, according to the colonialists, the caste-elites, especially the Brahmins, were the group who could attain higher learning in literature, natural philosophy, and mathematics.[16] In all the three universities that were established in India in the middle of the nineteenth century, there was no restriction, technically, for individuals from any caste group to join the institution. But the dominant castes overshadowed these institutions and continue to do so even in the twenty-first century.[17] Colonial education policy, especially in the late nineteenth and the early twentieth centuries, mapped the hierarchical caste system into a series of hierarchical educational institutions. The new universities were the place of dominant castes, whereas the industrial training centres were the proper place of artisanal castes.[18] In short, what we see as colonial knowledge by the end of the nineteenth century was already colonial–brahmanical knowledge in its content and form. Although in this period, the dominant castes in general and the Brahmins in particular were over-represented among the natives in the field of colonial knowledge practice, most of these communities did not engage in any form of knowledge production, be it traditional or modern. Historically, Brahmins *as a community* were never part of any field of knowledge, but individuals from their caste had been producing literature in fields like medicine, astrology, and art. The colonial discourse, which considered textual practice as the practice of knowledge production, authorized the Brahmin community as the sole carriers of traditional knowledge. The artisans and the agriculturalists (mostly oppressed caste groups) were excluded from knowledge-producing communities and became mere skilled workers.

In the process of mapping the hierarchical series of knowledge to the hierarchy of the caste system, the strategical use of different dichotomies as the top and bottom points played an important role. Textual and bodily practices, abstract and particular, universal and local, mental labour and manual labour, and objective and subjective were some of these dichotomies. By the end of the nineteenth century, both the 'modern' European and the 'traditional' brahmanical practices of knowledge production were situated in the former part of these dichotomies and, hence, the topmost position in the hierarchical series. The artisanal and agricultural practices represented the latter part of the dichotomies and were positioned at the lowest point in the knowledge series. I situate the former under the category of 'the production of knowledge' and the latter as 'the practices of knowing'. This separation is purely for heuristic purpose, and in practice, they have many common factors and overlapping spaces. I use this separation not as a binary of higher order in which the earlier mentioned dichotomies could be accommodated. In the category of production of knowledge, the *learning* is separated from the *production* of knowledge, which is considered a domain of expert researchers. This is reflected in the difference between educational institutions and research institutes. Learning is a process of slow distribution of and reception of already produced knowledge from the expert to the students, and only after reaching a certain level of hierarchy (for example, at the level of PhD research), one is allowed to take part in the production of knowledge. The higher your position in the hierarchy, the closer you are to the first part of the earlier mentioned dichotomies. In the top position, you are supposed to involve only in mental labour, in theorization, and in writing. In the category of practices of knowing, *doing* is the common activity of both learners and experts. There is no separation of mental and manual labour; both the novice and the expert involve in bodily activities and theorization. Here, knowing is a condition in the context of doing, and hence, 'knowledge' is not an 'outcome' of learning. Moreover, in this notion, knowing is a *located* and at the same time a universalizing practice. Hence, in the practices of knowing, the aforementioned dichotomies collapse or diffuse in the process and they become 'differences'; that is why the practice of knowing is different from but not an opposite of the production of knowledge.

In the production of knowledge, as the claim of universality is central, caste was not considered an element in the process. Scholars have already pointed out that the claims of universalization are always made by a particular local (say, Western or brahmanical) community to take control over other locals and sometimes to attempt to transform the other in the image of the self. Brahmanical claims of superiority, once these were located in the production of knowledge, attempted to erase the jati aspect of the claim and started appearing in the form of nationalistic and scientific claims. One can also say that jati was now interpreted more in secular terms such as division of labour than its ritualistic or social aspects. In the precolonial caste system, there existed specific understanding and rules regarding the relation of occupation and jati; however, this was not rigid or complete. For example, all Brahmins were not priests or scholars and all scholars and priests were not Brahmins. Still, Brahmins maintained their domination over other jatis. In the context of colonial–brahmanical production of knowledge, hereditary occupation attained a new status in the understanding of the caste system.

The question of hereditary occupation is central to the debate on caste practices in India. Colonial ethnographers and later nationalist historians and anthropologists used the theory of division of labour in an attempt to rationalize the origin of caste. In the 1871 census report, Surgeon-General William Robert Cornish observed that 'the present Hindu castes must all have branched out from a few parent stems; that from the first there must have been a primitive division of labour, and hence of caste, corresponding to the great division of labour now existing, i.e. Professional, Personal Service, Commercial, Agricultural, Industrial and Non-productive'.[19] Opposing Cornish's idea of caste, the author of *Malabar Manual*, William Logan, argued that caste was an Aryan invention of civil administration organized 'on the model of [the] well-regulated house hold'. Still, for Logan too, the division of labour was the criterion of stratification. Logan explained this model based on duties: 'The cook must attend to kitchen, the lady's maid to her mistress' attire; the sweeper must not interfere with the food, nor the water-man with the lady's muslin.'[20] As part of the project of writing the history of the nation as a unified entity, in the early twentieth century, the dominant-caste nationalists wrote the colonial interpretation of caste into that history. The idea that caste in its origin was the division of labour, the latter being universal, provided the nationalists a reason to support their claim as the representative of the whole nation and to ignore the critiques against the contemporary hierarchical and oppressive practices through caste.[21]

B. R. Ambedkar was the first scholar who challenged the aforementioned nationalist theory of caste and brought caste into the domain of power and politics. Considering the recent evidence based on DNA studies, one may find some gap in Ambedkar's theory of Shudras as originally Kshatriyas in the Indo-Aryan *varna* system.[22] However, Ambedkar historically located caste as a hierarchical exploitative system in its origins and throughout its existence. He did not attribute the domination and subordination in the caste system as a dichotomous relation but a graded hierarchy.[23] He also did not attribute the power of the Brahmins to their possession of knowledge, but to the nexus of ritualistic and political power.[24] He, however, recognized that in the colonial condition, the order of knowledge was always already colonial–brahmanical and that the depressed classes should break this by deliberately entering into the order of knowledge.[25] His insistence on social revolution before any political or economic revolution signalled to the need to challenge the reinforcement of colonial–brahmanical power in the 1930s and 1940s. He considered that caste overdetermined the politics of nationalism both in the Indian National Congress and in Indian communist parties.

It is interesting to note that most of the sociologists who studied caste in India in the second half of the twentieth century, even when critiquing the colonial conception of caste, continued their discussion in colonial and nationalist terms by ignoring and sidestepping Ambedkar's criticism. Here, their attempt was to find a theory applicable at the national level, typically through understanding rituals and caste practices based on concepts of purity and pollution from the brahmanical standpoint. Until the 1990s, this sociological scholarship interpreted caste practice through the lens of general theories of caste. If hierarchy and difference were the key explanatory devices in the classical work *Homo Hierarchicus* by Luis Dumont,[26] in other works, these varied from purity and pollution to ideology.[27] Irrespective of these differences, sociologists of caste made it a national phenomenon, something peculiar to Indian culture, civilization, and history, even while marking the utter impossibility of generalizing the caste practices at the level of the nation.

By the 1990s, historians, especially from south India, began questioning the nationalistic theories of caste by centre-staging region as the location of caste.[28] Prathama Banerjee observed that 'such histories have served to irreversibly disaggregate the dominant national story'.[29] The studies of caste in the last two decades by Indian sociologists also underscore the importance of the problem of generalized theories of caste as well as the separation of 'caste as culture' and caste as 'material practice'.[30] Following this criticism of the nationalist theory of caste, I argue that caste was imagined, inherited, and lived in different ways by different castes and that any general theory of caste fails to recognize the specific modes of these lived experiences. While the question of hereditary occupations cannot be disconnected from the question of caste, it is necessary to reframe the question differently from its colonial and nationalist versions in order to understand the ways in which caste was practised in the daily life. Ambedkar, as he was focused on the hegemonic aspect of the caste system—where every jati somehow believed in the brahmanical notion of graded hierarchy—did not elaborate much on the differences of self-understanding of jatis and the varied processes of world-making within each jati. In this book, I explore both the hegemonic aspects and the internal processes within jati worlds. To understand this difference, it is necessary to explore the question of caste outside its essence and transcendence and to closely understand how each caste is organized, through daily life practices, internally and with respect to the other castes. The meaning of 'belonging to a caste' varied between castes synchronically, and for a single caste group, diachronically.[31]

The entanglement of caste with occupation in the case of artisanal groups has been typically analysed by scholars situating this entanglement in the material domain or more narrowly in the domain of economic activity. One example for this approach is the comparison of caste with the European guild system, where caste is considered as a social regulatory mechanism of exchanges.[32] For the artisanal group in the Malayalam-speaking region, caste and occupation are denoted by a single signifier: their caste name. For example, Ashari is a caste as well as an occupation, like Thattan (goldsmith) and Karivan (ironsmith), which are also artisanal caste groups. While a majority of Pulayas were engaged in agricultural work, or, in other words, as a caste group, they were the experts in the field of agriculture, the caste name 'Pulaya' does not signify agricultural work directly; the association has to be brought in through further elaboration of the features of the caste. In the case of Pulayas and Ezhavas, this opened up a possibility of broadening the activities within the caste, although the dominant-caste groups vehemently attempted to regiment and limit this broadening of caste boundaries. It was possible for these caste groups to demand participation in the governmental institutions without abandoning their caste identities. However, in the case of Asharis, abandoning asharippani was possible only by abandoning their caste identity. If we translate this in Ambedkar's terms, Ashari migration to a different occupation was possible only in the situation of annihilation of caste, which is annihilation of all castes or the caste system itself.[33]

In the dominant versions of history, Asharis are part of the five artisanal jatis earlier known as Aynkammalar, which translates to 'five groups of handicraftsmen'. The category of Aynkammalar entered history through colonial ethnography, which was mediated through Brahmin interlocutors. Colin Mackenzie, who served in the British East India Company army and conducted a survey of south India in the early nineteenth century, mentioned five groups of artisans as part of Aynkammalar, namely, goldsmith, blacksmith, carpenter, sculptor, and leather-smith.[34] Francis Buchanan, who travelled through Malabar in the first decade of the nineteenth century, included Asharis in the category of Aynkammalar along with goldsmith, blacksmith, mason, and coppersmith.[35] Logan, quoting the 1881 census report, included Asharis in the category of Kammalar (handicraftsmen), which was again a group of five castes of carpenters, braziers, stone-masons, goldsmiths, and blacksmiths.[36] It is important to note that all these colonial ethnographers always collected information with the help of Brahmin interlocutors.

It is difficult to know whether, in the nineteenth century, Asharis in Malabar considered themselves as part of Aynkammalar. From the evidence in the available written and oral sources, one may observe that in the first half of the twentieth century, Asharis never mentioned being part of this group or establishing social or conjugal relations with any of these caste groups. Ashari, in sociological terms, was an endogamous caste group with kinship rules based on a patrilineal lineage system. Asharis considered themselves superior not only to castes like Pulayars and Parayars but also to the other four castes of Aynkammalar.[37] Another category to which Asharis were connected and to which a section of Asharis began identifying with in the last decades of the twentieth century is Vishwakarma, which in Sanskrit means 'the architect or creator of the universe'. In this sense, Vishwakarma replaces Brahma as the creator. But in some stories, Brahma is considered the originator of Vishwakarma. The five Vishwakarma castes trace their lineage to the five sages emerged from Vishwakarma. There are temples specifically designated to Vishwakarma, where artisans conduct rituals and prayers. Further, historians have noted that, in many parts of India in the precolonial period, people from artisanal castes had worshipped Vishwakarma through different forms of rituals. However, in the Malayalam-speaking region of Keralam, I was unable to find any historical evidence of Vishwakarma worship until recently, when Vishwakarma became an icon for the reform organizations of artisanal castes.

By the beginning of the twentieth century, the governing activities of the colonizers started penetrating the Ashari world through different channels. Even though the colonizers had initiated different improvements to artisanal practices all over India from the 1850s onwards, especially in the field of education, they had little effect in the world of Asharis in Malabar. In the early decades of the twentieth century, as colonial appropriations intensified through large-scale constructions of railways, roads, and buildings, asharippani (carpentry) became the organizing point of resistance to these colonial interventions. Asharis created a new space where they could distance themselves from colonial forces, bringing asharippani to the centre stage of everyday practice. The resistance was derived from the understanding that the colonial intervention would destroy the autonomy of asharippani, and hence, it was articulated in terms of defending asharippani as a unique practice of Asharis. Difference-making was the modality through which Asharis in this period created the distance between asharippani and the outside world. In this process, asharippani transformed from the status of a hereditary trade to that of a central organizing category of the jati Ashari.

In this context, I argue that different jatis understood, imagined, and practised caste in their own ways, each of which changed through time and space. Asharis in the early twentieth century understood caste as an effect to be produced by engaging in asharippani on an everyday basis. In other words, jati was not just a pre-established set of rules regarding customs and rituals, but also an active principle produced through engaging in asharippani. This does not mean that, at this period, Asharis imagined jati as a passive phenomenon or as an object that does not have any implication in their daily life. Contrarily, jati as the consequence of asharippani certainly produced its own effect in the everyday life of Asharis. The important point is that the capacity of jati to produce this effect was a function of both the practice of asharippani itself and the contexts in which Asharis conducted this practice. By privileging asharippani over *a priori* caste rules in order to understand the modalities of practices of knowing, this work attempts to underscore everyday practice as the central organizing feature of the jati Ashari.

By the last quarter of the twentieth century, the Ashari understanding of jati as a function of asharippani underwent a significant transformation, as they incorporated elements of colonial–brahmanical forms of knowledge production into asharippani. To begin with, the socio-economic changes in this period in general, and the reform organizations that Asharis formed in this period for negotiating with the state in particular, created new ways of understanding jati and asharippani. Reform associations encouraged the community members to learn and write history, which was one of the languages through which they could communicate with the state. As knowledge in the written form was a necessary condition for these negotiations, this compelled Asharis to transform asharippani into a production of knowledge from its earlier form of a practice of knowing. In this process, asharippani became the occupation of the caste 'Ashari'. In other words, by the end of the twentieth century, asharippani was no longer a determining factor of caste, which was now understood in terms of kinship, lineages, and blood relations. It became possible that even if one did not actually participate in asharippani, one could still be an Ashari, which was not the case in the first half of the twentieth century. Through the analysis of Ashari negotiations with production of knowledge in the twentieth century, I attempt to show the heterogeneity of the ways of knowing and how knowledge attained its present status as an element intertwined with power. Across the book, while the Ashari stories explain their struggles against the intrusion of disembodied objective knowledge, they also tell us how by the end of the twentieth century, features of production of knowledge made their entry into the world of asharippani.

While Ashari objections to production of knowledge stemmed from the fundamental contradiction between embodied and objective knowledges, the genealogy of Nampoothiri interaction with production of knowledge in the twentieth century traced a different vector of negotiations and transformations. The Nampoothiris of Malabar began their interaction with the colonial institutions at a later stage compared to many other Brahmin communities of different parts of India. By the early twentieth century, various new social forces that were part of the process of colonial knowledge production began challenging the domination of Nampoothiris in the social life of Malabar. The new economic opportunities were directly connected to colonial education, which came along with new social imaginaries and new moralities. The Nampoothiri interaction with colonial knowledge culminated in the reform movement in the 1920s and 1930s. This work, focusing on pre-reform and post-reform periods, explores the tension between the existing order of acharam and the emerging order of knowledge in the Nampoothiri world in the first half of the twentieth century. Acharam was simultaneously ritual and custom – that is, the everyday activities and the rules for performing these, respectively. For Nampoothiris in the first two decades of the twentieth century, acharam was the reference point for value and moral judgment and a guide for everyday life.

Historians and anthropologists have generally connected Nampoothiri acharams directly to the Vedic textual rules and assumed that the Vedic text is the reference point for acharam.[38] I argue that even though one could see resemblances between the prescriptions in the Vedic text and the everyday practice of acharam, the former was not a reference point for the latter. By this, I mean that when the question of values or morals was under dispute, they referred not to the texts but to precedents and authority based on experience. Hence, acharam in this work is not a mere reflection of the Vedic brahmanical ideology, but a performance which produces an effect of order in society. This order, which was produced through the rituals of everyday life, was the reference point for moral evaluations and judgments.

By the early twentieth century, the order of acharam confronted much opposition, especially from the young generation of Nampoothiris who were educated in colonial institutions. While this young generation thought that knowledge could be the basis of the well-being of a society, the majority from the community challenged this idea by pointing out the inseparable connection between the superiority of Nampoothiris and their daily performance of acharam. These ideas were dominant in the first two decades of the century, and as the community leaders were sceptical about the liberatory potential of knowledge, they postponed the question of education and reforms within the community. As the reform movement gained momentum by the third decade, it became impossible for the community to defer the question of knowledge anymore, which inaugurated not the destruction of the order of acharam but its reinterpretation and realignment.

Scholars of reform movements of various caste communities have noted the importance of the question of education for these movements. They considered reform a process of modernization or enlightenment through education.[39] Feminist scholars have questioned the conventional understanding of caste reforms as a transformation from tradition to modernity or as an element of the modernization process. Emphasizing the importance of understanding reform as a process of 'en-gendering', J. Devika noted that 'such an approach would be distinct from not only the liberal histories that celebrate women's liberation as part of modernisation, but also the critical efforts that seek to reverse the binaries of tradition–modernity or passive–active'.[40] Devika situated the question concerning gender as the central domain of the reform debate. On the other hand, many other scholars of reform movements focused on the issue of caste and explored the ways in which caste hierarchies continued in the new forms in the post-reform period.[41] My attempt in this work is to broaden the aforementioned analyses to the domain of knowledge production in this period, which will enable us to understand both the continuities and discontinuities of social formations, including those of caste and gender.

By the 1930s, Nampoothiris began reinterpreting acharam based on meaning, scientific fact, and history, all of which were categories adopted from the colonial discourse on the production of knowledge. They attempted to prove that the acharams were scientifically correct and could be justified through historical reasons. The oral tradition, which was an integral part of Nampoothiri acharams, lost its relative importance in comparison to the written text. For centuries, the learning of the Vedas, which was part of the childhood rituals of every Nampoothiri boy, did not comprise learning of the Sanskrit language or the meaning of the words. The basic objective of Veda learning was to memorize as many verses as possible and to learn their recital in proper tones and intonations. Even the well-known teachers never attempted to interpret the text, as they were not aware of the meaning of the words or the grammar of the language. Once *writing* became the legitimate form of representation of knowledge, the centres where the Veda learning was conducted lost importance in the daily life of Nampoothiris, though these continued to exist with less relevance.

Many scholars of religion who study brahmanical oral traditions have explained these as a form of transferring canonical knowledge in the Hindu tradition.[42] I argue that the colonial intervention not only transformed the mode of transfer of knowledge, but also made Vedic texts the source of traditional knowledge. It is important to note that although scholarly debates were very much part of brahmanical traditions, these debates were not the reference point for everyday life. What happened through the colonial discourse on knowledge was that knowledge became a measure of everyday activities of individuals and groups. Hence, the focus here is on the changing status of knowledge in the everyday life of Nampoothiris.

The Ashari and Nampoothiri stories from twentieth-century Malabar, as analysed in this book, enable us to trace the genealogies of production of knowledge and practices of knowing and the interaction between these two historical processes. By marking modern knowledge as colonial–brahmanical knowledge, this work participates in a politics that exposes the violent and oppressive nature of knowledge production that dominates contemporary societies all over the world.[43] At the same time, by mapping the trajectories of practices of knowing, this work underscores the possibility of other ways of understanding the world and being in it.

A User's Manual for the Book

This work, as all other academic histories (positivist, structuralist, or post-structuralist), is a historical fiction, as evidence, rational interpretations, intuitions, imaginations, dreams, and feelings are part of writing any historical narrative. The objective here is not to find out what Asharis and Nampoothiris exactly did in twentieth-century Malabar. Rather, what I attempt is to ask what the implications are and what we can learn if we juxtapose their stories to compare them. Hence, the invitation to read this book is not based on the claim of 'original arguments' but on the claim that I have arranged or assembled the narratives in an order that, I hope, might be interesting for some. I consider the arguments in this book less as logical–rational than as impressionistic. In other words, it is an invitation to listen to a storytelling session. Moreover, through this narrative (which itself is not different from many other academic histories), I wish the readers receive both certain ideas and feelings impressionistically, or even arrive at the unsaid moral of the story, during or after the reading process.

I also want to make some obvious but important clarifications regarding the way I formulated the narratives. This book is a result of my reading of several works, listening to many stories, and observing and being part of actions from different domains of life. It is difficult to pinpoint the source of each argument to any one of these actions. On occasions, while listening to Asharis, I remembered arguments from an academic writing that I had already read, and some idea erupted in my mind. On some other occasions, reading a poem clarified an aspect that had vaguely arisen earlier from an interview. At many other times, the ideas emerged not in my mind but in the text while I was typing the sentences. The author is sometimes an artist and at other times a curator, but always an interpreter of the stories. Hence, I have deliberately avoided citations (in the text or in notes) in many places, because I am not sure whether to refer a particular idea to, say, Martin Heidegger, Ambedkar, feminist and Dalit movements, Nanu Ashari, the unknown poet, the movie I watched ten years ago, or to a casual conversation with a friend. This is not to appropriate anyone else's argument as mine, but exactly the opposite: to emphasize that all my arguments are footnotes to the stories, told by many other actors involved in the process. I have put my name as the author of the book for selfish reasons; readers could consider it as a placeholder representing all the human and non-human actants involved in the network of production of this book: cleaning staff in the archives, scholars, activists, friends, enemies, computers, editors, printers, publishers, and many others.[44]

Even when we use citations in the conventional referential sense, these are used more in a ritualistic manner, as it is impossible not to exclude thousands of works already published in any given area. I want to emphasize that, ideally, the conventional form of referencing is well-intentioned: to pay tribute to those who paved the way for us and to respect their hard work, intelligence, and creativity. However, like many other rituals, referencing has become either a means for the authors to show how much they have read or merely a hollow and mechanical exercise, as at most times, readers tend to ignore these (especially in the endnote format). As I have mentioned earlier and in the acknowledgements, this work is greatly indebted to many social movements, the work of other scholars, activists, my teachers, and students. I do not want to limit my gratitude in notes, but express it through my whole narrative. Still, in this work, I use notes (there are several of them) for other reasons: first, I am not sure whether any reviewer or publisher would approve an academic work in history without notes; in that sense, they serve the impressionistic purpose! Second, and most importantly, I use notes to tell other stories that are not necessarily a part of my narration, while those who are familiar with these can relate or see the resemblance in them with the stories told in this book; this also serves the purpose of further exploration in the sense that those interested can refer to these in their own research. My hope is that a reader who does not want to be interrupted by notes or a person who has not read any academic work in this subject would still be able to get interested in this narrative and follow it. Note that while the Introduction, Chapter 1, and the Postscript could be considered as standalone chapters and could be read in any order the reader wishes, Chapters 2 and 5 and Chapters 3 and 4 are like couplets. Towards the end of every chapter, I reflect, in verse, on the arguments I made in that chapter.

Finally, on one of the most important and highly politically controversial topics in the contemporary times: the subject position of the author. For many, the following explanation may seem trivial or unnecessary; even if that is the case, I feel, it needs to be stated. Being brought up as a heterosexual male in Nampoothiri caste in Keralam, having learned about the colonial–brahmanical domination and exploitation in the field of knowledge production by being part of it as well as wanting to challenge this, how does one engage with the practice of knowing of a subaltern caste group (here, Asharis)? It would simply be a question of representation or appropriation if my attempt is to explain the Ashari practices even in 'their own terms' or to be an expert of the history of artisanal caste groups. Most of the criticisms of the dominant forms of knowledge production from within the privileged groups have either exoticized or ignored the subaltern criticism of the system. These projects (for example, many works in postcolonial studies or in the subaltern studies project) sometimes consciously and sometimes unintentionally attempted to recover voices of the subaltern or be the voice of the subaltern. My motivation, I believe, is very different; it stems from a conviction that the privileged who are part of the oppressive system, at any point, if they want to challenge the system, must listen and learn not from within but from the outside. The rich traditions of resistance by the subaltern groups are a lesson for the privileged who wants to be a follower of the resistance to the inhuman system. The focus here is the critique of the colonial–brahmanical system, for which the Ashari practice of knowing provides theoretical tools and valuable lessons of success (and failure) of using these tools for dismantling the oppressive caste system. My attempt here is to learn from Asharis and to communicate what I learned mostly to the privileged who are not yet familiar with these stories but interested in challenging the oppressive practice in their lifeworld. In other words, there is nothing about the subaltern communities in this book that they already do not know from their daily life experience and from their own theorization. However, I will be happy if they read the book and critically scrutinize how a person from a privileged group utilizes what he or she learned from them. Any author who has become aware of these factors would not justify his or her action just by his or her good intentions. My justification, which I learned from Asharis, is this: without action—without *doing*—there is no learning, and without learning, it is impossible to act in *other ways*: hence, this book.

Notes

1. Abhay Xaxa, 'I Am Not Your Data', Adivasi Resurgence, 13 January 2016, http://adivasiresurgence.com/2016/01/13/i-am-not-your-data/ (accessed on 1 September 2021).

2. Power–knowledge, as famously theorized by Michel Foucault, not only articulates a necessary connection between knowledge and power but also rejects the notion of power merely as destructive and knowledge as liberative. The following discussion is inspired by the various debates around Foucault's analysis of power–knowledge and is an attempt to historicize the relation of power and knowledge in a colonial context. See Michel Foucault, *Power/ Knowledge: Selected Interviews and Other Writings, 1972–1977*, ed. Colin Gordon (New York: Pantheon, 1980).

3. See Zaheer Baber, *The Science of Empire: Scientific Knowledge, Civilization and Colonial Rule in India* (Albany: State University of New York Press, 1996);

Joyce E. Chaplin, *Anxious Pursuits: Agricultural Innovation and Modernity in Lower South, 1730–1815* (Chapel Hill: University of North Carolina Press, 1993).

4. Tracing the relation between knowledge and power in the colonial context, Bernard Cohen analyses the 'investigative modalities' of the British Government in India. He explains that '[m]ost investigative modalities were constructed in relation to institutions and administrative sites with fixed routines. Some were transformed into "sciences" such as economics, ethnology, tropical medicine, comparative law, or cartography, and their practitioners became professionals.' Bernard Cohn, *Colonialism and Its Forms of Knowledge: The British in India* (New Jersey: Princeton University Press, 1996), 5.

5. Claude Alvares, 'Science, Colonialism and Violence: A Luddite View', in *Science, Hegemony and Violence: A Requiem for Modernity*, ed. Ashis Nandy, 68–112 (Oxford: Oxford University Press, 1988).

6. For explanation of science as a Western and European project, see Richard Olson, *Science Deified and Science Defied: The Historical Significance of Science in Western Culture* (Berkeley and Los Angeles: University of California Press, 1990); David C. Lindberg, *The Beginnings of Western Science: The European Scientific Tradition in Philosophical, Religious and Institutional Context, Prehistory to A.D. 1450* (Chicago: University of Chicago Press, 2007).

7. Kapil Raj, *Relocating Modern Science: Circulation and Construction of Knowledge in South Asia and Europe, 1650–1900* (London: Palgrave Macmillan, 2010).

8. For an analysis of the colonial invention of tropical diseases, see Helen Tilley, 'Ecologies of Complexity: Tropical Environments, African Trypanosomiasis, and the Science of Disease Control in British Colonial Africa, 1900–1940', *Osiris* 19 (2004): 21–38.

9. In the descriptions of Duarte Barbosa, Ludovico Di Varthema, and Francis Buchanan, all who travelled through Malabar at different periods between the early decades of the sixteenth century and the early nineteenth century, we can see the subjective elements of the production of knowledge becoming increasingly unspeakable and unscientific. See Ludvico Di Varthema, *The Travels of Ludvico Di Varthema* (London: Hakluyt Society, 1863); Duarte Barbosa, *A Description of the Coasts of East Africa and Malabar* (London: Hakluyt Society, 1866); Francis Buchanan, *A Journey from Madras through the Countries of Mysore, Canara and Malabar* (London: Cadell & Davies, 1807).

10. Lorraine Daston argued that though different notions of objectivity were part of the discourse on production of knowledge, it attained the specific meaning which it has in the present parlance only in the second half of the nineteenth century. Daston observed that the idea of objectivity as disinterestedness, as the distancing of the observer from the phenomenon observed, or as the value-neutral approach of the scientist was a result of the internationalization of science in the mid-nineteenth century. Lorraine Daston and Peter Galison, *Objectivity* (New York: Zone Books, 2010).

11. Laura Marks pointed out that while the visual and cultural turns in the scholarship on knowledge and aesthetics have contributed towards the criticism of positivism, 'the turn has left in place the sensory hierarchy that subtends Western philosophy, in which only the distant senses are vehicles of knowledge'. Even in the West, it was not the visual that was always privileged; this privilege has undergone numerous changes from the time of Plato to the early modern times. It was the post-Enlightenment society that started privileging visual and aural senses by removing touch, smell, and taste from the process of production of knowledge. Laura Marks, 'Thinking Multi-sensory Culture', *Paragraph* 31, no. 2 (July 2008): 123–137.

12. In his study of Nambkwara society in Brazil, Claude Lévi-Strauss observed how the introduction of writing among this indigenous group created new forms of power relations and new forms of inter-subjective violence. Criticizing Levi Strauss for his attempt to 'safeguard the exteriority of writing to speech', Jacques Derrida asked: 'Is there a knowledge, and above all, a language, scientific or not, that one can call alien at once to writing and to violence?' Derrida's attempt to question the Western metaphysical tradition of privileging speech over writing is important, but it fails to consider the specific historical situations where the colonialists privileged writing over speech, the act which had severe violent consequences in the colonial world. Claude Lévi-Strauss, *Tristes Tropiques*, trans. John Weightman and Doreen Weightman (New York: Penguin, 1975); Jacques Derrida, *Of Grammatology*, trans. Gayatri Chakravorty Spivak (Maryland: John Hopkins University Press, 1974), 127.

13. Kay Anderson has argued that humanism based on nineteenth-century scientific theories of human species did not assume homogeneity or equality among all human beings; instead, these theories essentialized the racial differences based on biology and justified hierarchical stratifications based on race. 'The colonial difference' practised by the colonial governments in colonies was not an aberration, as Partha Chatterjee puts it, of the universal theories practised in the Metropole. From the very beginning, universalism was a practice of the hierarchical ordering of objects and human beings. Kay Anderson, *Race and the Crisis of Humanism* (London: Routledge, 2007); Partha Chatterjee, *The Nation and Its Fragments: Colonial and Postcolonial Histories* (Princeton: Princeton University Press, 1993).

14. For an analysis of the role of museums and exhibitions in colonial governmentality, see Gyan Prakash, 'Science "Gone Native" in Colonial India', *Representations* 40 (October 1992): 153–178.

15. For example, James Mill, in his six-volume work on British India, depicted the Brahmins as despotic and uncivilized. H. H. Wilson, on the other hand, objected to the general view among the colonial officers that Brahmins were 'crafty and cunning'. Wilson argued that Brahmins and their Sanskritic tradition were part of a great civilization upon which the whole history of India was built. James Mill, *The History of British India* (London: James Madden and Co., 1840);

H. H. Wilson, *Essays: Analytical, Critical and Philological on Subject Connected with Sanskrit Language* (London: Trubner and Co., 1865).

16. Both the orientalists like William Jones, who favoured the promotion of Sanskrit-based education, and the utilitarian thinkers like John Stuart Mill, who was a strong proponent of English education, considered Brahmins and other dominant castes as the proper native group who could be 'educated' and enlightened through the colonial educational institutions. For an analysis of the colonial education policy and the privileges and preferences of the utilitarians and the orientalists, see Bart Schultz and Georgios Varouxaki (eds.), *Utilitarianism and Empire* (Oxford: Lexington Books, 2005).

17. For an analysis of the role of caste in the history of education, see Sabyasachi Bhattacharya (ed.), *Education and the Disprivileged: Nineteenth and Twentieth Century India* (New Delhi: Orient Blackswan, 2002).

18. Alfred Chatterton's study of industrial education is an example of how the colonialists mapped the caste hierarchy onto a hierarchical system of education and training. He attempted to assign each caste group a specific form of education depending on their traditional occupation and a supposed historical relation with knowledge. Alfred Chatterton, *Industrial Education* (Madras: Government Press, 1901). See also George Birdwood, *The Industrial Arts of India* (London: Chapman and Hall, 1884).

19. Quoted in William Logan, *Malabar Manual*, vol. 1 (Madras: Government Press, 1887), 109.

20. Logan, *Malabar Manual*, 112.

21. While he was totally against the hierarchical positioning of the status of various castes, M. K. Gandhi defended the benefits of division of labour based on caste. M. K. Gandhi, *Hind Swaraj and Other Writings* (Cambridge: Cambridge University Press, 1977). However, many other nationalistic writers considered that jati as a hierarchy based on the division of labour is natural, universal, and historically justifiable. For example, Bal Gangadhar Tilak severely opposed Jyotirao Phule's attempts to end caste-based occupations and argued that it will destroy the nationality of Hindus. See Parimala V. Rao, 'Educating Women and Non-Brahmani as "Loss of Nationality": Bal Gangadhar Tilak and the Nationalist Agenda in Maharashtra', Centre for Women's Development Studies, 2008, http://www.cwds.ac.in/OCPaper/EducatingWomen-Parimala.pdf (accessed on 17 January 2021).

22. For a recent work on Aryan migration based on DNA analysis, see Tony Joseph, *Early Indians: The Story of Our Ancestors and Where We Came From* (New Delhi: Juggernaut, 2018).

23. See B. R. Ambedkar, *Who Were the Shudras?* (Bombay: Thackers, 1949).

24. See B. R. Ambedkar, *Annihilation of Caste* (New Delhi: Samyak Prakashan, 2013).

25. Ambedkar, in his various speeches, emphasized the importance of education for the depressed classes usually through the phrase 'Educate, Organize, Agitate'.

This phrase became the motto of the institution Bahishkrit Hitkarini Sabha, which was established in 1924 under his leadership. See B. R. Ambedkar, *Dr. Babasaheb Ambedkar: Writings and Speeches*, vol. 17, part. 2 (New Delhi: Government of India, 2014 [2003]).

26. Louis Dumont, *Homo Hierarchicus: The Caste System and Its Implications* (Chicago: Chicago University Press, 1980).

27. See, for example, G. S. Ghurye, *Caste and Race in India* (London: Routledge, 1932); Dipankar Gupta, *Social Stratification* (Delhi: Oxford University Press, 1992).

28. For analyses of caste from various regions of India, see E. Zelliot, *From Untouchable to Dalit: Essay on Ambedkar Movement* (Delhi: Manohar, 1992); Shekhar Bandopadhyay, *Caste, Protest and Identity in Colonial India: The Namashudras* (Richmond: Curzon Press, 1997); G. Arunima, *There Comes Papa: Colonialism and the Transformation of Matryliny in Kerala, Malabar, c. 1850–1940* (Hyderabad: Orient Longman, 2003); Dilip Menon, *Caste, Nationalism and Communism in South India: Malabar 1900–1948* (Cambridge: Cambridge University Press, 2007); M. S. S. Pandian, *Brahmin and Non-Brahmin: Genealogies of Tamil Political Present* (New Delhi: Permanent Black, 2007).

29. Prathama Banerjee, 'Caste and the Writing of History', in *Dalit Assertion in Society, History and Literature*, ed. Imtias Ahmad and Shashi Bhushan Upadhyay, 214–238 (New Delhi: Deshkal Publications, 2007), 223.

30. Surinder Jodhka, enumerating various theoretical conceptualizations of caste, marks the complexities of answering the question, 'What exactly is happening to caste?' He explains that 'there are multiple and varied experiences of caste in today's India. The answer is likely to depend on the context in which the question is asked. It may also depend on whose experience of caste is being considered while answering the question. There could be, and there are, more than one answers to a question like this'. Surinder Jodhka, *Caste in Contemporary India* (London: Routledge, 2015), 1. See also, Balmurli Natrajan, *The Culturalization of Caste in India: Identity and Inequality in a Multicultural Age* (New York: Routledge, 2011).

31. Grace Carswell and Geert De Neve's analysis of the transformation of the caste in the neoliberal condition is helpful in theorizing caste as a changing relational hierarchy and towards highlighting the importance of studying this relation in the context of a specific caste context, which I am attempting to do in this work. Grace Carswell and Geert De Neve, 'T-shirts and Tumblers: Caste, Dependency and Work under Neoliberalization in South India', *Contributions to Indian Sociology* 48, no. 1 (2014): 103–131.

32. For a comparison of the European guild system and the artisanal manufacturing systems in India, see Tirthankar Roy, 'The Guild in Modern South Asia,' *International Review for Social History* 53, Supplement S16 (December 2008): 95–120. See also Irfan Habib, 'Potentialities of Capitalistic Development in the Economy of Mughal India', *Journal of Economic History* 29, no. 1 (1969): 32–78.

33. Ambedkar, 'Annihilation of Caste'.

34. *The Mackenzie Collection: A Descriptive Catalogue of the Oriental Manuscript*, India Office Library, London, B 21: 12, 1(828), 28.

35. Buchanan, *A Journey from Madras*, 231.

36. Logan, *Malabar Manual*, 115.

37. Interview with Achuthan Ashari (20 June 2008). Also, note that across this book, all translations from Malayalam to English, unless otherwise mentioned, are by me.

38. For example, Marjatta Parpola, in her ethnographic work on Nampoothiris, explains Vedic texts as both the imagined and actual reference point for the rituals in the daily practices of Nampoothiris. Marjatta Parpola, *Kerala Brahmins in Transition: A Study of a Nampoothiri Family* (Helsinki: Finnish Oriental Society, 2000).

39. See Ashok Swain, *Struggle against the State: Social Network and Protest Mobilization in India* (Burlington: Ashgate Publishing Company, 1988).

40. J. Devika, *En-Gendering Individuals: The Language of Re-forming in Early Twentieth Century Keralam* (Hyderabad: Orient Longman, 2007), 17.

41. For an analysis of continuing influence of caste in economic inequality, see Ashwini Deshpande, 'Does Caste Still Define Disparity? A Look at Inequality in Kerala, India', *American Economic Review* 90, no. 2, Papers and Proceedings of the One Hundred Twelfth Annual Meeting of the American Economic Association (May 2000): 322–325.

42. For a debate of canonical knowledge and the status of the Vedas in Hindu tradition, see the essays in Laurie Patton (ed.), *Authority, Anxiety, and Canon: Essays in Vedic Interpretations* (Albany: State University of New York Press, 1994).

43. For a study of the persistence of caste in the twenty-first century, see Amaresh Dubey and Sonalde Desai, 'Caste in 21st Century India: Competing Narratives', *Economic and Political Weekly* 46, no. 11 (March 2011): 40–49.

44. The way a new concept emerges from the ideas that already exist cannot be exactly mapped through notes. When we see a painting or read a poem, we recognize the 'influences' but do not complain about the painter or the poet not giving exact references to these influences. The claim that academic writings are completely different from arts and fiction is coming from a positivist perspective of objectivity and rational thinking in opposition to subjectivity and feelings. Many of the times (except if it is a question of plagiarism), the complaints about not providing the references are in the form of, 'You have not referred to the authors I have read, whom I consider important.' The concept of key authors is always subjective, and it is more important to focus on the text itself, imagining that the author is already dead.

1

An Ashari World of Knowing

In early twentieth-century Malabar, Asharis inhabited an 'Ashari world' that was constituted and reconstituted through daily life practices.[1] *Asharippani* (carpentry)[2] was the central organizing category and activity that determined the process of the constitution of this world. Asharis also engaged with many worlds outside their own, such as the world of plants, worlds of other *jati*s, and the world of the *sayip* (the white man). Imagining and constituting a world involves two actions: defining the boundaries and detailing the inner space–time of the world. This means that creating and sustaining a world is a simultaneous process of reproducing difference with the other worlds and sameness within one's own world. Jati was the crucial aspect in this boundary-making or difference-making process, and this process was very much connected to the defining and redefining of the internal constitutive elements within the Ashari world. Asharippani was understood as the defining activity of forming a unique Ashari world and, at the same time, it was also considered the activity that separated the Ashari world from the other worlds.

Asharis imagined that the meaning and essence of humans, plants, animals, and objects varied according to two important factors: the location or the world of the knowing subject and the position or the world of the object of knowing. This also meant that the facts and truths that were applicable to one world might not be valid in a different world. Jati boundaries limited the degrees of generalization of truth, and these boundaries determined not only the possibilities of belonging but also the very being in any world: a tree which originally belonged to the world of plants became a different entity when it was brought into the world of Asharis. Similarly, an object perceived from the Ashari world and the same perceived from the Nampoothiri world have very different essence or existence.

In this chapter, I compare the Ashari practices with contemporary scientific and technological practices and also with the academic scholarship on indigenous practices; no need to mention that the descriptions of the Ashari perspectives are my interpretation of Ashari narratives. Through this analysis, I attempt to point out that the categories such as modern and pre-modern as a prefix to knowledge are not useful in understanding various practices of knowing in the colonial world. Ashari practices included many elements that were similar to the modern forms of technological practices, such as objectification and abstraction; but, as I explain in the following paragraphs, this similarity does not establish any direct connection or influence between these two practices.

There is no consensus among scientists or philosophers of science on the questions, 'what is science?' and 'what is scientific method?'. However, most of them agree that science is an activity of producing generalized and generalizable rules and laws; in other words, theories.[3] Thus, science is generally understood as a process of arriving at universally applicable rules from particulars, whereas technology is understood as a movement from the general to the particular or as applied knowledge. From this perspective, the limitation of pre-modern or traditional knowledge is that it is always local and particular, and practitioners of traditional knowledge are incapable of abstraction. Scholarship on indigenous knowledge accepts that these are local knowledges, but considers their localization not as a constraint but as an advantage. In contrast, in the following sections, I argue that the Ashari practice of knowing did include abstraction and generalization. Sometimes, the generalization of certain facts could be even understood as similar to the idea of universal truth; however, the universe here was the Ashari world. In academic scholarship, abstraction is understood as a process that happens through the exclusion of differences and the reduction of multiple objects into a noun, category, or concept. The abstraction is conducted in the world of ideas and concepts, not in the material world; objects in the material world are particulars. Ashari notions of abstraction extended not only to the world of ideas but also to that of objects. An object could be simultaneously a particular and an abstract entity. Explaining the practice of asharippani, I show that it was a process that always oscillated between the particular and the general.

The chapter also engages with the role of experience in understanding Ashari practices. Most of the existing scholarship on artisanal practices foregrounds the role of experience, which is considered an accumulated memory in the mind or body and that acts as a reference point for the actions in the present.[4] Based on the concept of *knowing as doing*, I argue that *experiencing*, not experience, is a better category to explain artisanal forms of practices of knowing. From the discussion of sensing and experiencing, I conclude that the Asharis did not use their experience that was already residing in their body but engaged in experiencing, which was central to their knowing as doing.

The chapter then dwells with Ashari engagements with the other worlds in the first three quarters of the twentieth century. As mentioned earlier, jati was the boundary condition that separated different worlds, and these boundaries also limited both the possibility and the desirability of knowing. For example, not only was it impossible to know the truth of a tree in the world of plants but also it was not desirable to inquire about this. At the same time, when a tree was brought into the Ashari world, the truth of the tree was possible and allowed to be investigated. This idea that it was ethically not correct to investigate the truths of other worlds did not prevent Asharis from engaging with the outside world. The boundaries of different worlds were not impenetrable but had pores and had even overlapping time–spaces. In the later part of this chapter, I explore Ashari engagement with three outside worlds: plants, jatis, and colonialists. The following section lays down the basic principles through which Asharis engaged in different worlds.

Knowing in the Ashari World

Methodologically, Asharis explained knowing as doing, the implication of which was a complex theory of practice of knowing and practice of learning. According to this theory, the objective of knowing was not to understand the immutable essence of an object or a phenomenon but to engage in a process of mapping and locating its current condition and its effects, assuming *change* as the fundamental nature of living and non-living beings. This is different from the scientific way of inquiring, where the objective is to arrive at facts that remain the same upon repeating the experiment. The laws or the explanations of science are an extraction of the material world outside of the constraints of time, and they anticipate sameness without change.[5] Change in the material world is explained within the scientific paradigm as a transformation from one essence to another. For example, consider the scientific statement that 'a water molecule contains two atoms of hydrogen and one atom of oxygen'. This means that a water molecule always was, is, and will be a combination of two hydrogen atoms and one oxygen atom. The very definition of water in scientific terms depends upon the sameness—the unchanging nature—of this combination. If we now modify the above sentences into the statement, 'today, a water molecule contains two atoms of hydrogen and one atom of oxygen', its implications are very different from the former statement. This could imply either 'I will test it again tomorrow and will tell you whether water is formed with the same atoms' or 'Who knows what it will be tomorrow!' This, however, is incompatible with a scientific explanation of the objective world. In the Ashari modes of inquiry, the question 'What is water?' was articulated in the form of another question: 'How does water look like now?' Here, one could argue that the use of the term 'now' already assumes that water has a certain essence at least for the time defined as 'now'. Any explanation that describes a condition as it 'is' assumes an essence irrespective of the duration ascribed to the condition, whether that is short (this moment) or infinite (eternal). However, in the latter question, water appears as a relation between the process of looking by the Ashari and the process of self-revealing by the water: Asharis' action on water and water's action on Asharis. In other words, the question Asharis asked was, 'What is water as far as we are concerned now?' Here, obviously, the epistemological and ontological aspects are intertwined, and the ontological aspects are limited to the time of engaging with water. If 'What is water?' is a scientific question, then the very act of looking (a subjective action) is not important, because the 'water is', whether we observe or not. One could even argue that the objective of scientific inquiry is to state what water is, especially when we are not observing it.[6] Here, the inner truths, once revealed forever, remain as such, and there is no need to reinvent the wheel, which is a waste of time and an inefficient practice. It was not that the Asharis doubted the existence of water without their presence. They assumed that, at a particular time, water was different in different worlds and that it was also different at different times even in a given world. In short, there was no such thing as 'water as such'. Here, the difference between the existence and the essence is that the former is independent of the practice of perceiving or knowing, and the latter is dependent on the particular act of knowing.

There is another implication of knowing as doing. In scientific explanation, the truth of water remains the same, irrespective of its quantity and certain qualities. For example, water in a river, water in a well, and water in a bucket are the same in their essence, and even the essence of steam is the same as that of water (that is, two atoms of hydrogen and one atom of oxygen), even though the former is vapour and the latter is liquid. In the Ashari perspective, river water and well water had different essences because they were in different worlds and acted differently. In other words, the essence of an object was defined not just by its 'content' but also by its location and the relative conditions in the network of connected objects. The sameness of river water and well water can only be established by isolating the water (for example, in a lab or in concept) from its earlier surroundings or breaking its connections with other objects. The Asharis agreed that there was some amount of sameness in river water and well water or normal and boiling water; however, the process of knowing ignored the commonness or considered it an uninteresting subject of inquiry. During an interview, when we were discussing how Asharis understood various material objects in the world, Keshavan Ashari, a chief carpenter from Mukkam, asked me: 'What is the point in saying that rain, pond, well, and this bucket contain water? In each situation, water works in different ways. So why do we care that all of these contain water?'[7] If the question of 'what water *does*' determines the answer to the question of 'what water *is*', then the premise itself is that normal and boiling water are two different entities. In scientific inquiry, the premise is that both are the same but act differently at different conditions. In the Ashari ways of knowing, the action was the defining condition of the essence of an object, whereas in the scientific understanding, action follows the essence.

The ontological status of objects was dependent on the network in which it dwelled and the possible effect the object could produce. At the same time, for the Asharis, this status was also dependent on the perspective of the world from which it was perceived. They recognize that the answer to the question 'What is a tree?' depended on the standpoint from which you were answering it; in this case, the standpoint was a location determined by jati. *What a tree does* was very different for an Ashari than for a Nampoothiri, and hence *what a tree is* was also different for different jatis. Equally important was the idea that the essence of a tree was different when it was in the world of plants and when it was brought to the Ashari world. The Ashari interaction with trees in the world of plants is described in the next section. Here, I explore the situation when a tree was brought into the Ashari world. Trees entered the Ashari world mostly as cut wood, and they were scrutinized and categorized according to their utility. This categorization was conducted through action: by working on the wood piece. Ravi, from Mundur, who is working in a furniture shop described to me how his grandfather explained to him about the power Asharis had over raw materials:

> He [grandfather] told me that Asharis have the right to do whatever with the wood piece, but that we must act responsibly and discretely. If Muthappan [the creator God] has full rights over the creation of Asharis, Asharis have the full control over the things in our world; they are made for our purpose.[8]

One must note the anthropocentric approach here, with the constraint that it was not a general human-centric approach but rather an Ashari-centric perspective. Within the Ashari world, the wood was objectified and used in an instrumental way.[9] It would be incorrect to exaggerate this aspect, as this anthropocentrism was applicable only within the Ashari world and that too regarding what we may call raw materials. However, this aspect, on the one hand, shows that Asharis did not always consider themselves as just another element in the wide network of an inclusive world of humans, non-humans, ancestors, and gods. Plants or ancestors did not belong to the Ashari world; they belonged to the world of plants and to the world of ancestors, respectively. Asharis hold certain power over the objects in the Ashari world, and this power was absolutely necessary for the successful practice of asharippani. On the other hand, this also meant that Asharis did not hold power over plants, animals, or objects outside their world. Even within the Ashari world, the tools had a very different status from the raw materials, the function of which was mostly instrumental.

Tools, which belonged to the Ashari world, had their own agency, and asharippani was the co-action of hands and tools.[10] Asharis assigned different statuses to different tools, and their agency varied according to their status. Tools, similar to human beings, had jati—tools of one jati were not allowed to be used by a person from outside that jati. For example, the wooden measuring scale was considered as the symbol representing the Ashari jati. Mannans (stone masons in south Malabar) also used the wooden measuring scale, but they were made and marked differently. The *veethuli* (the wide chisel) was the most respected tool, and only the elder Asharis were supposed to handle it. The plaining tool was the lowest in this hierarchy and the first tool that beginners used when they started learning asharippani. Asharis considered tools as a means for an end only as much as their bodies were a means for the end goal of producing an artefact. While tools and Ashari bodies together conducted asharippani, they were not reduced to an instrumental status.[11] On the other hand, a piece of wood that was brought into the Ashari world was always considered as an object awaiting Ashari use. The raw materials were not marked by jati, and they moved across the jati boundaries, though in varied shapes and forms. Hence, tools and raw materials could not be explained together by the term 'object'. In other words, while Asharis *used* the wood, they did not just use the tools but acted along with them—as the hand gave direction to the chisel to move on the wood, the chisel also gave directions regarding the movement of hand. The reason for accidents and mistakes were often explained in terms of not following the direction of the chisel or not acting in concert with it. The idea was not that hands use chisels and chisels use hands, but that both co-acted and conversed with each other. Action itself was not just a means to an end; it was the way an Ashari was supposed to be in his world. Hence, an action was not defined or evaluated in terms of the quality of the end product or efficiency of the procedure. For example, tools were designed not for quick results but with a consideration that they co-acted with the hand in perfect symphony; time-saving methods were not an important concern.

The tools were also not an extension of the body in general or the hand in particular. The scholarship on handicraft has often expressed the idea that tools themselves start sensing the material on which they act and so become an extension of the hand.[12] Here, the tools transform into a part of the body and even disappear as an object. In other words, when tools act or have agency, they are understood in anthropomorphic terms and they lose their essence as an object. However, the Asharis considered tools as having independent agency, and in action, tools did not become part of the body but remained non-Ashari. While tools were not inanimate and passive objects, they did not behave like humans; in other words, in order to postulate the agency of the objects, it was not necessary to assign human-like qualities to objects. As mentioned earlier, even the notion 'object' itself was not a category in this schema. The tools and the wood on which Asharis worked were objects, but they were never considered as having similar properties. Wood, while having its own agency, was subordinated or was put under the control of the hand and tools—that is, in academic language, subjected to objectification. Hence, the category 'object' was not universal in the Ashari world. Similarly, 'human' was not a universal category but 'Ashari' was; here, each world was a universe, and universalization was limited to the boundaries of each world.

The process of generalization and abstraction was not limited to ideas or concepts. Asharis considered building a temple or making a table simultaneously a process of particularization and a process of abstraction. In the academic scholarship, the abstractness is attributed to the concept or to the word 'temple' or 'table'. The word 'table' is that which represents all tables but the one which does not exist as an object. It becomes an abstract by excluding the differences of each table and representing what is common in all tables. The abstractness is related to the possibility of representing. Asharis considered their action as a process of abstraction, and hence, the result of the action was simultaneously a particular and an abstracted object: every table they made was unique and abstract. Krishnan Ashari, a chief carpenter from Ampalappara, whom I interviewed, described this as follows:

> When we are asked to make a chair, we do not imagine the final form of it at the beginning. It is *pani* [work or action] that leads to the particular form. In other words, details are decided during the work, and so each chair will be different. But again, it is pani that leads us while we make the chair so that everybody sees it as a chair; during the pani, we don't have to repeatedly think that 'I am making a chair'.[13]

The initial reference point here was not an already abstracted image or drawing or even the word 'chair' as an abstract. The word 'chair' was a just a signal, a pointer, that moved the action of the Ashari in a particular direction. However, once the action began, the word or the concept 'chair' was no more a reference point during asharippani; the doing was self-referential.[14] It was in this doing that, as the process of abstracting, the object 'chair' was formed. The abstraction happens not just in thinking or language but also in action and in the object: the work of transformation of wood to a chair itself was a process of abstraction, and the object chair (which was not independent of the concept chair) was an abstracted object. Asharippani, a practice of knowing as doing, begins with the word chair, leaves the conceptual realm, and moves to a particular piece of wood that is then transformed to a chair, which is simultaneously a particular and an abstract object: particular in the sense that each chair is a unique object separated from all other chairs and abstract in the sense that each chair represents all the chairs that the Asharis made.

Asharippani, when described as a skill, technical knowledge, or expertise, is considered something that is acquired, stored, or deposited in the body, whereas when explained as doing, it is an activity in which the body is continuously engaged in knowing, and each time, something new emerges. In the former explanations, we follow a similar model wherein we define technology as applied science; here, the knowledge is created before the action. Asharis definitely had a notion of expertise, but it was similar to the notion of the expertise of a painter, a dancer, or a swimmer rather than an engineer. The technology the engineer is associated with clearly demarcates the knowledge aspect and the execution aspect. The engineer is the one who knows the science; his or her learning process is a journey from the general to the general: from one theory to another. The particulars he or she engages within the laboratory or in the workshop are just *examples*. He or she does not need to dwell in these examples. He or she may be involved in the production of the model, which is a physical representation of a conception. However, the model itself is an abstraction, and engineers are mostly not part of the physical production of even the model. In the self-description of modern technology, the factory workers who physically produce a car or the workshop assistants who identify and repair a problem in an engine have skill but are considered to not necessarily have knowledge; the division of labour is also a division between knowledge and skill, and the worker always engages with the particular. Asharis assumed that arriving at a theory, learning it, and applying it cannot be separated. There is no division of labour equivalent to the factory production. For example, theories of using wood for different purposes according to its hardness or malleability were created, learned, and applied only in doing. One may argue that Asharis knew beforehand which tree (mango, teak, mahogany, and so on) should be used for which purpose (furniture, roof frame, door, and so on) and that this was an acquired theoretical knowledge; however, in the Ashari understanding, this was just information (*vivaram*), not knowledge (*arivu*). The actual knowledge of appropriateness cannot be predetermined. This was because the essence of the mango tree was not defined by its species but by the properties of the individual tree in a particular context. To repeat an earlier argument, knowing a mango tree was to know what it does in a particular context. This knowing happened only in doing, and hence, asharippani, which was knowing as doing, included the simultaneous production of knowledge and its application. This also meant that learning asharippani was not a process of acquiring knowledge but a preparation of the body in a proper outward disposition for knowing—in short, *experiencing*.

The category of experience is central to the critique of claims of objectivity in knowledge production and in understanding the practices of knowing of subaltern communities. Experience has the pivotal role in the theorization of standpoint theories of knowledge and feminist criticisms of knowledge production. Questioning the notion of objectivity—which presupposes the knowledge of an objective reality of the outside world as a given—it was argued that different experiences create different realities.[15] The location of the person determines the experience of a person. Here, experiences are formed by processing sensations, or, in other words, they are an after-effect of this processing. People have different experiences because they process the sensations differently depending on their location. In other words, the difference in experiences is usually located in the processing of the sensations rather than the process of sensing itself. The eyes, ears, skin, and nerves work in the same way for all human beings, but the brain works according to the context. This concept—that sensing organs work in the same way for all—is the result of neuro-biological theories which pre-supposed a generalizable human body where the context is relevant only when the brain or mind is involved, which is again a continuation of the dichotomous conception of mind and body. In the recent times, however, even the neuro-biological theories consider the actions of the human body itself, not just the actions of brain, as located and contextual.[16] This implies that the process of experiencing itself differs according to the contexts; how the sensory organs act and react, how these sensations are processed, and how we act on the processed sensations vary according to the context of the training of the body. These latter theorizations resonate with the Ashari notion of experiencing. In short, for our purpose, we can conclude that, according to the Asharis, the way their hands sensed was different from the way the hand of a dominant-caste person sensed.

In the Ashari world, the concept of sensing was not limited to the five sensing organs. The idea of five sensing organs is important in both the Western and Sanskritic traditions of understanding the body and its interaction with the outside world.[17] While Asharis had the notion of five senses, they did not regard these as acting independently. In the Ashari way of knowing, in addition to the multiple permutations and combinations of the five senses, it also involved the hand and mind as sensing organs. The objective of the training in asharippani was to combine the sensing process of all these organs according to the context. For example, without focusing the mind on a particular object, it was not possible to clearly see the object, and only when the eye was focused on the object could the hand sense it properly. In certain other instances, such as while testing the hardness of a piece of wood, the ear should focus on the sound that the hand makes, and the sensation of touch and sound was processed together.

Asharis considered the mind as an organ which can extend to the outer world on its own without the help of the other sensory organs. They did not consider it as only the location of thought or as the control centre for bodily actions. The mind has the widest reach and access, and hence, controlling the mind was very important in learning asharippani. A conversation I had with Appu Ashari from Calicut was enlightening in this regard. According to Appu Ashari, 'In its natural state, the mind is always a wanderer, and only through practice, one can learn how to focus the mind on a particular object.'[18] The sensation that the mind received was not ideas or thoughts but impressions. While there was no specific term that described the corresponding sensation of the mind, such as *seeing* or *hearing*, the term *sraddha* (focus) was used on most occasions to describe how the mind related to the outside world. When you apply sraddha, the outside world impressed itself on the mind. This impression could be in the form of feeling or/ and thinking. The separation of feeling and thought was not necessary in this concept and the mind was not always the place where thinking was happening. I will explain the notion of the 'thinking hand' in the following part, which further clarifies the notion of the mind as an organ similar to other sensory organs. The way the mind focused on a place or on an object was through sraddha, and it could operate on its own or mixed with other sensations. Through the five sensory organs, one can extend sraddha to an object, an idea, or a place even in the absence of sensation; one can sense an object by the mind without seeing, touching, listening, and so on. One could also extend sraddha to intensify the sensation through other organs; for example, the mind could be extended to an object you are looking at and intensify the sensation of seeing.

The aforementioned notion of the mind did not completely reduce the mind into the body, which is clear from the absence of the concept of mind as a physical organ located at a specific part of the body. In some stories, the mind was the same as the heart; in some others, the mind was located in the chest; and in yet some others, inside the head. In conclusion, the mind, unlike other sensory organs, was not physically in contact with the outside; however, the mind can directly reach out to the outside world through sraddha. Feeling and thinking were considered similar to the acting or movement of the body, and hence, thinking and doing were not oppositional categories. Feeling was not a passive action of the mind where it just happened; it was also an act of the mind similar to thinking. Appu Ashari theorized the mind as follows:

> You may have specific feelings or thoughts even when you do not wish for those particular ones. This means that the mind is active, but sraddha [the focus of the mind] is somewhere else. The mind can but only be active except when you are unconscious or sleeping. In those situations, the mind is passive. Learning asharippani means learning to move sraddha into the places where the hand directs it to focus. When you have sraddha, then you can act without thinking in the mind.[19]

Asharis considered the sensing process as an active process of interaction between the body and the outside world. The mind, the five senses, and the hand extend to the outside world, which created impressions on the body, and the body acted according to these impressions. The sensing process was not a receiving process but a mutual engagement of the body and the outside world. Studies in handicraft have already explored much about the thinking hand. The attempt generally in this scholarship is to understand the action of the hand, which happens without the conscious directions from the brain. Based on the neurobiological studies, they argue that the action of the hand is the result of the interaction among the object on which the hand works, the hand itself, and the brain.[20] This is to challenge the idea of the brain being the control board of action, where it receives the signals from the outside world through nerves, processes it, and then directs the muscles to act. Here, the emphasis is on the role of the object and that of the hand.

In the Ashari world, the hand was an organ that could sense, feel, think, and act. While it could act independently, as mentioned earlier, without sraddha, all action would be improper. Here, the hand was not controlled by the mind; both acted together. The sensing of the hand was not completely explained by the sense of touch. It could again be understood as the impression created by the movement of the hand and the object it handles. The hand could store, recover, or use these impressions according to the context. Appu Ashari's deliberation on this was as follows:

> People say that we cannot consciously control the hand when we work. What they mean here is that the mind is not controlling the hand. This does not mean that the hand is like a machine which runs automatically once it is switched on. The hand thinks on its own and acts accordingly. When we learn asharippani, we are also learning how to make the hand think on its own.[21]

The concepts of muscle memory and the thinking hand are similar but not the same. In both the cases, there is a notion that the conscious mind is not involved in the process of action. The difference is that in the former, thinking is attributed to the brain and the hands act automatically without the involvement of thinking; in the latter, thinking is not necessarily the characteristic of the mind or brain alone—the hands, independent of the mind, could think and act. The action of the hand was not something automatic, but a thought-out, calculated one. Here, thought was more similar to impressions, which are not limited to concepts or ideas. An impression might be indescribable in words, and hence, scholars have explained the learning process in handicrafts as 'tacit knowing' or 'learning by doing'. Tacit knowledge is usually understood in contrast to learning from books or learning as a mental activity. Michael Polanyi's famous articulation, 'We can know more than we can tell', has become the axis around which much of the debate on tacit knowing has been revolving, and the major question in this debate is whether the knowledge that is communicable could be called 'tacit knowledge' at all. [22] If we understand tacit knowledge in this manner, then, from the Ashari theories of knowing, the idea of tacit knowledge has limited explanatory power because of the way in which the idea of 'telling' was conceptualized. Telling or communicating involved signs, not necessarily linguistic signs. Even when language was involved in creating impressions (as in listening to spoken words or observing a marked measure), it was not in the mind alone, where the learning or memorizing was happening. Here, the learner understood the meaning in impressionistic ways, which was memorized not just by the mind but also by the hand, the eyes, the ears, and so on. For example, listening to the teacher and memorizing the spoken words is an embodied action, same as observing the teacher's movement of their hand with the chisel and imitating it. The objective in learning asharippani was not to train the hand to act automatically without conscious thinking; it was to train the hand to think and act appropriate to the context.[23]

The basic principle of learning asharippani in this period can be summarized by the proverb 'Kannum manassum kayyil aayaal kazhukkolil kai vekkaam', which can be roughly translated as 'You can start the major works when your eyes and mind are within the control of the hands.' The coordination of the eye and the hand is considered fundamental to all craft practices. This coordination involves controlling the sensation through eyes within the reach of the hand. This also means that sight was not a dominating sensation over touch. However, the sensation of the hand cannot be completely understood in terms of touch, because the particular movements of the hand also influenced this sensation.

For example, the manipulation of the fingers, the relative strength of a grip, the part of the hand that was involved in the touch (that is, whether it was the back of the hand, the fingers, or the palm), and the directions of the movement were important to the way in which sensing happened through the hand. The learning of asharippani involved training in a particular way of sensing as well as processing of the sensations. Jati rules determined the possibilities of touchability and untouchability, what could be seen or looked at, what could not be, and so on. This particular way of training in sensing was limited to the Asharis. The boundaries that limited the sensing process were created by the jati rules, which means that jatis produced not only unique experiences but also unique methods of experiencing.

In the process of learning asharippani, the focus was not on knowing but on making the body ready for knowing. The objective was not to accumulate experience but to impart training in experiencing. Since learning was also a process of doing, knowing was part of this learning; still, what was learned was the capacity to experience. Here, Ashari concepts challenged the brahmanical notions of naturalness of experience or naturalness of capabilities as given at birth and argued that to experience something, one must learn how to experience. Asharis considered their experiencing as different from that of other jatis and that this difference had to be continuously produced; hence, the jati as difference was achieved rather than ascribed. An individual became an Ashari not just by being born in the Ashari jati; he became one through training. This Ashari conceptualization challenges the argument of merit in the current discussion of 'reservation versus merit', which demands that only those who have merit should be admitted for training (for engineering, medicine, and so on), assuming that the merit comes before training. Ashari understandings emphasized that the crucial aspect of capability is proper training. This also implied that reproduction of jati difference was crucially linked to the difference in the training.

The notion of difference in the Ashari practice of knowing needs to be further elaborated for understanding its concepts of singularity, binariness, and multiplicity. Philosophy (Western, Sanskritic, Chinese, and so on) has thrived by creating, questioning, and deconstructing binaries, and creating more of them throughout history, and many of them assume that binariness is a fundamental principle in which language, consciousness, and even the unconscious are structured.[24] Theologies based on the unity of God consider multitude as the binary opposition to the singularity of God. Advaita philosophy, in its multiple versions, spent its whole energy on the binary by questioning it and arguing for a singular essence.[25] The anthropological scholarship on indigenous knowledge also created a notion of unity through the notion of holistic perspective.[26]

My own argumentation regarding the non-binary thinking of Asharis is developed in the tradition of modern academy and hence uses a binary logic.

The Ashari practice of knowing ignored the binary as a fundamental principle and theorized difference as a relation between multiples. For example, their relation with any one of the other castes was always positioned not in the form of a binary relation (of opposition) but as a link in the network of jatis, and hence, any characteristic of the link was understood only in relation to many other adjacent links in the network. The oppositions, resistances, and compliances to forces were understood not in dialectical but in multilectical terms, and comparison—which was fundamental to any practice of knowing—always involved more than two instances or entities. The essence of a particular object—that is, what it does—was understood in comparison with more than one other objects. This was because, according to them, any qualitative or quantitative measure understood as degrees of difference was meaningful only if there were more than two entities. Nanu Ashari from Parali, with whom I had long discussions on different subjects on several occasions, has a detailed theory of how Asharis used comparative methods in asharippani. He explains:

These days, it seems that five is the number of Vishwakarma. They say that there are five jatis included in Vishwakarma, there are supposedly five Vedas, there are five elements with which we engage, five senses, and so on. In my childhood, three was the important number for Asharis (laughs). My grandfather always reminded that to confirm anything, we need to repeat it at least three times. If anyone gives you only two options, you should think a third one in mind and compare all the three. People may ask you, 'Which wood is appropriate for making a door—mango tree or teak?' If we assume that the most important aspect of a door is its strength to resist push and pull, then we are asked here to compare the hardness. One can say that teak is harder than mango tree. But is teak much harder and mango tree much softer than required? In order to understand that, we need to bring another one, say, jackfruit tree. Do you get it—you seem to be confused! Okay, I will give another example that my father told me. He asked me, 'Why do we need a measuring scale at all?' I said that it was to measure the gap between two things. He then explained, 'If we want to know the distance between two points, we can use any stick. But in asharippani, the question is always, "Is this distance too big or small?" For this, you need two other distances to compare, and for that, we need two more sticks. The measuring scale is a combination of multiple sticks in one wood piece.' You see, if there are only two pieces, we can still say which is taller or shorter, but if you need to know how much taller or shorter, you need a third piece; don't you see? You are not convinced, are you? This is the thing: Asharis are not good at explaining in words. Even I clearly understood what my grandfather and father told me only when I did the actual comparison during work.[27]

I will explain the emergence of five as the number of Vishwamkarma in the fifth chapter. Whether five or three is the key number is not crucial for our discussion; what is important is the idea of difference as compared on a scale rather than the difference between two entities. The difference between two entities brings in binaries, dialectics, and dichotomies, whereas the difference on a scale implies multiple degrees, networks, and forces acting from multiple directions, functioning as a three-dimensional hierarchical series. Nanu Ashari explains the consequence of this for asharippani. The identities, the self, and the essence, or, in general, all the notions of singularities, depended not on a single (oppositional) other but on the relationship with multiple other entities in the network, and, according to him, the minimum number for multiplicity was three. He struggles to explain this to me, whom he rightly understood as coming from a world where the binary is a fundamental principle of categorization. He also points out that language itself is not sufficient to express the multilectical epistemology of asharippani. Doing, which was usually considered a singular event or as an *example*, was the proper domain of this multilectical approach. Doing always incorporates an object not as a unique object but as an object in a network and, hence, always approaches it in a multilectical dimension. Here, the difference of Ashari knowing was not that Asharis were not dealing with concepts but objects. The concept of hardness was very much present during their work on a wood piece, but it appears among hardness of other wood pieces, not as a property but as a comparative notion as well as being entwined with the object itself: in short, as an impression. Nanu Ashari, in order to communicate to me, was struggling to translate an impression into a concept; in other words, he was trying to convey an impression, not just the meaning, through words. Knowing was an impressionistic process, and hence, words, concepts, and ideas were not separate from sensations and feelings, and all these came together to compose an impression.

So far, we have discussed knowing as doing within the Ashari world. How was it different when Asharis ventured into other worlds? On the one hand, the modalities of experiencing, which were formed by training in the jati world, were applicable in the outside world as well. However, the notion of what were knowable and what were unknowable determined the difference between knowing inside and outside of the Ashari world. The difference, in this sense, was determined more by ethics than methods.

Knowing in Other Worlds: The World of Plants

Asharis engaged in knowing in their own world according to specific conventions, which were not applicable when they entered the other worlds, where there were strict conditions for engaging in knowing or in positioning oneself in an 'inquiry mode'. The rules of this positioning varied, depending on which world they were engaging with. In order to understand the practice of knowing that Asharis engaged with in these different worlds, we need to explore two aspects of knowing that they considered important: methodological and ethical. The first defines the concept of knowing itself and the second defines the boundary conditions of knowing. We already discussed the methodological aspect of asharippani in the Ashari world, where the ethical question was expressed as the duties of Asharis: engaging in pani while following appropriate procedures such as respecting elders, respecting tools, using only the prescribed tools for specific works, and so on. In an outside world, knowing was further limited because, as an outsider, dwelling in that world was temporary or partial. An Ashari as an outsider to the world of plants needed to respect the rules of that world when engaging with it. It was not possible and desirable to know these rules completely, and one had to respect and accept the sovereignty of this world. One of the songs about entering the world of plants explains the rules of engagement with the elements of that world. It begins with a notion of unfamiliarity as well as undesirability of knowing everything and hence the need to listen carefully what that world tries to tell the outsider.

> Do not seek the inner truths,
> Ought not know the words that were told by,
> (Fore)fathers and mothers and gods to them
> Should not look into the inner entanglements,
> Pass through with humility,
> They are the rulers and they are superior,
> Listen and follow the path they whisper.[28]

These lines from a song popular among older generations of Asharis in northern Malabar explain the limitation of knowing in the world of plants. The conceptualization of animals and plants as not part of our own world needs to be emphasized in the context of sociological and anthropological theories of indigenous worlds, which, in their attempt to establish radical alterity with the modernist notions of a human-centric world, assume living, dead, human, and non-human as part of the same world.[29] The question of alterity is important, but not at the cost of (wrongly) imagining a simplistic holism at best or a kind of anthropomorphic world at worst. The idea that indigenous societies believe in a world where humans, animals, plants, and inanimate objects are integral parts of the same universe and are ruled by the same rule is just a reverse-anthropomorphism—the idea that everything in the nature is similar and human beings are not different from plants and animals—which is not correct, at least in the case of the twentieth-century Ashari world. The difference with the modern human-centric world in this case was less about holism, or incorporation of humans as a part of plant and animal worlds, than about an ethical positioning regarding knowing and not knowing. However, this idea of undesirability of knowing completely did not prevent the Asharis from acting in that world. Then, the question is, how does one act with partial knowing? The song further explains how to act in this condition. The first step is to take permission from the tree to approach and ask forgiveness if any kind of pain is imparted by improper actions:

> With the blessing of the forefathers
> Accepting the humble request to follow my own duty,
> Allow me to approach you,
> You are the only one to decide and,
> You are the only one to help.
> Forgive me when I act improperly,
> Lead me in my action to propriety.[30]

To reiterate, the idea of sovereignty of plants in their world was considered as given, and there was no attempt to understand the secrets of that world. Asharis believed that it was important not to enter the depths of the world but to engage with the periphery. They could not understand the way a tree 'thinks', and even if that were possible, it was not ethically desirable. There was a principled disengagement with that world, and the act of knowing had limitations in this situation. There was a belief that the plants and animals are powerful enough to protect themselves and that humans were not superior beings who could control their world. In this imaginary, if an Ashari could convince a tree that it was absolutely necessary for him to cut it to fulfil his own duty, there was no reason for the tree to resist it. At the same time, it was important to make sure that he was acting in a principled manner and that the tree was not resisting. The next section of the song mentions how one could convince the tree by listening to it:

> From a distance, see the tree,
> See the branch and leaves.
> When you are four feet close
> Touching by back of the hand,
> Listen to the words the tree utters.
> When you squeeze the leaves,
> It will give you the odour.
> When you mix all together in mind,
> The facts will emerge into light.[31]

The use of touch, taste, and smell for knowing is obvious here, and this has been much discussed in the scholarship of indigenous practices. However, as mentioned earlier, this scholarship does not engage sufficiently with the question of how one learns to 'sense', because of the idea that sensing is somehow a natural capacity. The aforementioned song, on the other hand, is an attempt to teach how to sense in a different or other world, similar to learning in the Ashari world. What was important here was the idea that in the world of plants, Asharis positioned themselves on the 'receiving end', and for ethical reasons, they withheld the active interventional form of knowing. This did not prevent them from interacting with the plant world and knowing what was already revealed. Further, to know what was revealed was not natural but needed training. The focus of the training was mostly on reading the signs, which meant a comparative analysis of colours, movements, tastes, hardness or softness, wetness or dryness, and so on.

Asharis, like scientists, attempted to understand the 'forces of nature' through sensing (in terms of making sense of it), but unlike the engineers, they did not attempt to control the 'forces of nature' but to tap into the forces to manipulate them. The difference here is similar to the difference between the windward movement of a ship with sails and that of a ship with a steam engine. In both cases, the law of nature is learned and utilized to create movements; however, in the former case, the attempt is to manipulate the natural force (the wind), whereas in the latter, the idea is to create an oppositional force that can overcome the natural force. Needless to say, the latter creates far more possibilities of travel with less use of bodily labour.

The tree that the Ashari cut was considered a gift handed over to him and not something he possessed using his knowledge. The humbleness might have reduced the effectiveness, now conventionally measured in the domain of modern technological production, as a ratio of output (the product) to the input (time and labour); however, the efficiency increases when it is measured in terms of economy of ethical negotiation and responsibility towards other worlds. Asharis, according to these terms, were only partially responsible for cutting the tree. The efficiency increases in other ways as well, as the availability of wood required was drastically reduced due to ethical limitations, which motivated a desire to produce more from less, mostly in qualitative terms. For producing more from less, you need to invoke more creativity and imagination. In conclusion, Ashari interaction with the world of plants was based on a relation of revealing and accepting, of reading and analysing the language of the plant world, and of accepting the ethical responsibility of not knowing.

Knowing in Other Worlds: The World of Dominant Jatis

In the engagement with the worlds of other jatis, Asharis had to invoke different strategies depending on whether those worlds were that of dominant castes or further subordinated ones. Due to the rarity of accessible narratives, my description of the relations between Asharis and other subaltern jatis is limited. My focus will be more on the engagement of Asharis with the world of dominant castes in general and Nampoothiris in particular. Asharis entered in the dominant-caste world only in the context of asharippani. Nampoothiris rarely directly supervised asharippani; it was usually delegated to the *karyasthan*s (managers), who were from the other dominant castes like Variyars or Nairs. Nampoothiri appropriation of asharippani was mediated through other jatis, which were in the middle of jati hierarchy between Asharis and Nampoothiris. When a member from the Nair jati gave directions and supervised the Asharis' work, the Asharis had to recognize not only that this manager was from a dominant jati but also that he was representing a member of the Nampoothiri jati, which was dominant to both his jati and that of the Nairs. Articulation of hierarchy and difference as theorized by many scholars was central to the mutual engagement of different jatis. However, this is a more accurate description of both how dominant castes understood caste in general and their view of relation to the oppressed castes in particular.[32] Ambedkar was questioning this notion when he stated that the jati system is a graded hierarchy. The dominating power and resisting forces in the jati system were not in dialectical opposition; the system was a network of forces which pulled and pushed from multiple directions. The metaphor of the vertical ladder in which each jati was arranged neatly on a step with one jati above and another below explains only one aspect of domination within the jati system. For example, if we consider the production of knowledge in a jati system, the metaphor of concentric circles in which the Brahmins at the centre exploited the knowledge produced by the other jatis through centripetal forces of acharam may be more appropriate. When we consider the question of mobility and untouchability, jati worked simultaneously as a repulsive force that kept the oppressed jatis away and as a compressive force that bound them inside their jati boundaries. It was inside this boundary, for example, within the Ashari world, that the oppressed jatis attempted to build their limited autonomy, which always required a force of resistance in order to just survive within the boundary. For Asharis, asharippani as a practice of knowing provided a force of resistance, which might not have challenged the jati domination but prevented their degradation to absolute slavery; surviving itself was resistance, and for this, they needed capabilities to produce forces, which in the case of Asharis were provided by their practice of knowing.

Unlike many other oppressed jatis, the physical workplaces of Asharis, such as houses and temples, were mostly within the world of the dominant jatis. Here, constructing an opaque world was more difficult for the Asharis compared to the case of other oppressed jatis, and it was through limiting themselves in pani that they attempted to create this opacity. Shanmughan Ashari from Mundur, with whom I had conversations on different occasions, explained to me that the basic principles of engaging with the dominant castes were to keep distance, minimize conversations, and avoid direct questions. He mentioned that his grandfather was more concerned about how to teach the grandchildren to 'keep distance' or avoid engagement with the 'Thamprans' (lords) at the workplace than teaching them the actual work. Literally and figuratively, the children had to learn a new language, because language was overdetermined by the hierarchical jati relation. In the instance of an Ashari conversing with a person form a dominant jati, *veedu* (house) had to be translated into *kuti* (poor house), *uppu* (salt) into *veluthaaram* (the white thing), *njaan* (I or me) into *adiyan* (your servant), and so on. The body language also had to be submissive and respectful. These caste practices are already well discussed in the sociological scholarship. According to Shanmughan, the more interesting aspect about learning this new language was that by the time you were permitted to enter an adult conversation among the Asharis, the focus would shift from 'actually respecting' to 'showing respect'. It was also a lesson in how to use the 'weapons of the weak'. This learning happened through listening to the sarcastic comments made by the elders outside the workplace, murmuring, and sometimes mentioning thampran with curse words (for example, in toddy shops, when dominant-caste people were not present). The ability to express contempt mostly came from the awareness that the dominant castes were dependent on them for knowledge practice.

Rajan, whom I met in Palakkad, is a middle-aged Ashari who is very enthusiastic in collecting proverbs used by Asharis. He mentions two phrases that he had heard in his childhood about the dependence of the dominant castes on oppressed castes. Both phrases hint at the recognition that Asharis were superior to the dominant castes in the hierarchy of knowledge but inferior to them in power relations. The first one is a direct statement of this parallel hierarchy: 'Ashari palaka virikkum, thampran paaya virikkum'—the Ashari spreads the wooden plank (metaphor for making a couch) and the lord spreads the bed. The second one is more about the direct dependence of the dominant castes on Asharis for constructing a roof over their heads: the phrase 'Ashari uli vecha Nairude thalayil mazhayum veyilum'—when the Ashari puts down his chisel, the sun and rain fall upon the Nair's head. The claim of superiority in knowledge was central to the

Ashari understanding of the negotiation with the changing world of dominant castes and the colonialists. However, in this period, such a claim was not made by other oppressed castes about themselves in their respective narratives. The fact that the superiority in knowledge did not translate into higher status or superior power shows that knowledge as a discursive category and as a practice was not central to the operation of power in the caste system. This will become clearer when I analyse, in the third chapter, the Nampoothiri claims of superiority based on acharam at this period.

Jati was simultaneously dominant in certain situations and hegemonic in certain other situations. Here, dominance is understood by the oppressed castes more as their acceptance of the possibility of the oppressive castes deploying a superior force over them than as a conviction in the values that enabled those forces, whereas in the case of hegemony, the oppressed accepted the dominant values as well. Asharis recognized the power of the dominant jatis to exert violence over them. It is this fear that forced them to accept the domination, and in spaces where this possibility was absent, they expressed their contempt freely. The shift from paying respect to showing respect was an activity of resistance towards the domination. The situation of hegemony, on the other hand, involved the conviction of a superior force, which created the hierarchy other than that of the dominant caste and the acceptance of the values of that superior force. Asharis at this period considered that jati as a system was pervasive and predetermined; each jati had to follow their own jati rules and follow the vocations attributed to them. This belief could also be explained as a belief in acharam. Acharam (which is detailed in Chapter 3) combined daily rituals and their justificatory norms that enabled the hegemonic brahmanical principles of the jati system. This did not mean that Asharis were convinced by the brahmanical stories or myths of origin of jatis. This was more about understanding a situation where negotiation was impossible unlike the situation of dominance. The difference between the two aforementioned situations determined their strategies in engaging or not engaging with the dominant castes. Asharis in the first three quarters of the twentieth century did not question the hegemonic principles of acharam, even though they resisted in limited ways the dominance of the opressive jatis. Asharippani provided certain power and limited autonomy to Asharis; however, this was subordinated by the hegemony of acharam. In a later period (after the 1970s), as analysed in Chapter 5, once the hegemony was lost and dominance continued, they started to challenge the dominance in different ways than those in the former period.

Knowing in Other Worlds: The World of the Sayip

The Ashari engagement with the colonial world was framed based on the idea of epistemological differences but was formed as a triangular relation with the dominant caste acting as the third angle. The method of work and training was a major area of contestation between the Asharis and the colonialists. This was also mediated through the new discourse on knowledge of the reforming dominant castes. The colonial understanding of jatis, their relations, and the idea of 'traditional occupation' was influenced by the narratives created by the dominant castes in this period. The mapping of the colonial concepts of various kind of intellectual and manual labour to the existing caste hierarchies positioned the artisanal castes at the lower level of this hierarchy of knowledge. From this perspective, Asharis were not capable of abstract thinking and their training is basically a training in skill.

The report of the industrial education conferences held in various provinces in India during 1901–1902 revealed the objectives and the anxieties of the colonial administrators in transforming the methods and training processes of artisanal practices.[33] As preparation for the industrial education conferences, the education department of the Government of India distributed a questionnaire to government officials, industrial school administrators, and private businessmen. Through this questionnaire, the government sought to collect information regarding the native methods of training and the possibility of reform of the native system. The questionnaire asked the informants to provide their opinion regarding the advantages and disadvantages of the native systems of training of artisans over the British system of industrial training schools, regarding the possibility of improving the native system, and about the desirability of including native methods in industrial training schools. Another question was whether the native system could be 'influenced by outside expert suggestions, advice, or interference, and how best'.[34]

These questions, on the one hand, expressed the intentions of the colonial state to translate and bring artisanal production activities into the field of the 'mapped' and controlled territory of colonial governing practices. On the other hand, the questions also showed that the government did not desire to transform the artisanal production into the factory production system; rather, the colonialists wanted to transform artisanal practices into a (modernized) traditional knowledge practice. The colonial officers in the field made these intentions clear through the answers to the questionnaire. The superintendent of the Madras School of Arts, Alfred Chatterton, submitted a detailed reply to the questionnaire.[35] In this reply, he opined that the native system as such cannot survive without the modernization of tools and methods, especially in competition with the factory production system. He mentioned that 'artisans are cut off from the rest of the industrial world and continue to pursue the most antiquated methods of working notwithstanding the fact that they have long been superseded everywhere else'.[36] According to Chatterton, the best procedure to reform artisanal practice was the method followed by the Madras School of Arts. The school, as a first step, provided training in drawing to new apprentices of all trades. Drawing is the 'most important step in learning how to produce standard patterns', a method about which the 'native artisans are completely ignorant'.[37] Chatterton underscored the learning of basic arithmetic and the English language as well because this would help Asharis in converting their trade into a business.

The Principal of the Madras Engineering College, H. D. Love, rejected the idea that the artisans should gradually be transformed into factory workers. Even though he supported the reformation of artisanal practices, he insisted that it should not be at the cost of the skills 'that produced wonderful artifacts of the yesteryears'.[38] Further, he differentiated between the practices of trained artisans and engineers, which he thought should co-exist in the contemporary industrial scenario in India. Artisans 'pick up knowledge of their father's craft' at an early childhood 'in the same way as they learn their mother tongue'. Engineers learn the trade 'as one studies a foreign language through the mother tongue'. [39] The advantage of the latter was that an engineer attains 'not only the capability to talk (that is, to actually execute the work) but also an expertise in the grammar of the language (that is, the knowledge of what he executes)'.[40] In other words, according to Love, the reformation of artisanal practice should focus on increasing the skill of the artisans, not on imparting knowledge about their practice.

The aforementioned report contained several other colonial administrators' suggestions regarding the reformation of artisanal practice, and most of them reflected the views of Chatterton and Love. These suggestions can be summarized as a proposal for the institutionalization, standardization, and modernization of artisanal practices. It was exactly these attempts that the Asharis tried to both oppose and ignore in reforming their trade according to contemporary requirements. As mentioned earlier in this chapter, asharippani was not a practice of applied knowledge, nor was it a unidirectional movement from the abstract to the concrete or vice versa. For Asharis, the abstract was not an already formed idea, drawing, or any other fixed sign system. For colonialists, this was not only a methodological issue but also a problem of control.

The director of the Public Works Department (PWD) of the Madras government issued a directive in 1910 that the engineers should exactly follow the drawings and plans for all the buildings constructed by the department in various towns.[41] While the preparation of drawings was already an existing practice among civil engineers, in many cases, for practical reasons, the actual construction did not follow the plans or drawings. As a result, there was always an escalation in the estimated cost of construction. It was in this context that the director issued the aforementioned directive. In a reply to this, the Assistant Engineer of PWD at Kozhikode, M. J. Reed, submitted that he needed more time to implement this directive.[42] According to Reed, the masons or carpenters were incapable of working according to a drawing or a plan. It would take time to train them in reading drawings and to teach them to work according to the plans. Reed observed that 'the carpenters still measure using their own measuring scales which are marked in units of fingers and feet'. There were standard conversion tables converting fingers and feet into inches, but Asharis did not follow them. Reed stated that 'the carpenters here are reluctant to abandon their traditional measuring practices' because 'they consider these practices as part of their religious belief'.[43] It is obvious that what Reed named a 'religious belief of Asharis' was actually the belief in caste practices.

The issue of the use of drawings was not just a question of whether Asharis could learn to read the drawings; it was a question of the stark difference between the two kinds of practices. In the colonial form, knowledge *represents* something outside itself and it is always a knowledge *of* something. This conception separates the object of knowledge from the knowledge about the object. The use of models and drawings are knowledge in the form of representation. Within colonial practice, it was difficult even to begin a task without this knowledge. In an article in the fifteenth issue of the *Journal of Indian Art*, B. C. Temple, a colonial officer, expressed his surprise over the native system of building construction, which never used drawings or models. He wondered 'like many other Englishmen, what manner of men, they were who raised grand buildings, the remains of which we see in India'.[44] He observed a temple construction at Karli (a town near Pune in present-day Maharashtra) and reported the conversation he had with the overseer of the construction about the chief mason:

'How long had he [the mason] been at it?'
'Oh a long while—many months.'
'How much longer would he be?'
'He could not say, there is no need for hurry.'
'Had he any plans?'

'Yes.'

'On paper?'

'No, why should he have [them] on paper?'

'But how do you know what it will look like?'

'The master mason knew, he just gives directions to others. I will know when it finishes.'[45]

For Temple, it was seemingly impossible to begin construction work without drawings. Even after witnessing the native method of construction, he was not convinced that the native masons or carpenters were reliable for anything other than simple works:

> They may be safely trusted to make a reasonably good house, to bridge a small stream, or road on special circumstances with reasonable intelligence; but, unless directed, they will not make a plan or an estimate. There are some *mistiris* [contractors] who understand plans, but many, and by no means the most incompetent in the practice, when asked to explain details, gaze at them helplessly for a while and then look up wishfully saying '*Garib Parivar* (poor family)!!'[46]

In the hierarchical series of knowledge, colonialists positioned practices significantly below theoretical or written knowledge. They believed that theoretical knowledge can always represent practice. Drawings and plans were such knowledges which represented the construction practices. For colonizers, this knowledge was important to control, order, or, in short, to govern the practices of the natives. The Asharis clearly attempted to escape from these governing practices to keep their authority over asharippani. P. C. Kuttikrishna Menon, who was a Sanskrit scholar and a *vydya* (native medical practitioner), noted in his autobiography that Asharis (in the 1930s and 1940s) consciously decided 'what kinds of reforms should be accepted and what should be rejected'.[47] While constructing a new house, Menon sought the help of an engineer from Kochi for designs and drawings. He gave the design supplied by the engineer to the chief carpenter, who in turn asked Menon to explain the drawings. After Menon's explanation, the *moothashari* (chief carpenter) asked Menon, 'You know what type of house you want, and I know how to construct it. Then what is the purpose of these drawings?' Menon stated that 'no one referred to those drawings after these conversations, but they still lie in the attic of the old house covered with dust and smoke'.[48]

Menon added, 'The chief carpenter was not ready to compromise on the relative proportions of the rooms, but he easily accommodated modern facilities in the kitchen and the front room according to my demands.'[49] Also, in his construction, the moothashari used many objects which were relatively 'modern', such as iron nails for joints and clay tiles for roofs. However, he was resistant in modelling his practice according to the drawings and plans prepared by an engineer.

Asharis did not completely reject the materials that emerged in the colonial world. The accommodation of new objects into existing methods of asharippani requires creativity, flexibility, and openness toward changes. The introduction of the two objects mentioned earlier—the iron nail and clay tiles—demonstrates these features of asharippani during the first half of the twentieth century. Till the end of the nineteenth century, Asharis designed the wooden frames for the roof in such a way that pegs or nails had very limited application. Even for complex assemblies, they used the lap joint, box joint, or dovetail joint techniques, which limited the use of fasteners and pegs.[50] The British engineers introduced iron nails to the Asharis in Malabar in the 1840s during the construction of a government guest house at Kozhikode. However, even in the beginning of the twentieth century, as there was a very limited availability of iron nails, Asharis continued their earlier methods for making joints and couplings.[51] By the 1920s, the availability of iron increased, especially in the form of scrap from the railway workshops, and many small industrial units began manufacturing iron nails along with many other fabrication materials such as bolts, nuts, and screws.[52] The Assistant Engineer in the PWD at Kozhikode, E. W. Thomason, wrote in 1923 that the carpenters in Malabar have started using iron nails, 'but only as an additional reinforcement for joints'. He added that the carpenters, as they were still an 'uneducated and ignorant class', could not fully accept 'the significance of modern construction materials and reform their practices accordingly'. [53]

If this was the colonial interpretation of selective adoption and adaptation of changes, Asharis viewed themselves as flexible but cautious regarding the changes in that period. In a conversation with Karuppan, a chief carpenter, P. Govinda Variyar described the attitude of Asharis towards the changes in the construction filed.[54] Karuppan considered himself as a person who was ready to experiment. According to him, Asharis always observed external conditions, including weather and time, and hence, they easily sensed the pulse of the moment. Karuppan further explained how, disregarding his father's concerns, he has started using a new form of joint using iron nails. Even his father started using it after he found it simple and convenient. For Karuppan, the criterion for accepting a new practice was that it should 'allow the combination of proper measure and beauty'. If the measure was not proper, 'he [an Ashari] would be nailing not the wood piece, but the body of his forefather. Asharis can do only asharippani. One can do a new thing, if and only if it is asharippani'. [55] Karuppan here assumed that all Asharis knew what asharippani was. According to him, the reference point for evaluating the propriety of a new material or method was the caste rules—such as the aprropriate use of of tools and raw material as explained earlier—which defined asharippani. The assimilation of clay tiles for roofs is another example in which Asharis incorporated the changes within the norms of asharippani.

By the end of the nineteenth century, the Basal Evangelical Mission established various industrial units all over Malabar. The mission opened three tile factories in the Malabar district at Palakkad, Kozhikode, and Kannur. Even though tiles were available from the early decades of the century until the last quarter of the nineteenth century, only a few houses, such as those of the local rulers, had tiled roofs. This was because the custom prevented even the smaller landlords from having tile-roofed houses.[56] By the end of the century, however, we can observe that the custom was relaxed, and many rich landlords started roofing their houses with clay tiles. Clay tiles brought two important changes in the methods of roof construction. A new kind of frame was required to hold the tiles properly. Asharis invented a new model of frame that was a long, square wooden pole, which replaced the old round-shaped bamboo poles. The older bamboo poles were usually tied to the main frame of the roof. In the case of new poles, Asharis started using iron nails to fix them to the frame.

The clay tiles and iron nails were factory products, and their sizes were measured in inches. Asharis had to adapt to the new material and to a new measuring system. Even though the colonial and Ashari systems of measuring had feet as a standardized measure for length, the actual length of a foot was different in these two systems. The colonialists attempted to standardize all the units of measurement and make them uniform all over India. The Government of India in 1905 appointed a committee to reform the use of weights and measures and to suggest standardized measures. Earlier, in 1865, W. H. Bayley had submitted a report with suggestions to improve the measuring systems then in practice. While considering the reform initiative in 1905, the Director of the Department of Weights and Measures opined on Bayley's system that, though it 'may not be scientifically the most perfect, [it] is practically the best in the present circumstances'.[57] Further, the Director suggested that 'the time has come to create a system which is both scientifically and practically the best'.[58] While the members of the committee were not in unison in their opinions regarding the reforms, they suggested that 'the government can implement the English system causing least inconvenience to people'.[59]

While generally agreeing with the committee, W. T. Denison, an officer with the Madras government, observed that the system proposed by the committee would be the 'simplest mode of getting over a difficulty without running too much counter to native ideas, fancies and prejudices'. According to him, the general principle should be that the 'name [of measures] shall be general and that the measures will be easily assimilated to the English standards'.[60] Denison, on the one hand, thought that the native systems of measures should be homogenized and made comparable with the English systems. On the other hand, he also believed that this should be executed in a manner that would be acceptable to the natives as well. This colonialist attempt was part of the general effort to make native practices visible, knowable, and controllable.

The conflict between the colonial and native systems occurred mainly in transactions between the natives and the government, such as in tax payments and government purchases or in commerce between the natives and the Europeans. Asharis generally did not engage in any transactions, commercial or otherwise, with the government or with the European traders until the second decade of the twentieth century. After the introduction of new construction materials such as iron nails or clay tiles, Asharis began using measures such as inches in their practice. Even then, as we saw earlier, Asharis incorporated the new measures by translating them into the unit of fingers.

Achu Ashari, a chief carpenter from Palakkad, remembered how his grandfather used to engage in arguments with the latter's elder brother (most probably in the 1930s) regarding the translation of inches into fingers.[61] The grandfather used clay tiles from the Basel Mission Tile factory at Olavakkod as a standard for inch (a tile was twelve inches in length), and he converted 3 inches as equal to five fingers. His brother thought that it was more accurate to equate 6 inches with ten-and-a-half fingers, in which case an inch would be slightly longer than in the former case. Even though they differed in opinion regarding the length of an inch, this difference did not create any problem for them to work together. Achu Ashari's point was that it was not a precalculated conversion method that determined the practice. Both his grandfather and his brother determined the width between the two wooden frames which supported the tile using the tile itself as a measure.

Using the tile itself as a measure is a perfect example for understanding the difference between the Ashari ways of knowing and the colonial methods of knowledge production. In the Ashari practice, knowing and using that knowledge was a single activity; in other words, knowing was doing. The processes of measuring and understanding the unit of measure were simultaneous. Hence, the separation of representation from practice, which was one of the fundamental characteristics of colonial knowledge, was not relevant for Ashari practices. In other words, by keeping the colonial separation in abeyance, Asharis avoided the intrusion of colonial knowledge into their practice. It is important to note that Asharis were not incapable of generalization or abstraction. The *muzhakkol* (the wooden measuring scale that Asharis used) itself was an object of abstracted measure. In the colonial form, the production of knowledge started from the particular and ended in the general (which is the only form of knowledge) through abstraction. In the Ashari practice, the movement between the particular and the general was a reversible action. On the one hand, an abstract measure was present in the form of muzhakkol, but an Ashari learned or understood the measure through the action of measuring. The continuous movement between generalization and particularization constituted the practice of asharippani. In other words, Asharis avoided the colonial intervention not by abstaining from the process of abstraction as such but by negating the separation of abstraction from the process of particularization. In the early twentieth century, asharippani as a practice of knowing played a crucial role in the Ashari engagement with dominant colonial practices. To conclude:

> The hand pours rhythm into the chisel,
> The eyes drive the hands to the wood,
> Between the hands and the wood,
> The chisel dances in swirls,
> The hands keep knowing,
> And the wood twirls into a door,
> And the door transmutes into the one and the many.[62]

How did the epistemological aspect of practices of knowing as explained in this chapter relate to the sociopolitical aspects in this period? How did Asharis politically negotiate with the colonial–brahmanical interventions into their practices? The next chapter explores these questions centred on the concept of ignoring as a form of resistance.

Notes

1. The period mentioned in this chapter is roughly between the 1870s and the 1970s. Hence, the generalizations made in this chapter are applicable only to this period; readers may add 'in this period' for every conclusion made here. Ashari worlds before and after this period were very different, and hence, the theories elaborated in this chapter regarding Ashari practice of knowing should be understood as a changing phase of the Ashari world. In short, this particular world was created in the context of jati domination and colonial intervention in the aforementioned period. When the context changed, this world disappeared and a different world emerged, which is explained in Chapter 5.

2. Asharippani at this period involved designing, organizing, and conducting various aspects of temple and house constructions: finding the best location, planning the design according to the caste and economic status, conducting all the woodwork for the construction of a house or a temple, such as windows, doors, and, most importantly, the roofs, and so on. Also, Asharis were in charge of directing the masons who built the walls and floors.

3. From positivists to relativists, there are infinite incommensurable definitions of science, but most of them agree that what we expect from science is a theory about the material world. Richard Feynman, one of the most popular philosophers and propagandists of science, writes: 'Science means, sometimes, a special method of finding things out. Sometimes it means the body of knowledge arising from the things found out. It may also mean the new things you can do when you have found something out, or the actual doing of new things. This last field is usually called technology.' Richard Feynman, *The Meaning of It All* (Boston: Addison-Wesley, 1998), 3.

4. In the discussion of experiential learning, John Dewey proposed a concept of continuum of experience. Here, he argued that the previous experiences influence the current experience and, therefore, that experience is not just a product of some external action but itself an actor which can cause change in further experiences. For him, experience is not just personal but an ensemble of subjective elements of the experiencing subject and the social factors or environment that enables an experience. Here, he was hinting towards the issue of different ways of experiencing. However, his focus was not on the moments of experiencing but what was experienced and how it effected the future experiences. Similarly, Sundar Sarukkai in his inquiry about the relation between experience and knowledge brings a separation between 'experience as choice' and 'lived experience' which is given. In both cases, the focus is on what is gained as experience, not the process of experiencing. See John Dewey, *Experience and Education* (New York: Touchstone, 1997); Sundar Sarukkai, 'Understanding Experience', in *The Cracked Mirror: An Indian Debate on Experience and Theory*, ed. Gopal Guru and Sundar Sarukkai, 46–70 (New Delhi: Oxford University Press, 2012).

5. According to Karl Popper, a statement is scientific when it is falsifiable but not yet falsified. This implies that for a theory to become scientific, it should withstand without change under proper experimentation. If there is disparity between the evidence and a theory, then the theory is falsified. What makes a theory scientific is its capability to represent the reality upon repeated experiments, without any change. For Popper, particular theories may change, but a theory is constant within the duration in which it is scientific. Karl Popper, *Conjectures and Refutations: Growth of Scientific Knowledge* (New York Routledge, 2002).

6. Those who are familiar with George Berkeley's arguments on perception and ideas (especially the much-discussed question of pain analogy) may find some similarity with the Ashari notion of action-dependent essence. However, both the Ashari notion of the possibility of ideas and sensations being located outside the mind and the Ashari separation of existence and essence contradict

Berkeley's idealist notion of mind-dependence of ideas and sensations and even his notion of the existence of objects. George Berkeley, *A Treatise Concerning the Principles of Human Knowledge* (New York: Dover Publications, 2012).

7. Interview with Keshavan Ashari (20 January 2009).

8. Interview with Ravi (1 February 2009).

9. For Heidegger, the appropriation of objects into standing reserves is a feature of modern technology and is a departure from the earlier concepts of handicraftsmen. Heidegger seems to differentiate the difference in conceptions of objects only between two worlds: that of the pre-modern and the modern represented by handicraftsmen and engineers, respectively. According to him, handicraftsmen did not imagine the natural world as standing reserve. For Asharis, all humans were not occupying the same world, and plants were in a different world of their own. In the Ashari understanding, plants in a forest were not a standing reserve, but they became standing reserve when they were brought into an Ashari world. At the same time, objects such as tools, which by definition are standing reserve, had a different status than the raw material like a piece of wood. Some of the objects within the Ashari world were standing reserve, and some were not. See Martin Heidegger, *Question Concerning Technology* (New York: Garland Publishing Inc., 1977).

10. Karl Marx, on his discussion of transition from handicrafts to manufacture, considered the machine as a tool where the motive of power is shifted from humans to mechanical power. He wrote:

> On a closer examination of the working machine proper, we find in it, as a general rule, though often, no doubt, under very altered forms, the apparatus and tools used by the handicraftsman or manufacturing workman; with this difference, that instead of being human implements, they are the implements of a mechanism, or mechanical implements. Either the entire machine is only a more or less altered mechanical edition of the old handicraft tool, as, for instance, the power-loom or the working parts fitted in the frame of the machine are old acquaintances, as spindles are in a mule, needles in a stocking-loom, saws in a sawing-machine, and knives in a chopping machine.

Marx's focus was on the implication of shifting agency from human to machine; the agency of the tool itself was not a factor in this. Marx considered the machine as a humanized object, whereas tools were instrumental, whether powered by humans or by machine. Karl Marx, *Capital: A Critique of Political Economy* (London: Penguin Books, 1976), 494.

Early anthropological studies of so-called non-modern cultures had noted the idea of agency for non-human beings and objects as part of describing their belief systems. Here, the objects and actions were understood in structural functionalist approaches and were positioned antithetical to the modern. See Bronislow Malinowski, *Magic, Science and Religion and Other*

Essays (Illinois: Free Press, 1948); Claude Levi-Strauss, *Myth and Meaning* (London: Routledge, 2001). The agency of non-humans is now extended to the modern world as well in the field of science and technology studies and particularly in the studies of material cultures. The actor–network theory is one of the important examples in this regard. See Bruno Latour, *We Have Never Been Modern* (Cambridge, MA: Harvard University Press, 1993); and Bruno Latour, *Reassembling the Social: An Introduction to Actor-Network-Theory* (Oxford: Oxford University Press, 2007). The recent studies from this perspective incorporated the new findings in neurobiology in order to establish the connection of tools, raw materials, hands, nerves, and the brain as a network that enables any action. For example, Lambros Malafouris points out that 'while agency and intentionality may not be properties of things, they are not properties of humans either: they are the properties of material engagement, that is, of the grey zone where brain, body and culture conflate.' Lambros Malafouris, 'At the Potter's Wheel: An Argument for Material Agency', in *Material Agency: Towards a Non-Anthropocentric Approach*, ed. Carl Knappett and Lambros Malafouris, 19–36 (New York: Springer, 2008), 22. In this view, all objects have equal possibilities of having agency, though they may act differently in different networks. In the Ashari contexts, tools have a very specific kind of agency different from that of the raw material. Hence, the agency is not attributed to all objects in the network.

11.   Tim Ingold, analysing 'skill' in its minute details, explains: 'In sawing, as in rowing, … I am working *with* the instruments and materials at my disposal rather than *against* them (emphasis original).' Tim Ingold, *Being Alive: Essays on Movement, Knowledge and Description* (New York: Routledge, 2011), 55.

12.   The scholarship inspired by Marshall Macluhan's theorization of media as an extension of the sensory mechanisms of humans attempts to understand tools not merely as instrumental objects but as having independent agency of creating impacts. Marshall McLuhan, *Understanding Media: The Extensions of Man* (Cambridge, MA: MIT Press, 1994). However, most of these theories understand agency similar to human agency in using a means to an end. For example, see David Le Breton, *Sensing the World: An Anthropology of the Senses* (London: Routledge, 2017); and David Howes and Constance Classen, *Ways of Sensing: Understanding the Senses in Society* (New York: Routledge, 2014).

13.   Interview with Krishnan Ashari (13 August 2008).

14.   Ingold explains the first stage of sawing a wood piece as 'setting out'. He points out that 'this moment of setting out, however, is also marked by a switch of perspective, from the encompassing view of the umbrella plan to a narrow focus on the initial point of contact between tool and material'. This could be considered a movement from the abstract to the particular. He also underscores that in practice, 'it is not the image of the end product that governs the phase of finishing off. By the time this phase is reached, any deviations from the initial plan will have been either accepted or corrected'. In other words, in each stage

of the process (although not at the phase of finishing), there is movement back to the abstract, and this abstract need not be the one with which the process had begun. Ingold, *Being Alive*, 54–55.

15. The standpoint theories, especially the feminist studies of science based on standpoint theories, foregrounded the epistemological importance of experience in knowledge production. Sandra Harding noted that 'we have come to understand that what took to be humanly inclusive problematics, concepts, theories, objective methodologies, and transcendental truths are in fact far less than that. Instead, these products of thought bear the mark of their collective and individual creators, and the creators in turn have been distinctively marked as to gender, class, race, and culture'. Sandra Harding, *The Science Question in Feminism* (Ithaca: Cornell University Press, 1986), 15. Also see Janet A. Kourany, 'The Place of Standpoint Theory in Feminist Science Studies', *Hypatia* 24, no. 4 (Fall 2009): 209–218; Alison Wylie, 'Feminist Philosophy of Science: Standpoint Matters', *Proceedings and Addresses of the American Philosophical Association* 86, no. 2 (November 2012): 47–76; Ashley Glassburn, 'Settler Standpoints', *William and Mary Quarterly* 76, no. 3 (July 2019): 399–406. In the feminist debate around standpoint, experience is not just a subjective phenomenon but an effect of social practices in a hierarchized world. Hence, the focus was more on the social formation of experience rather than the experience itself.

16. It is not a surprise that even when studies in neurobiology recognize the agency of the material object one handles and its influence in the action of brain, the influence again is understood as a bodily property applicable to all human beings. For neurobiological interpretations, see Allan Wing, Patrick Haggard, and Randall Flanagan, *Hand and Brain: The Neurophisiology and Psychology of Hand Movements* (California: Academic Press Inc., 1996); Michael G. Lacourse, Elizabeth L. R. Orr, Steven C. Cramer, and Michael J. Cohen, 'Brain Activation during Execution and Motor Imagery of Novel and Skilled Sequential Hand Movements', *NeuroImage* 27, no. 3 (September 2005): 505–519. What is interesting to note is that most of the anthropological studies that situate senses in the cultural context also focus on the patterning or processing part of sensing and how meaning or the making of senses varies across cultures. For example, David Howes writes: 'The anthropology of the senses is primarily concerned with how the patterning of sense experience varies from one culture to the next in accordance with the meaning and emphasis attached to each of the modalities of perception. It is also concerned with tracing the influence such variations have on forms of social organization, conceptions of self and cosmos, the regulation of the emotions, and other domains of cultural expression.' David Howes, 'Introduction: To Summon All the Senses', in *The Varieties of Sensory Experience: A Sourcebook in the Anthropology of the Senses*, ed. David Howes, 3–21 (Toronto: University of Toronto Press, 1991). See also Francois Laplantine, *The Life of the Senses: Introduction to a Model Anthropology*

(London: Bloomsbury, 2005); and Constance Classen (ed.), *A Cultural History of the Senses in the Age of Empire* (London: Bloomsbury, 2014).

17. Jack Goody noted that 'human societies in general recognise the same senses of sight, hearing, touch, taste, smell, as we do'. He pointed out that the Ayurvedic tradition explained the five senses under the category of 'rasas' and they are connected to the concepts of the five elements that the universe is made of. We can see similar grouping of five senses in the Chinese tradition from the third century BCE and in the Greek tradition, especially in Aristotle. Jack Goody, 'The Anthropology of the Senses and Sensations', *La Ricerca Folklorica*, no. 45, Antropologia delle sensazioni (April, 2002): 17–28; Fiona Macpherson (ed.), *The Senses: Classic and Contemporary Philosophical Perspectives* (Oxford: Oxford University Press, 2011).

18. Interview with Appu Ashari (28 May 2009).

19. Interview with Appu Ashari (28 May 2009).

20. See note 13.

21. Interview with Appu Ashari (28 May 2009).

22. Tacit knowledge, in this debate, is articulated sometimes against all knowledges expressed in language and other times by posing bodily knowledge, muscle memory, and so on against conscious thinking or, in general, mental activity. See Michael Polanyi, *The Tacit Dimension* (Chicago: Chicago University Press, 1966).

23. Polanyi has already discussed this in relation to the gestalt psychology. He pointed out: 'Gestalt psychology has assumed that perception of a physiognomy takes place through the spontaneous equilibration of its particulars impressed on the retina or on the brain. However, I am looking at Gestalt, on the contrary, as the outcome of an active shaping of experience performed in the pursuit of knowledge. This shaping or integrating I hold to be the great and indispensable tacit power by which all knowledge is discovered and, once discovered, is held to be true.' Polanyi, *Tacit Dimension*, 6.

24. Socrates and Plato in their dialogues emphasized the importance of dialectics. The influence of Pythagorean principle of opposites such as limited–unlimited, plurality–one, male–female, and so on had critical influence in Greek philosophy for a long time. The binary of Civilised Greeks and Barbarians was central in the Greek political thought, especially after Aristotle. Paul Cartledge notes that 'the hypothetical opposition between custom or convention (*nomos*) and nature (*phusis*) was the special contribution of the so-called Sophist to Greek cultural debate as a whole'. Paul Cartledge, *The Greeks: A Portrait of Self and Others*, 2nd edition (Oxford: Oxford University Press, 2002), 14. See also Irad Malkin, 'Postcolonial Concepts and Ancient Greek Colonization', *Modern Language Quarterly* 65, no. 3 (September 2004): 341–364; G. E. R. Lloyd, *Polarity and Analogy: Two Types of Argumentation in Early Greek Thought* (Bristol: Bristol Classical Press, 1987). Peter Elbow argued that 'there's no hope of getting away from binary oppositions given the nature of the human mind and situation.

Binary thinking seems to be the path of least resistance for the perceptual system, for thinking, and for linguistic structures'. He pointed out that binaries as such are not problems but what we do with the binaries is the more important question. He agrees with post-structuralist critic of the Hegelian form of dialectical thinking, which suggested a transcendental unity after the synthesis of the dialectical opposites erasing the difference altogether. However, Elbow explores the possibility of keeping binaries and at the same time having 'situations of balance, irresolution, nonclosure, nonconsensus, nonwinning'. Peter Elbow, 'The Uses of Binary Thinking', *Journal of Advanced Composition* 13, no. 1, Special Issue: Philosophy and Composition Theory (Winter 1993): 51–78. Robin Wang in his analysis of the famous Chinese concepts of yin and yang explored the varied and complex uses of this binary in Chinese thought. 'Yinyang is not only offered for matters of basic health but also for the highest levels of self-cultivation.' Robin R. Wang, *Yinyang: The Way of Heaven and Earth in Chinese Thought and Culture* (New York: Cambridge University Press, 2012), 2. The critic of binary in Chinese thought was mostly based on the transcendence of binary and arriving in unity. See Edmund S. K. Fung, *Intellectual Formations of Chinese Modernity: Cultural and Political Thought in the Republican Era* (New York: Cambridge University Press, 2010).

25. In the Sanskritic tradition, the Samkhya School was known for their defence of *dvaita* (dualist) principles. While there was great variance in the opinion within the school regarding what constitutes the opposite part of the binary, the operative principles were always binaries such as *vyaktha* and *avyaktha*, *sath* and *asath*, *prakruthi* and *purusha*, and so on. The Advaithis positioned themselves against the Dvaitha school and hence they used binary language, as negation was an important operator in their arguments against dualism. The prefix 'अ' used for negation of a nominal item (for example, *advaita*, *avarna*, and so on) or 'न' as absolute negative are fundamental to the binary modality of Sanskrit language in general. However, for Advaithis, this is not just a rule of language but also an ontological and epistemological principle. Also, Advaitha as a philosophy of unity aspired to reduce all difference into the ultimate reality of a single unifying entity. See Anima Sen Gupta, *Samkhya and Advaita Vedanta: A Comparative Study* (Calcutta: Sanskrit Pustak Bhandar, 1973); Pulinbihari Chakravarti, *Origin and Development of the Samkhya System of Thought* (New Delhi: Oriental Books Reprint Corporation, 1975); Gerald Larson and Ram Shankar Bhattacharya (eds.), *Encyclopaedia of Indian Philosophies*, vol. 4: *Samkhya, a Dualist Tradition in Indian Philosophy* (Princeton: Princeton University Press, 1987); Sthaneswar Timalsina, *Consciousness in Indian Philosophy: The Advaita Doctrine of 'Awareness Only'* (New York: Routledge, 2009); Arvind Sharma, *The Experiential Dimension of Advaita Vedanta* (Delhi: Motilalal Banarasidass Publishers, 1993).

26. For example, see F. LaFlesche's description of one of the native American communities: 'The Osages saw the cosmos as a highly integrated and unified

system in which humans were only one factor.' 'Traditional Osage social, political, and religious institutions were so highly integrated that they constituted a single unified system.' F. LaFlesche, *The Osage and the Invisible World: Civilization of the American Indian*, vol. 21 (Norman, OK: University of Oklahoma Press, 1995), 30, 68. Similarly, Scott Fatnowna and Harry Pickett mention: 'Spirituality in an aboriginal sense is encompassing and holistic in nature.' 'Objectivity as a notion is culturally inappropriate and should not be linked to Aboriginal spirituality and holistic wellbeing.' Scott Fatnowna and Harry Pickett, 'Indigenous Contemporary Knowledge Development through Research', in *Indigenous Knowledge and the Integration of Knowledge Systems: Towards a Philosophy of Articulation*, ed. Catherine A. Odera Hoppers, 209–236 (Claremont: New Africa Books 2002), 214. See also Julian T. Inglis (ed.), *Traditional Ecological Knowledge: Concepts and Cases* (Ottawa: Canadian Museum of Nature, 1993); and Raymond Pierotti, *Indigenous Knowledge, Ecology, and Evolutionary Biology* (New York: Routledge, 2011).

27. Interview with Nanu Ashari (17 July 2014).
28. 'Akamporul thedaayka,
    avarude thantha thalla daivangal
    othikkodutha porul arivayka,
    akathe kettikoottam kaanaayka,
    thaanu vanangathe pokaayka,
    avare thampuran avarkke melkkai,
    avaru manthrichothum vazhiye mathram nadakka.'
29. See note 23.
30. 'Munne vanna karanavanamar thuna,
    kalppicharuliya panikale cheyyendathinvare
    aduthukoodan kaniyenam,
    neeye thuna, ninakke kalpana kaaryam,
    pizhayellam porthu vazhikaattanum neeye thuna.'
31. 'Akalannu maram kaanam,
    naaladiyil kompum ilayum kananam,
    puram kayyaale thottu maram
    chonnathe kelkkanam,
    ila pizhinjaal manam tharum,
    cherthu vechellam ganikkam
    ulle theliyum neru.'
32. See the Introduction.
33. *Report on Industrial Education* (hereafter, *The Report*), part 2, Education Department (Calcutta: Government Press, 1906).
34. *The Report*, 3.
35. *The Report*, 143–171.
36. *The Report*, 162.
37. *The Report*, 164.

38.   *The Report*, 159.
39.   *The Report*, 161.
40.   *The Report*, 162.
41.   Proceedings of the Public Works Department, Government of Madras, 1910 (Madras: Government Press, 1911), 23–25.
42.   Proceedings, 31.
43.   Proceedings, 32.
44.   R. C. Temple, 'A Study of Modern Indian Architecture as Displayed in a British Cantonment', *Journal of Indian Art* 15, no. 15 (March 1890): 57–61.
45.   Temple, 'A Study of Modern Indian Architecture', 59.
46.   Temple, 'A Study of Modern Indian Architecture', 61.
47.   P. C. Kuttikrishna Menon, *Pinnitta Pathakal* (The Treaded Paths) (Thrissur: Vidya Vijayam Publishers, 1957), 76.
48.   Menon, *Pinnitta Pathakal*, 82.
49.   Menon, *Pinnitta Pathakal*, 78.
50.   For a detailed description and drawings of the joints that Asharis use in the construction of roof frames, refer to Keshavan Achari, *Prayogika Vastu Vidya* (Practical Architectural Knowledge) (Kodungalloor: Jyothi Books, 1993), 34–56.
51.   Keshavan Achari claims that, according to his knowledge, in the 1930s, one Appu Achari of Kunippara invented new forms of joints, which assimilated the use of iron nails and clay tiles into the proper measures of asharippani. Achari, *Prayogika Vastu Vidya*, 34.
52.   See K. Ramakrishnan, *Theevanti Malabaril: Oru Charithranweshanam* (Railway in Malabar: A Historical Inquiry) (Shornoor: Kripa Publishers, 1987).
53.   Proceedings of the Public Works Department, Madras Government, 1923, Tamil Nadu State Archives 34, nos. 29–31.
54.   P. Govinda Variyar, 'Marunna Nattinpuram (Changing Rural Area)', *Keralapathrika* 2, no. 4 (May 1928): 38–45.
55.   Variyar, 'Marunna Nattinpuram', 40.
56.   Until the last decades of the nineteenth century, caste and power status determined the nature of the house one could build. See P. Bhaskaranunni, *Pathompatham Noottantile Keralam* (The Nineteenth Century Keralam) (Thrissur: Kerala Sahithya Academy, 1988).
57.   *Report of the Committee on Weight and Measures*, Proceedings of the Home Department (October 1907), no. 61–63, National Archives of India.
58.   *Weight and Measures*, 21.
59.   *Weight and Measures*, 22.
60.   *Weight and Measures*, 26.
61.   Interview with Achu Ashari (14 August 2008).
62.   Translated by Bindu Menon.

2

An Ashari World of Ignoring

By the end of the nineteenth century, various caste groups in the Malayalam-speaking region of Keralam began actively participating in the colonial educational institutions. Historians of the region have mapped various caste communities' interactions with colonial knowledge under the category of 'community reform'.[1] Education was central to all the modern social reformers throughout India, starting from Jyotirao Phule to Ayyankali to dominant-caste Bengali reformers. However, a close observation of the Ashari world in the first half of the twentieth century tells us a different story. In this period, Ashari as a *jati* was an oppressed community and simultaneously aware of the emergence of the colonial modernity; however, by actively ignoring or avoiding the opportunities provided by the colonizers, Asharis resisted the temptations extended through various colonial institutions. Asharis neglected or avoided colonial intervention by maintaining carpentry as a practice of knowing, rather than transforming it as a process of knowledge production.[2] This chapter explores the strategies through which Asharis mobilized the practice of ignoring and its affects and implications on the daily life of the community.

Ignorance and Ignoring

As discussed in the Introduction, the knowledge–ignorance binary was central to both the claims of domination of the colonialists and to the discourse of reform of various caste communities. The colonialists considered artisans highly skilled but ignorant of the modern ways of using tools and technology. According to Alfred Chatterton, Director of Industries, Madras, 1900–1908, 'Caste restrictions, combined with *ignorance* and intense dislike to change of any kind have kept the artisans to their hereditary methods', which he considered as obsolete and to be reformed through 'external help'.[3] E. B. Havell, a friend of Ananda Coomaraswamy and Abanindranath Tagore, and who can be considered a committed orientalist, was more appreciative than Chatterton of the capabilities of Indian artisans. He opined that the 'most valuable industrial asset' India possessed was 'the skill of her handicraftsmen'.[4] He explained:

It is of vital importance for India to retain all the *accumulated skill of hand and eye*: the problem for India is how to use the labour saving appliances not as a substitute for but as an auxiliary to handicraft—so that handicraft may be developed instead of being crushed out by the inventions of modern science. (Emphasis added)[5]

Havell attempted the modernization of Indian handicrafts through the Schools of Arts in Madras and Calcutta, of which he was the superintendent at different points of time. For him, the 'Anglo–Indian educational system has no ideal beyond that of imparting to the Indian students the intellectual impressions of Oxford, Cambridge, Aberdeen and London'.[6] While Havell did not consider skill as something inferior to knowledge, the dichotomy was important to him. He attempted to bring the traditional artisans into the modern form of schooling and improve their skills to adapt to the emerging needs in the country. This was the general colonial policy in that period, and it was exactly this attempt that Asharis bypassed through an innovative strategy of ignoring, which resulted in making the community comparatively opaque, but not bounded or isolated.

The practice of ignoring is usually considered as a privilege of the dominant, and hence, in the historical and sociological scholarship, as an action of the dominant, it serves the purpose of exclusion. In the modern form of politics, starting from the form of memorandums and appeals to the authorities, the major pleas by the aggrieved groups were against ignoring particular issues or conditions of their community by the State. For example, the Malayali memorial, submitted to the Thiruvithamkoor government in 1891, complained that the government was ignoring the Malayali Nair and Brahmin communities in the appointment to the government service, privileging the foreign (Tamil, Mysore, and Andhra) Brahmins. A similar memorandum submitted in 1896 by Ezhava community leaders complained about the practice of ignoring the Ezhavas by the Thiruvithamkoor state. In the aforementioned cases, ignoring was more a non-action than an action, and it was the non-deployment of forces that was criticized in these situations. However, when imagined as a 'weapon of the weak', ignoring enables different possibilities of actions such as those practised by Asharis. For Asharis, ignoring was a way of sustaining *asharippani* as a practice of knowing. In other words, for a subaltern community, ignoring means actively mobilizing certain forces and diverting its activities towards the community's intent and not yielding to interventions by a dominant community.

The practice of ignoring can find its similarities in James Scott's notion of 'art of being not governed', where communities attempted to move away from the access of the State and created partially autonomous spaces. Ignoring in this sense is to move away from the purview of the State's accessibility by keeping oneself away from the institutions of the State. However, the Asharis did not attempt to create an autonomous space in the periphery of the colonial governance. The Ashari act of ignoring, on the one hand, was an attempt to keep the State at an arm's distance, as Scott argues. On the other hand, this was located very much within the interstice of the State's activities, and the community did not isolate from the surrounding transformations initiated by the colonialists and the nationalists.[7] In other words, the articulation of ignoring was premised not on the notion of separation from the outside world but on the notion of a unique identity of asharippani, different from other practices. Hence, the idea of difference was central to the narratives of Asharis about their community and work in the first half of the twentieth century.[8]

Ignoring also resonates with the idea of 'forgetting' in Friedrich Nietzsche, which 'is essential to action of any kind, just as not only light but darkness too is essential for the life of everything organic'.[9] In Nietzsche, forgetting may be read as a result of the survival instinct, but simultaneously, it is a conscious action for a healthy life rather than being the simple lack of memory.[10] Similarly, ignoring is not something arising from the lack of knowledge of what is ignored, but from a conscious scrutiny and the resultant decision to not engage. It was caste, as analysed in this chapter, simultaneously as a belief and practice, which produced the necessary forces that enabled Asharis to consciously ignore the dominant assimilation techniques. In this process, caste also transformed in such a way that asharippani became the central organizing category of caste, which is explained later in this chapter.

Asharis used different strategies to uphold asharippani as a practice of knowing. First, they created a spatio-temporal location called *desham*, within the boundary of which they limited their practices. Asharis imagined desham as the limit of action and experience, which were the two major elements of asharippani. This imagination was a part of Asharis' resistance against colonial attempts to bring them into cities or towns. Second, Asharis refused to participate in colonial educational institutions or to assimilate the methodologies used in these institutions into their practices. In this period, the attempt of the colonizers to standardize measures, instruments, and products was a failure at least in the case of the Asharis in Malabar. Further, Asharis did not incorporate into asharippani the objectification process—such as the use of drawings or modelling—which was fundamental to the production of colonial knowledge. However, at the same time, they reformed their tools, included new production materials, and implemented their own new methods within the practice of knowing. In short, ignoring was an active process of resistance in order to protect what Asharis considered as the interest of the caste community at that period.

Historical Conditions for Ignoring

The Ashari process of negotiation with colonial institutions of knowledge differed fundamentally from the reform process initiated by other oppressed-caste communities in the Malayalam-speaking region around the same period. During the late nineteenth and the early twentieth centuries, the Pulaya (the former agricultural slave caste) and Ezhava (another subaltern-caste community) reformers strongly urged their members to participate in colonial educational institutions. These leaders attempted to use colonial education as a means for the struggle against brahmanical oppression. The reform leaders urged the community to relinquish the hereditary occupation and to seek jobs in government service, a move which they thought would bring respectability and progress to the community.[11] These oppressed-caste communities, similar to Asharis, engaged in practices of knowing such as agriculture or toddy-tapping.[12] The Ashari community in this period, however, considered modern education a strategy of the *sayip* (white man) designed to intervene in their autonomy and freedom of practice. It is difficult to pinpoint a reason for the difference in the responses of Asharis and those of other subordinated-caste communities towards the emerging colonial institutions. Still, we can map some of the contextual factors that enabled Asharis to avoid the colonial intervention.

Brahmins considered agricultural work and toddy-tapping, which were the 'traditional occupations' of the Pulaya and Ezhava castes, respectively, as menial physical work and impure practices. The Christian missionaries and the colonialists, influenced by the brahmanical discourse, espoused these derogatory notions regarding occupations in their understanding of various caste practices.In their evangelical mission in the late nineteenth and the early twentieth centuries, the missionaries in Malabar preferred artisanal practices rather than agricultural work or toddy-tapping as occupations in which the newly converted natives could be trained to develop their moral and material skills.[13] The annual report of Basel Evangelical Mission in the first decade of the twentieth century observed that the mission should 'encourage the downtrodden to join the industrial centres' because 'the traditional occupations, they are currently involved in, are driving them towards slavery and disrespect'.[14] Carpentry, unlike agricultural work or toddy-tapping, was not an impure or disrespectable occupation within the colonial and brahmanical discourses of the early twentieth century. Hence, at this point of time, there was neither an incentive for nor a moral pressure on Asharis to renounce their occupation or to join in colonial institutions like other subaltern-caste communities had.

The economic changes in the first half of the twentieth century also helped Asharis to remain in asharippani rather than shift to a different occupation.

In Malabar, the Nampoothiri and Nair landlords were the Asharis' main employers. In the nineteenth century, Nairs and Nampoothiris resided as large joint families, and the family property was undividable. The *karanavar* (the eldest male in the family) controlled the income and expenditure of the family, the main source of which was agriculture. It was impossible in this circumstance for an individual member of the family to build a new house for themselves, owing to lack of resources and given the fear of the displeasure of the karanavar.

By the late nineteenth and the early twentieth centuries, several members of the Nair community, who were educated in colonial educational institutions, joined middle-level government service and started earning private incomes. The new occupations also created in this generation of Nairs an urge for independence from the karanavars and to build their own households outside the joint family. In 1923, the Madras legislative assembly passed the Madras Marumakathayam (Matriliny) Act, which endorsed individual rights on the joint family property of Nair households and which 'guaranteed the legitimate partition of joint property and provided for individual inheritance'.[15] The legal and social intervention under the leadership of the educated young generation of the Nair community catalyzed the shift from matrilineal joint family households to patrilineal nuclear families. Corresponding to this shift, the requirement of new houses and demand for Asharis increased throughout the first half of the twentieth century.

Analysing the reports of the industrial survey conducted by the Madras Government in 1926, F. Fawcett noted that 'the carpenters and masons are the two groups relatively less affected by the flooding of domestic and imported industrial products in the market, compared to weavers, black smiths and potters'. The survey evidenced that the carpenters in the Malabar district have significantly improved their 'economic and social status, compared to the other artisanal communities'.[16] V. N. Kurup observed in 1934 that 'the trend and fashion of the time compel every married person to move into a new house. The time will tell whether this is a healthy tendency or not, but for the carpenters and mason, this has provided an ample opportunity to remain in their hereditary trade'.[17] V . Keshavan Achari is a chief carpenter from Thirur who is also researching on history of Vishwakarmas. He remembers that his grandfather was the first Ashari in his and neighbouring deshams to work simultaneously on more than one house. 'Nairs and Nampoothiris started dividing their property and moving into new houses. This was a good opportunity for Asharis, as we got for the first time a sufficient income to survive.'[18] The status of asharippani as a respectable profession and the prospering economic opportunities served as the two most important factors that enabled the Ashari avoidance of the colonial intervention. Asharis utilized the economic opportunities that emerged in their respective deshams; at the same time, they rejected another set of opportunities that the colonizers extended to them as part of the governing process of the colonial state. The genealogy of this colonial intervention in artisanal practices extended back to the middle of the nineteenth century.

Colonial Attempts of Assimilation

By the middle of the nineteenth century, the British colonial government in India established new governing practices which differed significantly from the earlier forms of colonial administration. David Scott, using the Foucauldian notion of governmentality, describes this as a transformation from the 'rule of force' into the 'rule of law'. In this new form, population became the basic unit of the governing process, and self-governance, the ultimate form of governmental control.[19] Though the military and the police still had important roles in controlling the population, education became one of the major activities of governing. This transformation was part of a wider colonialist recognition of knowledge as the organizing category of governance and for arranging individuals and groups in a hierarchical order in both the metropole and the colony. A new political rationality and a new order of knowledge co-emerged and mutually constituted each other. This order assigned a specific position for each section of the population in a hierarchical series according to their assumed historical relation with knowledge.

It was in the colonial attempt of ordering the population in the hierarchical series of knowledge that artisans became the target of governing processes. In this attempt of governing, we can mark two important tactics developed by the colonialists. First, the colonial government encouraged the artisans to migrate from their supposedly natural locations in the villages to the institutional spaces in the cities and towns. Through this process of institutionalization, the government hoped to bring artisanal practices under the visibility of the state and to transform these into a formal and regulated process. Second, the government initiated different programmes to standardise artisanal practices all over the country by implementing uniform methods and measures in artisanal production.

The colonial government assigned Asharis an important role in its project of development based on towns and cities. In 1883, analysing the prospect of industrial development in the Madras state, Havell argued that the native handicraft industry, rather than large factories, should be the central feature of the development of cities and towns. He observed that there were very few workshops and training centres in urban localities and the government should focus on providing economic support for carpenters and smiths to migrate into

Madras city and into other small towns.[20] The committee that conducted a nationwide survey as part of the industrial education conferences in 1901–1902 (see *The Report* in Chapter 1) concluded that though large-scale industries should be part of the long-term plan, developing small, handicraft-producing workshops and trading shops in towns was the best option for the Indian socio-economic situation at the time.

Public works initiated by the government was another site of state intervention in artisanal practices. In 1875, the Madras government founded a new department for conducting and supervising public works. The Public Works Department (PWD) initiated the construction of roads, railways, bridges, and buildings, for which the colonial officers in charge attempted to recruit traditional artisans and to train them in using modern tools and methods. The government established a series of technical education institutions which would accommodate different sections of the population. While the colonialists considered general education a suitable domain for the 'upper castes', they imagined technical training as the proper and pertinent method of governing artisans. The Madras government attempted to recruit Asharis for the carpentry works related to railway, bridge, and building construction under the PWD. The Education Department established various institutions such as schools of arts, industrial training centres, and technical schools for training carpenters in modern methods of carpentry. All of these institutions and work sites were located in towns and cities.

From different colonial documents, we can see that both the aforementioned attempts—relocating artisans to the workshops in cities and recruiting artisans to PWD-related institutions—did not succeed in general. Chatterton, who was the superintendent of industrial development in the Madras government in the early years of the twentieth century, explained the reluctance of artisans in joining factory production:

> We have found that the hand weavers of Salem like the hand-weavers of Madras object to working in a factory, and although their wages were good their attendance is unsatisfactory. This is mainly because the weavers prefer to work in their own home, assisted by their women and children and dislike being subjected to the discipline and regular hours of working which must necessarily prevail in the factory.[21]

Many colonial officers made similar remarks in the context of recruiting artisans into the colonial institutions. Havell, when he was the superintendent of the Madras School of Arts, saw a connection between the failure of the various departments in the school in imparting quality training and the 'shortage of apt students from the traditional castes for appropriate trades'.[22] In 1910, the

Director of the Department of Public Instruction of the Madras Government reported that the technical training schools, especially those in small towns, 'serve no purpose because they completely failed in enlisting the children of traditional craftsmen such as carpenters, smiths and potters'.[23]

The colonial documents of this period underlined Ashari adherence to their desham as one of the major reasons for this failure. In Malabar, like many other places in the colony, the colonizers 'targeted' artisans and initiated different plans to relocate them to new institutional locations. For example, the colonial officers in Malabar planned different strategies to recruit Asharis for PWD work and technical training in the early decades of the twentieth century. W. Francis, the District Collector of Malabar, in 1907, recommended that the government should use the traditional authority of the educated landlords or 'upper-castes' to 'convince the artisans of the advantages of joining in government works'.[24] He sent a detailed note to the subordinate officers explaining the importance of improving traditional artisanal practices. After one year, he reported to the government that he 'is still waiting for definite results of the new initiatives'. A number of village-level officers reported that Asharis were not ready to leave their village because by doing so, 'they feared that they [would] become outcastes and [would] not be able to go back to their villages'.[25] The collector assured the lower-level native administrative officers under his authority that the artisans who were ready to work in the PWD would be able to perform 'the daily rituals they have to conduct according to their caste rules', unless it violates 'the rule of law and existing norms of work'.[26] This clarification did not help much in convincing Asharis.

Six months later, the same collector reported to the government that he was now in contact with the Christian missionaries who had established workshops in Kozhikode and Kannur, where they imparted technical training to the non-artisanal subaltern-caste converts to Christianity. The protestant Christian missionaries who were active in Malabar were already using technical training as a method to teach the pagan natives the importance of hard work and punctuality and the troubles of laziness. For the missionaries, physical industriousness was the first proof a native had to show in order to be accepted into the mission and into Christianity. The Basel Mission Church of Kozhikode established a number of carpentry, weaving, and pottery workshops, the training in which was compulsory as probation for the new aspirants for conversion into Christianity.[27]

Colonial officers were reluctant to accept the newly trained and baptized workmen from the missionary workshops for the works of the PWD. The Malabar Collector mentioned that he 'is worried about the quality of these workers, because they are not from the traditional craftsmen castes'.[28] Here, the colonialists' concern may seem purely economic. However, their attempt was not merely to create a labour force suitable for their economic policies. On the one hand, in India, the so-called modernization projects were already cast through the prism of caste. Caste was an important parameter in the economic policies of the colonial government. On the other hand, colonialists initiated these projects not simply as economic activity but as a process of governing in which no section of population could be left out.

Strategies of Ignoring: Locating Asharippani in Desham

Many Asharis remember that their grandfathers were invited to work in towns for the government and that they had refused it for fear of losing their caste. Velayudhan, an eighty-year-old chief carpenter from Kozhikode, remembered his grandfather's advice that he should never leave his desham, which was told to him in a proverbial form: 'The moment you leave the desham, the *charatu* [the measuring string Asharis use] will break.'[29] According to Krishnan, a chief carpenter, his grandfather considered 'sayip as evil' and that 'they reside in towns'. [30] Several Asharis I interviewed remember similar stories, told by their grandparents in their childhood. The moral of these stories was the necessity of rejecting the temptation of the town, or the importance of locating oneself at a place to which one belongs: the desham.[31]

Desham as such did not emerge as a new space in the early twentieth century. Even in the pre-colonial period, it was the lowest administrative region and a familiar location for different sections of the society. The landlords and the agricultural labour castes were 'located' in the desham for the obvious reason of settled agriculture. However, Asharis, until the early twentieth century, shifted their location from one desham to another for various reasons. William Logan, while challenging the traditional wisdom that Indian villages were always self-sufficient in material production, noted the mobility of artisanal practitioners. He observed that the mere fact that the different sections of the population speak in different accents—and sometimes in totally different languages—underscored the mobility of the population. Logan specifically mentioned that 'in many occasions, the artisans and the lower-caste people shifted their locations mostly for the reasons of survival'.[32]

While describing the procedures of a temple construction he witnessed in Malabar in 1897, W. Arbuthnot observed that 'the architect, a carpenter, who is originally from a neighbouring village, has settled with his family near the temple for the purpose of the construction'. Arbuthnot noted that once the construction was over, 'he may make this village as his permanent location or may move into a different place', depending on the demand for his expertise.[33] C. A. Innes and F.B. Evans also observed that though large-scale migration of labour was an unknown phenomenon in the late nineteenth century, workers, 'especially carpenters and smiths, were not hesitant to shift into a new village according to the opportunities available to them at different periods'.[34] These observations show that on the one hand, jobs that were within a desham were not sufficient to survive and hence Asharis had to move places, looking for opportunities. On the other hand, it also shows that in this period, Asharis did not consider moving out of their desham a violation of custom or caste rules.

By the turn of the century, we start observing Ashari articulations in which desham becomes the only genuine space of asharippani. In a reply to W. Francis, the Collector of Malabar, the Amsham Adhikari (Village Officer) of Purathur wrote about the difficulty of recruiting Asharis for the PWD. He explained:

> One of the major objections they [Asharis] raised was based on their affinity to their desham. In one case, I pointed out to a chief carpenter that it was only thirty or forty years ago that his grandfather and his maternal uncle had moved from the neighbouring village to the present one. His reply, which was not convincing for me, was that they took a long time to settle in the new locality. Now, it is difficult for him to start again in another place because to work efficiently, he has to know the peculiarities of that desham.[35]

The village officer in the case discussed previously, who mainly wanted to justify his failure before higher authorities, depicted the Ashari arguments as historically incorrect. In a report in 1915, S. W. Johns observed that though 'the spirit of progress we brought into this country has reached even in the remotest villages ... the parochial nature of the caste artisans has been increasing year by year'.[36] The colonizers noted that the Ashari claims regarding their affinity to the desham was a new phenomenon, but they considered this a mark of the backwardness and inherent parochial nature of the community.

Asharis cared less about the historical correctness of their argument than about a strategy that would help them preserve their authority and independence over their practice. They based their reluctance to move into towns by emphasizing the importance of the desham as the location of asharippani. Desham in this context was not only a geographical space but also an imagined social space. Asharis in this period thought of asharippani as a *located* practice, bounded by the space of the desham, crossing which would disable their knowing or practising capacities. By locating asharippani in desham, Asharis connected knowing and space, which was incommensurable to the colonial idea of universal knowledge.

Two written Ashari sources from the first half of the twentieth century shed some light on the relation between desham and asharippani. *Ashari Vrithantham* (The News of Asharis) is an unpublished palm-leaf manuscript written by Neelakantan Achari.[37] Neelakantan Achari learned reading and writing in Sanskrit and Malayalam from a dominant-caste teacher named Govinda Variyar. He finished the writing of this particular work in 1932.[38] It is important to note that even though paper and printing were popular by this time, Achari wrote on the traditional palm leaves. In the pre-colonial period, scholars and experts wrote the Sanskrit texts, horoscopes, and almanacs on palm leaves. When paper and printing became the dominant mode of writing, people started associating palm-leaf manuscripts to sacred, traditional, or ritual knowledge. Invoking a traditional method and form of writing, Achari might have been attempting to make his work authentic through the traditional medium. However, the work itself did not follow any traditional narrative practices. It is in the form of a dialogue between a father and son described both in prose and *sloka*s (verses). Thus, the content itself was not mythical or ritualistic but about the contemporary social situation.

In Achari's story, Koman, the son, plans to migrate to Kozhikode town, where he can find a job in the railway workshop. Kandan, the father, in attempting to discourage his son's wish to relocate, highlights the importance of secluding themselves in desham:

> An Ashari out of his own desham
> Is like a fish out of water.
> He knows only about his desham
> And only that desham knows him.
> Outside desham,
> He doesn't know East or South,
> He doesn't know the wind or water,
> Doesn't know the tree or measure.[39]

Kandan connected Ashari and desham through knowledge. According to him, the Ashari practice of knowing was limited within the geographical space of desham. Unlike colonial knowledge, which once produced can be exported to any place, knowing requires continuous experiencing, and hence the knower should be located in a space for long periods. By creating a relation between space, experience, and knowing, Achari indirectly made a distinction between asharippani and the colonial modes of knowledge production. It is important to point out that Asharis' emphasis was on the locatedness of their practice, not on making it a local practice of a particular desham.

The second source on the relation between desham and asharippani is a travelogue titled *Deshamahima* written by Govindan Ashari in the second or third decades of the twentieth century, which expresses a similar kind of connection between Asharis and desham.[40] Govindan Ashari left his home near Thalasseri in North Malabar in the early years of 1910s and travelled through the southern part of the Malabar district and through the neighbouring princely state of Kochi. He returned home after three years, started writing this travelogue most probably in the late 1910s, and finished it in 1921.

The travelogue begins with the description of his re-entry into his desham. The moment he crossed the bridge at the boundary of his desham, he retransformed into his earlier identity as Ashari. 'During the travel, I was mere Govindan, and at this moment, I became Govindan Ashari again.' Even though he enjoyed his travel, he was 'naturally happy' only in his desham because 'it is only here that I can do my own work, which is the responsibility rested on me by the directions of my forefathers'.[41] He also explained how in different deshams, Asharis exercised very different procedures and methods. According to him, this was another reason for an Ashari to remain in one's own desham. For Govindan Ashari, his own desham was always the reference point for comparing the peculiarities of other deshams. The desham in his description was not a space that was always already existing for him. It was his travel that made him aware of the connection between Ashari and desham, and this awareness became important to him in the new circumstance of the sayip's intervention. He wrote this travelogue mainly to explain this new situation where Asharis had to understand the importance of desham.

Knowing as doing required a certain sustained process of experiencing and training, which further necessitated being in a place. The body was trained for knowing through this exposure to the surrounding for a substantial time period, and a particular disposition of the body was related to that of particular networks and forces enacting in that surrounding. Hence, desham was an important actant in the network of Ashari practices, and belonging to a desham was one of the necessary conditions for practising asharippani. The relation of Asharis to desham was not similar to either love towards one's mother country (patriotism) or a sense of belonging to a particular geographical space with a unique history and culture (nationalistic feelings). Affinity to a particular desham was part of the practice of knowing, and hence, it was not the history or 'culture' of that particular desham that was important; rather, it was the present and the presence that were crucial in this process. This again points towards the earlier mentioned notion that asharippani was a located practice, not a local one.

Asharis imagined desham through the axes of asharippani. Desham was the boundary of their experiencing and hence the limit of their practices. The relation between desham and asharippani was not exhaustive so that asharippani could be explained completely by the parameters of desham or vice versa. Still, this relation played an important role in the Ashari articulation of difference in the first half of the twentieth century. The Ashari imagination of desham was different, say, from that of Brahmins in the same period. For Brahmins, desham was an administrative region or mark of certain controls and powers.[42] As we observed earlier, Asharis started invoking desham in the early decades of the twentieth century typically by connecting it with asharippani. We may then assume that it was at this time that Asharis situated themselves in desham, and it was then that desham became a space of belonging and a space of difference-making.

Desham as articulated by Asharis was not the same as *gramam* (village), which was one of the central themes of the nationalist discourse, especially in M. K. Gandhi's imagination of the nation. In the nationalist narrative, village and artisans were inseparably connected. By the beginning of the twentieth century, artisans became an important figure in the national movement dominated by the dominant castes. The Indian National Congress, which was the major organization in the nationalist movement, championed the revival of handicrafts of India which were being made extinct by the colonial policy of importing industrial products from England. Gandhi's campaign for self-reliance imagined artisans as the central figure of material production. Analysing the central-staging of craft in the nationalist movement, Abigail McGowan pointed out that in the early twentieth century, 'crafts stood in for India as a whole economy, society, culture and politics'. She explained that this was 'the result of struggles by Indian elites and British officials to establish authority over the lower classes as well as the state itself'.[43]

Both the colonialists and the nationalists imagined gramam as the natural location of artisanal production in opposition to the city, which was the site of industrial production. Gandhi's idealization of India as a federation of self-reliant villages incorporated the British orientalists' romanticized views on the structure and functions of Indian villages.[44] Asharis, who refused to relocate into the cities, did not accept the romantic space of gramam as their location; it was desham that they considered the place of belonging.

The descriptions of Kuttippurathu Keshavan Nair about his village in the 1920s indirectly explained how the nationalist imagination of gramam and the Ashari imagination of desham were different. Nair was famous for his verses which romanticized the natural beauty of gramam in opposition to treacherous and pretentious cities. In an article in 1921, Nair explained that 'if there is anything valuable about the city, it is the fact that its emergence helped everyone to recognise the beauty of the village'.[45] This beauty was also part of the recognition that his village 'is not an isolated and remote place, but part of a nation, the culture of which is formed in thousands of similar villages'. It was only when this connection (that is, through the idea of being part of the nation) was established that the beauty itself would be revealed. He contrasted this with the imaginations of 'innocent and poor villagers who have never travelled outside their village. They are unfortunately unable to see their village as beautiful'.[46] For example, the carpenters see the village as their place of work. Appunni, an elderly carpenter in Nair's village, told him that 'one should walk only where one can learn and one should work only where one can learn this work by walking around the place'.[47] According to Nair, the river at the boundary of his desham was the limit of Appuni's walking. For him, that world was 'a place for working and remaking, not an object for the eyes to gain immeasurable pleasure'.[48] Nair's descriptions showed that while for Asharis, desham was the world of work, for the dominant-caste nationalist, gramam was a world of beauty and innocence.

Strategies of Ignoring: Colonialism as a Vicious Time

If space was one of the important parameters though which Asharis avoided the colonial invitations, time was equally an important factor in this avoidance. Asharis in the early decades of the twentieth century recognzsed the presence of a new time which was different in form and behaviour from other times in the past. To understand how Asharis interacted with this new time, we must first explore the Ashari ways of engaging with time in general. *Kalam* was the general name that was used to represent different forms of times at different periods. The prayer quoted as follows, which is known to many Asharis even now, illustrates certain generalized notions of kalam as Asharis understood it:

> Oh Kalabhairava!
> Didn't you see that
> A kalam with all its vicious intentions
> Has captured me and leads me
> Through paths which are not mine?
> Use your powers and help me
> In escaping from its tightening embrace.
> I don't know where it came from,
> I don't know whether I deserve it.
> If I do, I don't know

How many days it will continue.
Please show mercy on me and
Send this vicious time
Far away from me,
Hey Kalabhairava.[49]

Asharis especially recited this prayer in a ritual attempting to exorcise bad omens. Unlike the colonial notion of time, kalam was not an omnipresent phenomenon in which everything else was located. Nor did it progress in a linear path from the past through the present to the future. Kalam, while being a measure of duration, was also an object or a person-like entity which had its own behavioural patterns and effects on other objects and individuals. Since it was an object-like entity, humans could interact with it, be located inside or outside of it, resist it, or just distance themselves from it. Since it was also a human-like entity, a powerful person could change the characteristics of a particular time for good or bad ends.

It was within this general notion of temporality that Asharis invoked the presence of a new time in the early decades of the twentieth century. Kunjan, a carpenter in his eighties from Keralasseri in the southern part of Malabar, described the time of his childhood during the 1930s in a manner similar to that of several other old Asharis who were interviewed.[50] According to Kunjan, 'Time is like an intelligent person who behaves in different manners with different people.' His childhood was such a period when time was angry with all Asharis. 'Evil forces were active everywhere. In that situation, one had to act carefully and cautiously.' To my question of the form in which the evil forces manifested in that period, Kunjan answered that the evil forces acted mainly in the form of temptation to violate caste rules. As Kunjan's grandfather knew the strategies to overcome the evil forces of time, they did not face any major catastrophe. According to Kunjan's grandfather, the most important rule was that one should not travel to any unfamiliar places, especially out of desham, during *kashtakalam* (bad time).

Kunjan's story is an example which shows how Asharis understood the period when the colonial intervention shook the fundamental structures of caste and asharippani. In *Ashari Vrithantham*, Neelakantan Achari explained the characteristic of the new time through the dialogue between Kandan, the father, and Koman, the son. In their discussion about the desirability of travel, the son argued that travel was not against caste rules by pointing out the example of the great grandfather who had moved from another desham to the present one. To this argument of his son, Kandan replied:

One has to decide when and whether one should travel according to his time. The present is obviously a difficult time for Asharis. Who will protect asharippani other than Asharis? During the bad time, we have to stick to desham and *pani* like a scared baby who sticks to the chest of its mother. That should be the *new* prayer of Asharis to Chathan [one of the gods]. If we travel out of the desham during an evil time, we will not come back. (Emphasis added)[51]

In this narration, we can glimpse a shadow of fear of the imminent threat to asharippani from some undisclosed sources. In this new circumstance of bad time, Kandan saw a necessity of a new prayer for holding on to one's own desham and work. The Asharis in my interviews only indirectly explained the colonial intervention as a reason for the bad time in their childhood, but *Ashari Vrithantham* directly refers to the nexus between the new and old *thamburakkanmar* (lords) as the evil force in the form of bad time. The Brahmins were the old lords and the white men were the new lords in this description. Achari, through his character Kandan, described the relation between the new and the old lords as intimidating and uncontrollable:

Earlier too, under the old thamburans [that is the earlier generations of the landlords], we had had many instances of bad time. But our forefathers knew how to overcome those unkind forces which were mostly otherworldly forces. When the old thamburan [native landlord] in desham met the new thamburan [the white man] from the town, he was tempted by the latter with earthly pleasures and succumbed to it. They together changed the world around us, and now we Asharis have ended up in the clutches of an evil time.[52]

Neelakantan Achari's analysis of the contemporary forces of domination noted not just another period of bad time but a new variety of bad time, which was the result of the alliance between the colonialists and the oppressor castes. In other words, time, like an individual, could behave in totally unprecedented ways and one has to be creative in deciding strategies to overcome bad time. As we saw earlier, the first rule that Kandan prescribed to his son was that of locating oneself in desham when one was under the influence of bad time. The second rule, which was equally important, was that one should slow down every activity, including asharippani:

You can see, there is an urge in everyone and everywhere to rush towards fulfilling our desires. Ashari, in order not to fall down in this rush, has to bring time under his control. When there is doubt, he has to slow down, even though others may not appreciate it. If earlier, one has to touch the wood once to sense it, now he has to do it twice to make sure; he should see twice and smell twice.[53]

Achari here prescribed a slowing down of work, which was clearly a strategy to oppose the colonial or missionary conception of work and industriousness. Asharis' 'slowness' was a very popular concept, especially among the dominant castes for whom Asharis built houses or temples. There are many proverbs from the early decades of the twentieth century which criticized Asharis for their lazy attitudes during the work. One proverb says that 'if the Ashari is in, then the *adharam* [document of the property] is out'. The proverb means that if an Ashari is working in a house, his work never ends until one has to pledge the document of the property to pay the expenses. Mention of the property document shows that the proverb emerged in the colonial period, where a property's ownership was established by the adharam.[54] The proverb 'It is like when you call the Ashari for the lunch' is premised on the opinion that, generally, Asharis worked very slowly, and when they were called for lunch, they pretended that they were busy in their work. It is important to note that this concept of slowness of asharippani was a relatively new notion that emerged in the context of Asharis' conflict with colonial notions of work and time.

In one of his early travel reports in 1889, Edgar Thurston described how he was surprised 'by the coordination and swiftness' of Asharis who worked 'without drawings or plans'. In Ponnani, he witnessed the construction of the roof of a house 'which was completed in a day's time by a group of proficient carpenters in an orderly manner'.[55] Havell considered carpenters 'efficient and hardworking'. According to him, the way Asharis executed their work was 'commendable for its precision, promptness and finish'.[56] We should remember that the colonialists generally considered natives lazy people who did not know the value of time. Even in that context, Thurston and Havell described Asharis as prompt and hardworking. Reading these colonial and dominant-caste narratives along with Neelakantan Achari's prescription of slowing down in an evil time, we may conclude that the so-called slowness or laziness of Asharis was not an ahistorical and essential characteristic of asharippani but a strategy in a particular context and period. The Ashari concept of desham and (bad) time were part of the strategies through which Asharis avoided the colonial attempt of relocation and assimilation. In other words, space and time were two of the important domains in which Asharis resisted the colonial intervention in their practices of knowing.

Strategies of Ignoring: Social Boycott of the Collaborators

As a child, Murukan Achari left his Malabar home in 1901—without the consent of his parents or the community elders—with a Christian missionary to Salem, where he joined a missionary school. As he was from the Ashari caste, the principal of the school enrolled him in the industrial training classes. After graduation, he joined as an instructor in the industrial training centre at Salem and later joined the Madras School of Arts. He came back to his desham in 1919 to visit his parents, and he also had plans of getting married to an Ashari woman. He wrote, 'Even though I had expected some kind of antagonism at home and in my village, I did not think that it would be to this intense degree.'[57] He tried to convince them that he had neither converted to Christianity nor moved to any trade other than carpentry. Even his father did not agree with him. They thought that he could not learn carpentry without training under a *moothashari* (chief carpenter). He might be 'working on wood, but it could be named only as *companyppani* (factory work)'. No Ashari family was ready to enter into a marital relation with a person 'who is practically not an Ashari'.[58] Within two weeks, he returned to Madras, in vain.

Asharis at this point socially boycotted those who left desham to join a colonial institution. Arumughan Achari, in an article, described a similar experience of his brother who joined the railway workshop at Perambur in the early 1920s.[59] Even though this brother used to visit the house once a year, he was excluded from all the important family functions. After many failed attempts of finding a woman from the Ashari caste, he married from outside the caste, which completed his expulsion from the community. It was mainly through the strategy of social exclusion that Asharis resisted the institutionalization process. The aforementioned were the instances where individuals left desham and where, in turn, the community used expulsion from the caste as an effective tactic to prevent such incidents. We already saw that technical education institutions generally failed to attract students from the traditional artisanal castes. This was not a general result of the ignorance of artisans about these institutions. At least in the case of Asharis, there were several instances where they actively tried to discourage the members of the caste from enrolling in these institutions.

By the 1950s, as the result of Indian political independence, colonial educational institutions came under the control of nationalist elites. Education became one of the major agendas of the union government, and following this national agenda, the state governments attempted to widen the network of educational institutions. By the late 1950s, almost all villages in Malabar had at least a primary school which enrolled students from all caste groups.[60] As education was now a national issue, the compulsion to join these institutions was far greater than in the early part of the twentieth century. For Asharis, it became difficult to completely ignore the social pressure of enrolling their children in schools.

The majority of Asharis I interviewed, who are between the ages of fifty and sixty, have studied at least up to fourth standard. However, only a few had passed the tenth standard, which was the qualification required for many government jobs in the 1950s. Gopalan, who studied till the ninth standard, explained that his father withdrew him from the school then, because those who passed the tenth standard never came back to asharippani. Shreedharan, who is now a schoolteacher, remembers that his father was totally disappointed when he decided to complete the tenth standard. As predicted by his father, he did not return to asharippani, but joined a teacher training course and later became a history teacher. A report on education in Madras state in 1951 mentioned about the Malabar district that 'though there is substantial improvement in the enrolments in the primary schools, the number of "dropouts" is increasing at an alarming rate'. The report pointed out that one of the reasons for the increasing dropout was the concern among parents regarding their children 'moving out from the hereditary occupations based on castes'.[61]

Cherukad, who was famous for his progressive novels and short stories, discussed the issue of dropouts from his experience as a teacher in the 1950s. He connected this issue with 'caste prejudices' and observed that 'the members of the lowest castes are comparatively more interested in education than the castes like Ashari or Karivan (carpenter and smith, both artisanal castes)'.[62] According to Cherukad, one could not blame the parents from these castes, because they were then able to provide their children with a solid training in a job which provided a stable income, whereas the school education did not provide any such training for any kind of job.

A sample survey conducted by K. Ravindran in Kozhikode district (which was part of earlier Malabar district) in the late 1960s shows that only 2 per cent of Asharis between the ages of sixteen and fifty had a matriculation degree (tenth standard) at that period.[63] Ravindran observed that usually students drop out from school when they continuously fail in a class three or four times. Many of the Ashari students, however, dropped out because 'their parents required more hands to finish the works they undertook'.[64]

From the discussion thus far, it is clear that Ashari students were dropping out from schools not necessarily because of their disinterest in studies. It was the silent understanding among the community elders that the educational institutions could not protect the interest of the community, thus compelling them to withdraw their children from the schools. In short, we can observe that from the early twentieth century to the late 1960s, Asharis resisted the attempts of institutionalization by the colonial and the post-colonial governments, which tried in similar ways to 'governmentalize' the population through educational institutions.

Strategies of Mobilizing: Conversations and Storytelling

The strategies of ignoring have left many traces in both memory and archives, which were the sources from which the earlier analysis was constructed. However, the actual deployment of these strategies has fewer traces, as it was part of the daily life practice of the subaltern community which did not 'make history'. It is not easy to answer the question of how Asharis actually mobilized and practised the politics of ignoring. Who told the individual Asharis that they should not associate with the colonial institutions? How did the idea of protecting asharippani become a common sense among the individual members? The reform movements of subaltern caste groups like Pulayas and Ezhavas in the early twentieth century problematized the caste oppression and organized resistance based on their caste identity. In this process, they formed caste associations like Sree Narayana Dharma Paripalana Yogam and Sadhu Jana Paripalana Sangham. They also started publications as a strategy of mobilization.

Unlike these caste communities who organized themselves under associations, the Asharis did not form a caste-community association. They did not start publications of newspapers or journals, which were the important domain of imagining caste as a community, in this period. When I posed this question to Asharis, most of them signalled to conversations and storytelling as practices of mobilization, which happened mainly at two locations: at workplace and at home. If the elder male Asharis initiated the conversations at the workplace, it was the older women who led the storytelling at home.

The different functions of storytelling in various stages of history have been analysed by historians and anthropologists. Most of these scholars underscore the aspect of teaching and transferring morals and knowledge as functions of storytelling.[65] Storytelling as a mobilizing strategy was not particular to the Ashari caste. It had a central role in maintaining the networks based on castes. In the case of Asharis, especially in the context of colonial attempts of intervention, storytelling was a political mobilization strategy as well. Narratives of elder Asharis included reporting and analysing of incidents or events, stories with moral lessons, new lessons in carpentry, 'fun talk', and so on. It was mostly women Asharis who visited the houses of relatives in other villages and brought news from these places. Similarly, occasions of wedding, death, rituals for dead ancestors, and so on were also the occasions of travel and collection and distribution of stories. In short, the mobilization was shot through a network, in which the narratives were the nodes, and the travel and gathering played the role of connecting links.

Raghavan Ashari is a practising carpenter at Baypore and was one of my interviewees. According to him, he learned the rules and customs of Ashari caste from his early childhood conversations with his grandfather. These conversations at workplace, he remembers, were not particularly directed towards children. These stories were either about the bad luck of those who left the village or about the boycott of such persons by the family and relatives. One of the popular stories in those days was about one Ashari named Kunjan, who left the village to join the railway workshop at Cheruvannur. Kunjan learned the skills of carpentry from a very early age and was blessed with a 'special hand'. His hands were swift and the 'finish' of his works was excellent. However, due to his special hand, 'he was not the one who could be on the other end of the saw' (which hints that he was not a group player).[66] Kunjan joined the railway workshop disregarding the elders; but within a year, he had a stroke and his right side was paralyzed. Raghavan Ashari remembers that, whenever he did something that interrupted the rhythm of the group work, his grandfather would scold him by shouting, 'Are you possessed by Kunjan?'

Raghavan Ashari, as a child, knew that some of the stories might be fictional, but he also knew that he should 'respect the stories because that is how you learn about the past and about the surroundings one inhabits'.[67] Here, he reveals many important aspects of storytelling as a strategy. The storytelling was important in organizing the conceptual world of Asharis; more importantly, its significance was also recognized by the participants who listened to the stories. Hence, what concerned the listeners was not about the facticity of the events narrated as such, but the question of why a certain story was narrated in certain situations. Raghavan Ashari pointed out that the storytelling was not continuous but always interrupted by other conversations such as 'giving directions or orders', 'silence' because of focusing in work, or interruption by other elders to add their own versions and anecdotes. Laughing loudly, he concluded, 'These work-time conversations were similar to today's TV; it has both news in stories and stories in news.'[68]

Asharippani and Gender and Caste Differentiation

The protection of asharippani as a practice of knowing, in the process of avoiding the invasion of colonial knowledge, created multiple effects on the daily life of Asharis and their imagination about caste and gender. In nineteenth-century Malabar, like most other places in the colony, caste and gender forces operated as a single force in an entwined manner.[69] At this period, gender identification was directly predicated on the caste identification of an individual. For example, the cloth or ornament an individual wore in the late nineteenth-century Malabar clearly indicated both their gender and caste identities.[70] In other words, the identification process as an Ashari and as a woman or man was a unified practice determined by the reproduction of these identities in the daily life. The dress codes, the manner of speech, the diet and eating restrictions, and the restrictions of movement and touch in daily life simultaneously reproduced gender and caste identities.

By the end of the nineteenth century, the gender identification process began separating from that of caste identification. The question of the status of women was the central question of the reform movements in India in general in the nineteenth and twentieth centuries. From the very beginning, the colonial and the dominant caste reformers deployed the female body as an object of reform discourse. In Malabar, both the Nampoothiri and Nair reform movements focused on the status of women in their reform efforts. Scholars have already shown that the community reformers never imagined a complete equality between men and women. The attempt was to transform women into a respectable position in the private space of the modern household, and they would manage this household and serve the educated, modernized husband in civilized ways.[71]

The fundamental principal of gender relations in the reform narratives was 'bio-logic', which was premised on an essential biological difference between the identities of men and women. According to this imagination, the whole future of a body is biologically determined, and a civilized society has to design practices that will reproduce, maintain, and naturalize the difference between the identities of the gender binary: man and woman. In other words, both the colonialists and the reform leaders justified the social practices that created the difference between the men and women based on the logic of the law of nature as well as on a concept of essentialized bodies. Bio-logic was not just a concept of differentiation of bodies based on biology. It was a process of the social construction of the very biological difference and the naturalization of that difference.[72] Hence, by bio-logic, we are not just mentioning the process of gender identification at birth; rather, it points towards the justification of gender difference based on biological difference. Asharis, in the first half of the twentieth century, refused to accept this bio-logic by centre-staging asharippani as the gender-differentiating category. This refusal was very subtle and complex, and it could be sensed only if we pay great attention to the nuances of the Ashari gender identification processes in this period.

Asharis, like any other community, identified a child as boy or girl at its birth. The different sets of male and female names are indications of this identification. One could consider this as differentiation based on biology. The difference between the Ashari identification of gender and the colonial bio-logic was that in the former case, gender difference was not reproduced or explained based on bio-logic but on asharippani. The song which was popular among Asharis in the first half of the twentieth century explains the relation between the gender differentiation process and asharippani:

> Protect me, Kaliyamme [the goddess Kali],
> Protect my pani [the work: asharippani].
> If I lose my capacity to work,
> I will be considered neither man nor Ashari.
> Oh, Kali, protect my pani.
> If my hand cannot hold the chisel,
> I will be among the womenfolk.
> Oh, Kali, protect my pani.
> If I cannot measure with the *muzhakkol* [wooden measuring scale],
> I will have to work in the kitchen.
> Oh, Kali, protect my pani.[73]

The song defined the manliness of an individual based on his capacity to engage in asharippani. It articulated the difference between the genders in the form of an affiliation to work: men engaging in asharippani and women working in the kitchen. If a specific dress code was one of the important markers of gender for most of the communities, it was the *kolum charatum* (the scale and the string which Ashari men were supposed to carry everywhere) that was the mark of the Ashari man. In the first half of the twentieth century, the Ashari man and woman wore the same kind of attire: a simple white plain cloth that covered the lower part of the body. Even the hairstyle of men and women was similar. Both tied their hair upwards and both wore similar earrings.[74] If the aforementioned song represented the internal conceptualization of Asharis regarding gender, Asharis gave a similar impression about them for outside observers too. W. Travers, a British colonial officer in Malabar, observed that 'among the five traditional artisanal castes, carpenters attract separate attention for their customs and practices. They are the only group in which women are not part of the hereditary occupation; for the other four artisanal castes, women are important part of their trade'.[75] Travers also mentioned that some of the natives informed him that earlier, Ashari women used to engage in producing kitchen utensils and small tools at home.

When he asked about this to a chief carpenter, he completely denied any such knowledge. Travers concluded that irrespective of the stories about the past, in the present, 'carpentry is a vocation of men', and for an external observer, 'outside the workplace, it would be difficult to identify their women from the men from their appearance'.[76]

This was true not only for a foreign observer but also for a native person outside the Ashari caste. K. V. Moosathu, a dominant-caste reform writer, who was a strong supporter of the reforms and modernization in the 1920s, wrote:

> After ten or fifteen years, if we tell our children about the dresses men and women were wearing in the Malayalam-speaking region in the wake of this century, they will consider it as ridiculous and some may think it as pure fiction.... Consider the example of Asharis. Even now, both Ashari men and women wear a mundu [a plain cloth] around their waist, which reaches a little below the knees. Both wear earrings and style the hair similarly. I am wondering how we will distinguish the men from women if the men stop asharippani and no longer carry the measuring scale and the thread![77]

In the description, it is clear that Moosathu observed asharippani as the major measure of gender difference for Asharis. It should be noted that Moosathu, who was trained in a colonial system of education, believed in the bio-logic of gender difference, and in the later part of his article, he directly expressed this belief. He observed that the educated classes 'are now aware of the basic difference between man and woman through scientific education'. These educated individuals expressed this understanding through their dress: 'Men wear mundu and shirt, and women wear mundu and blouse.' Moosathu reasoned that Ashari men and women were similar in their appearance because 'they have not attained the scientific awareness of the difference between the bodies of man and woman'.[78]

Questioning Moosathu's argument in the next issue of the same journal, another dominant-caste orthodox writer, Vasudeva Menon, observed that Asharis were not unaware of the bodily difference between man and woman. The difference between Asharis and the young, reformed generation was that 'Asharis have not yet started indulging in bodily pleasures like the contemporary educated young people'. According to Menon, Asharis still considered their body as a 'God-given instrument for divine work; through their work, they show that they are strong men'.[79] Menon connected the manliness of Asharis directly to the work. In a satiric article in 1932, an unknown reporter for the *Mathrubhumi* daily mentioned that 'for the educated new generation, it would be difficult to distinguish between men and women of the lower caste'. Again, this was because most of the 'lower-caste' men and woman wore the same kind of attire and engaged in similar work. 'Asharis and Mannans [mason caste] are exceptions; at least their men and women engage in different kinds of works.'[80]

The aforementioned discussion shows that in the first half of the twentieth century, Asharis deliberately projected asharippani as the organizing category of gender. This was not possible in the nineteenth century because Ashari women were also part of asharippani, though they worked only from home and their role was subordinated to that of men. Even in the last decade of the nineteenth century, we can see references to the work of Ashari women in the colonial records. In a report in 1889, Logan observed that 'Ashari women in Malabar are experts in making carved handles for knives and wooden utensils'.[81] We have already seen that when Travers reported on the carpenters thirty years after Logan did, he mentioned that 'they are the only one artisanal group in which women are not part of the hereditary occupation'.[82] Until the 1911 census, like other artisanal groups, Asharis were generally counted as families. This was because the colonialists considered carpentry, like other artisanal practices, as family work in which the whole family participates. From the 1911 census onwards, the government started using an individual occupational status for the Asharis for all comparative purposes. This indicates the shift in the gender aspect of asharippani, which is no more a family activity.

In an article in 1932, C. Raman Menon made a similar comment regarding the participation of women in asharippani. His grandmother told him that in her childhood, an Ashari woman living nearby, who used to make toys for her was also an expert in making kitchen utensils. When Menon inquired about this to a carpenter near his house, he was told that 'there are stories like that, but Ashari women were never allowed to touch a chisel'.[83] Despite the contradictory nature of these accounts, we can conclude from these that Ashari men at this period purposely took efforts to convince themselves and others that asharippani was always a male profession.

The Ashari ways of constructing gender difference through asharippani, in one sense, resisted the bio-logic of colonial knowledge. At the same time, it was not completely antithetical to this logic. For the dominant-caste educated classes, the Ashari interpretation was not surprising or unacceptable. Even when the colonial knowledge based its justification of gender difference in biology, the division of occupation based on gender was part of its practice of gender differentiation. The colonialists and the native reformers considered tailoring, nursing, and house management suitable occupations for respectable women. The criteria for this was the bio-logic, which reasoned that women's bodies can sustain only lighter jobs and also that by nature, women are not capable of highly intellectual deliberations.[84] In this circumstance, it was not difficult for the colonialists and the dominant castes to understand the Ashari interpretation of asharippani as a male profession. The difference was that Asharis did not use any bio-logic to justify the exclusion of women from the profession. For them, the gendered nature of the profession was not connected to the nature of the body that executes the work; rather, it was the reverse. In this logic, asharippani, by nature, was a male profession, engaging in which a child becomes a man. It was not the human being who was 'necessarily gendered'; rather, it was the work which was already gendered and which enabled the human being to achieve one's gender. It is necessary to underscore here that the point is not that Asharis did not assign any *a priori* gender to the body. The difference between the colonial and Ashari practices of gender differentiation was, rather, in the justificatory logic of the respective arguments.

As a central organizing category, asharippani not only was the ordering logic of gendering process but also became the defining factor of caste itself. Again, as in the case of gender differentiation, the difference from the earlier period was subtle and complex. Earlier in this chapter, we saw that Asharis used the threat of exclusion from their caste as a strategy against those who cooperated with colonial institutions. It was in this process that asharippani began determining the definitions of the Ashari caste. This argument should not be confused with the orientalist and Hindu revivalist argument that caste in its origin was a system of division of labour.[85] The functionalist argument in the latter case attempts to justify the caste system in its origin by considering the brahmanical domination as a later aberration. Our point here is that asharippani became the defining category of caste only in a historical juncture, where Asharis projected asharippani as something more than mere occupation in their resistance against the intervention of colonial knowledge.

We have already seen two cases where Asharis excluded men who joined the colonial institutions from their family and the caste. This indicates a tendency where Asharis started increasingly defining caste based on asharippani. In other words, the caste identification process, which had multiple dimensions, gradually narrowed down to a process based on asharippani. Francis Buchanan, a Scottish physician who surveyed south India in the first decade of the nineteenth century, noted the complexity of the process through which natives identified their caste. A child slowly recognized what his caste means through the location of their residences, food habits, dress codes, and specific ways of conversation with older and younger people within and outside the community. Buchanan observed that 'it is hard for a foreigner to recognise all the factors of caste rules', considering the fact that 'even the natives here do not know how the people outside their caste conduct their daily life'.[86] Buchanan's description shows that caste identification through daily life practices was a complex and multi-dimensional process.

By the 1930s, we could observe asharippani increasingly becoming a crucial condition for Ashari men to be part of the community. In *Ashari Vrithantham*, Kandan, the father, explained to his son that asharippani was not something that was limited to 'working on wood with a chisel and a hammer'. Asharippani was a dialogue 'with other worlds: the world of plants, the world of the five elements (earth, water, fire, air, and sky), and the world of forefathers'. It was through engaging with these five elements that one becomes an Ashari. According to Kandan, the white man could understand only one part of the dialogue of Asharis; 'they could never hear what we [Asharis] hear from the trees, waters, fires or forefathers. In the white man's working place, even we will not be able to hear these voices'. This was the reason that one cannot be an Ashari 'in white men's location'.[87]

Neelakantan Achari's philosophical deliberations on what it meant to be an Ashari in the first half of the nineteenth century clearly defined caste based on work. In Achari's story, the son who provoked his father with questions was a character who symbolized the temptations of the new world. The son asked his father, 'If Asharis are only those individuals who are engaged in asharippani, how does a woman born in the Ashari caste remain an Ashari?' The father replied, 'Men and women become Ashari by performing their duty. An Ashari woman's duty is to be in relation with an Ashari man [that is, to be in kinship relations in terms of sociology] and serve the Ashari men in her family. If she fails to do that, she is no more an Ashari.'[88] This explanation established the Ashari-ness of women through their connection to Ashari men, and men could be Ashari only if they are engaged in asharippani. Hence, if an Ashari was not submitting himself to his duties, he was risking not only his existence within the caste but also that of his immediate woman relative. In short, asharippani was the defining category of caste directly for men and indirectly for women.

The stories of the Ashari world in the first half of the twentieth century show the importance of different forms of practices of knowing in understanding the social forces of caste and gender. By the beginning of the century, for each caste community, the relation to knowledge became an important parameter in their changing understandings of caste and gender relations. In other words, knowledge became the reference field from where communities could evaluate their present and chart out their future. However, these evaluations and future programmes were already constrained by their corresponding position in the hierarchical series of knowledge created through the dominant colonial discourse on knowledge. The varied interaction of communities with the knowledge production resulted in varied understandings of caste and gender within each community.

Until the 1970s, Asharis successfully avoided or actively ignored the colonial–brahmanical forms of knowledge through various strategies and tactics. The Ashari interaction shows how difference-making, instead of dichotomous opposition, could be a way of creating distance from the intervention of the dominant forces. It also provides examples of how practices of knowing became central to caste and gender identification. It is also important to note that the transfer of power from the colonialists to the Indian elite did not have a direct influence on the transformation of practices of knowing for the subaltern communities. In other words, the independent Indian state continued the policies of colonial governments in the field of education and knowledge production. To summarize:

> In walking,
> There are many acts of knowing,
> The smell of leaves, the taste of trees;
> The westerly wind, the portent rains,
> The ways of the brook, the warmth of sunlight.
> Amidst those who divert us,
> Amidst those who lead us,
> We must separate,
> Find other paths.
> In misleading times,
> Let slowness set in,
> Let caution grow.[89]

What were the brahmanical practices related to knowledge and caste in the same period? How did the Nampoothiris—the Kerala Brahmins—negotiate with emerging colonial institutions? What was the role of knowledge in the Nampoothiri reform discourse of the 1920s and 1930s? The next two chapters explore these questions by comparing Nampoothiri practices with Ashari negotiations in the same period analysed so far.

Notes

1. For a discussion on caste community reform and education, see Govindan Parayil (ed.), *Kerala: The Development Experience, Reflections on Sustainability and Replicability* (London: Zed Books, 2000). For a discussion on the Ezhava

reform movement, see K. P. Chandramohan, *Development Modernity in Kerala: Narayana Guru, SNDP Yogam and Social Reform* (Chennai: Tulika Books, 2016); and P. R. Gopinathan Nair, 'Education and Socio-Economic Change in Kerala, 1793–1947', *Social Scientist* 4, no. 8 (March 1976): 28–43. Also see Rajan Gurukkal, 'Development Experience of Colonial Keralam', *Rethinking Development: Kerala's Development Experience* 1 (1999): 73–98.

2. See the Introduction.

3. Alfred Chatterton, *Industrial Evolution in India* (Madras: The Hindu Office, 1912), 9 (emphasis added).

4. E. B. Havell, *The Basis for Artistic and Industrial Revival in India* (Madras: The Theosophist Office, 1912), 12.

5. Havell, *Artistic and Industrial Revival*, 13 (emphasis added).

6. Havell, *Artistic and Industrial Revival*, 3.

7. James Scott, *The Art of Not Being Governed: An Anarchic History of Upland Southeast Asia* (New Haven: Yale University Press, 2009).

8. See Chapter 1.

9. Friedrich Nietzsche, *Untimely Meditations* (Cambridge: Cambridge University Press, 1996), 62.

10. Ashis Nandy, 'History's Forgotten Doubles', *History and Theory* 34, no. 2 (May 1995): 44–66.

11. Both Ayyankali, the Pulaya reform leader, and Sree Narayana Guru, the Ezhava reform leader, underscored the importance of (colonial) education in their writings and speeches. *The Ezhava Memorial*, a memorandum submitted to the Travancore government in 1890, pleaded with the Raja to reserve a certain percentage of government jobs for educated Ezhavas. Several articles in *Mithavadi*, the mouthpiece of Sree Narayana Dharma Paripalana Yogam (SNDP)—the reform organization of the Ezhavas—urged the members of the community to completely distance themselves from toddy-tapping and to seek government jobs. Sadhujana Paripalana Sangham, the reform organization under the leadership of Ayyankali, initiated steps to start schools for the children from the Pulaya community. For Ayyankali's contribution towards education, see M. Nisar and Meena Kandaswamy, *Ayyankali: Dalit Leader of Organic Protest* (Calicut: Other Books, 2007). For Sree Narayana Guru's deliberations on knowledge and education, see Sree Narayana Guru and Muni Narayana Prasad, *Sree Narayana Guruvinte Sampoorna Krithikal* (The Collected Works of Sree Narayana Guru) (Kottayam: DC Books, 2005).

12. Toddy is a juice extracted from coconut trees, and it has high alcoholic content. Tapping toddy from the coconut tree is a highly skilled job, and it was considered the traditional occupation of Ezhava men.

13. The main missionary organization in Malabar was of the German protestant missionaries of the Basel Evangelical Mission (BEM). Unlike the British protestant group such as the Church Mission Society (CMS) and the London Missionary Society (LMS), which were active in the neighbouring

Malayalam-speaking areas of Kochi and Thiruvithamkoor, the BEM did not believe in mass conversion. According to the manual of the BEM, each individual had to go through a certain period of probation before they were able to convert. But both the CMS and the BEM considered education an important step in approaching God. They urged the oppressed-caste people to join in mission schools and escape the tyranny of the Brahmins through knowledge. The missionaries recruited mainly Pulaya and Paraya community members; their attempt to convert people from artisanal castes was generally a failure. For the contributions of the LMS and the CMS, see P. K. M. Tharakan, 'Socio-Economic Factors in Educational Development: Case of Nineteenth Century Travancore', *Economic and Political Weekly* 19, no. 45 (November 1984): 1930–1938. For the work of the BEM on education of oppressed castes in Malabar see J. Raghaviah, *Basel Mission Industries in Malabar and South Canara (1834–1914): A Study of Its Social and Economic Impact* (Delhi: Gian Publishing House, 1990).

14. Basel Evangelical Mission Records, vol. 15, Mission Archives, Mangalore, 1899, 112.

15. For a detailed analysis of the changes in the Nair joint family in the nineteenth and twentieth centuries, see G. Arunima, 'Multiple Meanings: Changing Concepts of Matrilineal Kinship in Nineteenth and Twentieth Century Malabar', *Indian Economic and Social History Review* 33, no. 3 (September 1996): 283–307.

16. *The Report of the Industrial Survey of 1926*, Madras Presidency (Madras: Government Press, 1928), 132.

17. V. N. Kurup, 'Marunna Kudumba Kramangal (Changing Family Practices)', *Kerala Chandrika* 11 (1934): 34–37, 35.

18. Interview with Keshavan Achari (6 October 2009).

19. David Scott, 'Colonial Governmentality', *Social Text* 43 (Autumn 1995): 191–220.

20. E. B. Havell, *Report on the Native Industries in Madras Province* (Madras: Government Press, 1883).

21. Chatterton, *Industrial Evolution in India*, 81.

22. E. B. Havell, *A Report on Madras School of Arts* (Madras: Government Press, 1902).

23. *Report on Public Instruction*, Madras Presidency (Madras, 1910).

24. Proceedings of the Home Department 1909, Tamil Nadu State Archives, NO N, 12, 21.

25. Proceedings of the Home Department 1909, 25.

26. Proceedings of the Home Department 1909, 34.

27. For an analysis of the Basel Evangelical Missions practices of conversion in Malabar, see Raghaviah, *Basel Mission Industries.*

28. Proceedings of the Home Department 1909, 12, 23.

29. Interview with Velayudhan (6 June 2009).

30. Interview with Krishnan (27 June 2009).

31. Several people whom I interviewed repeated similar stories regarding cities or towns. Even in the contemporary situation, where a significant number of

Asharis are working in the furniture manufacturing workshops in towns and cities, they consider the city not a place of belonging but a temporary location. Almost all the elderly Asharis whom I interviewed had a story about the evil nature of the city and how their grandparents did not want to leave the desham.

32. Proceedings of the Home Department, Government of Madras, CRI, No 12–32B, 1887.

33. W. Arbuthnot, *A Journey through Malabar Coast* (London: Trubner & Co., 1901), 43.

34. C. A. Innes and F. B. Evans, *Malabar and Anjengu* (Madras: Addison & Co., 1905).

35. *Proceedings of the Home Department 1909*, Tamil Nadu State Archives, NO N – 12, 41 (original letter in Malayalam; my translation).

36. *Report of the Malabar Tenancy Committee, 1915* (Madras: Government Press, 1917), 154.

37. This palm leaf manuscript is now with V. Shreedharan, the grandson of Neelakantan Achari. Shreedharan, through consultations with his grandfather's younger brother, helped me read this manuscript and calculate the time period of the work. Also, note that there was no practice of numbering the pages of the palm leaves in this form.

38. In the Sanskrit tradition, the last line of the verse indicates the year in which the work is finished. Neelakantan Achari uses a similar method, but according to the Malayalam calendar year. Neelakantan Achari, *Ashari Vrithantham*, unpublished manuscript (1936).

39. 'Desham Vittoru Ashariyum,
    Vellam varnna meenum onnepol
    Deshathile ariyavoo, deshathine ariyavoo
    Deshathin purame velivaykayilla
    Kizhakketh thekketh
    Katteth, neereth marameth alaveth.'
    Neelakantan Achari, *Ashari Vrithantham*.

40. Govindan Ashari, *Deshamahima*, unpublished manuscript (1921). Govindan Ashari wrote these notes in a notebook, which is currently with his nephew, K. Manikantan. Though Manikantan made some effort to publish this work, it remains unpublished. The time of the work is calculated from the memories of Manikantan's grandmother, Kunja, and her brother, Gopalan.

41. Ashari, *Deshamahima*, 21–26.

42. Each Nampoothiri family, especially in south Malabar, was associated with specific deshams. They considered families in certain deshams as having a lower status than those in other deshams. For the relation of Nampoothiris with desham, see Kanippayyoor Shankaran Nampoothirippad, *Ente Smaranakal* (My Memories) (Kunnamkulam: Panchangam Pusthaasala, 1964).

43. Abigail McGowan, *Crafting the Nation in Colonial India* (New York: Palgrave MacMillan, 2009), 3.

44. For example, Gandhi's description of Indian villages and George Birdwood's analysis of Indian villages share many aspects, especially regarding the role of the artisans. For Gandhi's ideas about gramam, see M. K. Gandhi, *Mahatma Gandhi: Selected Political Writings* (Indianapolis: Hackett Publishing Company, 1996).

45. Kuttippurathu Keshavan Nair, 'Nattuvazhiyiloote (Through the Village Road)', *Kerala Nandini* 8, no. 2 (March 1925): 33–37, 36.

46. Nair, 'Nattuvazhiyiloote', 37.

47. Nair, 'Nattuvazhiyiloote', 37.

48. Nair, 'Nattuvazhiyiloote', 38.

49. Allayo Kalabhairava
    Kanunneele, dushtabudhi
    Kalathin pidiyil njaan ninakka vazhikalil
    Alayunnu, kaathukonteeduka,
    Avante kadumpidutham vittozhiche tharika.
    Vannathenguninnee kalam,
    Njano pizhachathenth, ariveela
    Ethra nal ivan pidiyil njanennum ariveela
    Karuna katti ivane akattuka doore
    Kalabhairavaa.'
    This song was sung to me by Shanmughan Achari of Mundur, who is a chief carpenter and scholar. According to him, 'Time is a powerful force like the flow of wind. If it is slow and cool, we call it breeze, which is pleasurable. But if it is strong, we call it a storm, which is destructive.' Interview with Shanmughan Achari (13 May 2010).

50. Interview with Kunjan Keralasseri (26 January 2009).

51. Achari, *Ashari Vrithantham*.

52. Achari, *Ashari Vrithantham*.

53. Achari, *Ashari Vrithantham*.

54. Specific documentation of individual landed property was not unknown in the pre-colonial period. This was mostly in the form of the king's order written on palm leaves. The specific word *adharam* (literally meaning reference) became the name of the land title in the colonial period. See K. N. Panikkar, *Against Lord and State: Religion and Peasant Uprising in Malabar 1836–1921* (Delhi: Oxford University Press, 1989).

55. Edgar Thurston, *Ethnographic Notes in Southern India* (Madras: Government Press, 1906), 358.

56. Proceedings of the Department of Industries and Commerce, Industries, March 1901, No. 1–21, National Archives of India (NAI).

57. Proceedings of the Department of Industries and Commerce, 24.

58. Proceedings of the Department of Industries and Commerce, 26.

59. Arumughan Achari, 'Asharimarum Acharangalum (Asharis and Customs)', *Vidyaposhini* 2, no. 6 (July 1943): 22–27.

60. For a history of the educational institutions in Malabar, see S. Subba Raman, *History of Progress of Education in Madras State, 1875–1960* (Madras: Sakthi Publishers, 1979).

61. *Education Reforms: A Report from the State of Madras* (Madras: Government Press, 1952), 126–127.

62. S. Cherukad, *Vidyalaya Chinthakal* (Thoughts on School) (Kozhikode: Mathrubhumi, 1952).

63. K. Ravindran, *A Study of Technical Education in Kerlam*, Industries Department, Government of Kerala, (Thiruvanathapuram: Government Press, 1964).

64. Ravindran, *A Study of Technical Education*, 23.

65. For example, see Rodolfo Maggio, 'The Anthropology of Story Telling and the Story Telling of Anthropology', *Journal of Comparative Research in Anthropology and Sociology* 5, no. 2 (Winter 2014): 89–106.

66. Interview with Raghavan Ashari (13 August 2014).

67. Interview with Raghavan Ashari.

68. Interview with Raghavan Ashari.

69. For analyses of entwinement of caste and gender, see Anupama Rao, *Gender and Caste* (Delhi: Kali for Women, 2005); Sharmila Rege, *Writing Caste, Writing Gender: Reading Dalit Women's Testimonios* (New Delhi: Zuban, 2006); Sharmila Rege, *Caste and Gender: Violence against Women in India* (Florence: European University Institute, 1996).

70. For the description of the dressing codes in the nineteenth century based on caste and gender, see P. Bhaskaranunni, *Pathompatham Noottantile Keralam* (The Nineteenth Century Keralam) (Thrissur: Kerala Sahithya Academy, 1988).

71. J. Devika discusses the reformation of patriarchy in the context of reform movements. Exploring the dominant-caste reform literature in the late nineteenth and early twentieth centuries, she shows that the elite-caste reform movements separated the public from the private and positioned women in the private space of family. The reform discourse articulated family women as virtuous and 'public women' as morally corrupt. J. Devika, *En-gendering Individuals: The Language of Re-forming in Early Twentieth Century Keralam* (Hyderabad: Orient Longman, 2007).

72. For a critical analysis of understandings of gender difference based on biology, see Oyeronke Oyewumi, *The Invention of Women: Making an African Sense of Western Gender Discourses* (Minneapolis: University of Minnesota Press, 1997).

73. 'Kaathukolkenne Kaaliyamme
Kaathukolken pani
Paniyariyathavan
Aanumaaka Ashariyaaka
Kalee pani kathukolka
Uli pidikkaatha njan
Penkoottathile pedum

Kolalakkaatha njaan
Aduppoothiye theerum
Kalee pani kathukolka.'

The song is included in C. K. Venugopal (ed.), *Natan Pattukalum Nattarivum* (Folk Songs and Folk Knowledge) (Thrisur: Mudra Publishers, 1997), 34–35. According to Venugopal, this song was part of the rituals for pleasing the goddess Kali which also describe various Ashari tools and instruments.

74. K. V. Moosathu, 'Acharavishengal' (The Peculiarities of Customs), *Vidyavinodini*, no. 12 (December 1929): 34–38.
75. W. Travers, *A Journey through Malabar and Mysore* (Madras: Higginbotham and Co., 1918), 29.
76. Travers, *A Journey Through Malabar*, 34.
77. K. V. Moosathu, 'Acharavishengal'.
78. Moosathu, 'Acharavishengal', 36.
79. M. Vasudeva Menon, 'Visheshamaya Acharangal' (Peculiar Customs), *Vidyavinodini*, no. 1 (January 1930): 43–47, 45.
80. Menon, 'Visheshamaya Acharangal', 46.
81. *Proceedings of the Home Department*, Government of Madras, 1889, Tamil Nadu State Archives, B – 156, No. 32–34.
82. Travers, *A Journey Through Malabar*, 47.
83. C. Raman Menon, 'Chila Nyayangal' (Some Justifications), *Kerala Chandrilka* 32, no. 6 (June 1932): 43–49.
84. For a discussion on how the reform discourse categorised different new occupation based on gender, see Devika, *En-gendering Individuals*.
85. B. R. Ambedkar, who was the champion of the downtrodden and then-untouchable castes, through his writings, exposed as fallacious the brahmanical justification of caste as originally a division of labour. To the contrary, Ambedkar argued that from the very beginning, caste was a hierarchical argument of power and brahmanical strategy of domination. See B. R. Ambedkar, *The Untouchables* (Delhi: Sidhartha Books, 2008).
86. W. Hunter (ed.), *Journal of Francis Buchanan, Mysore and Malabar 1821–22* (Madras: Government Press, 1907).
87. Achari, *Ashari Vrithantham*.
88. Achari, *Ashari Vrithantham*.
89. Translation by Bindu Menon.

3

A Nampoothiri World of *Acharam*

The claims of superiority by nations, races, and castes always accompany a constructed past where these claims find justifications. It is common sense in academic scholarship that often these histories as constructed pasts change according to the needs of the present, and new histories are constructed to match these requirements. In India, the claim that Brahmins were the authority of traditional knowledge and it is this authority that resulted in their dominance is such a claim. It is accompanied by descriptions of the Vedas and other Sanskrit texts explained not only as the source of traditional knowledge but also as texts that contained all important modern scientific knowledge. This chapter positions the changing claims of dominance by Brahmins in the historical context by explaining the social processes that necessitated the changes in the claims of domination.

Anthropologists and historians have explained brahmanical domination in India in relation to their economic, political, and ritualistic power. The European scholars of the colonial period generally explained the brahmanical domination citing the 'spiritual nature' of Hindu society and the importance of Brahmins in the ritual practices based on Vedic knowledge.[1] Ambedkar, while criticizing the caste system, challenged the authority of brahmanical knowledge and considered the Sanskritic textual tradition, which he called *shasthra*s, as the fundamental resource for caste practice.[2] In the beginning of the second half of the twentieth century, M. N. Srinivas and Louis Dumont raised serious questions regarding power and status in relation to the dominance of a caste in a locality. Srinivas in his early work on dominant caste explained that 'a caste may be said to be "dominant" when it preponderates numerically over the other castes and when it is also wields preponderant economic and political power'.[3] In a later work, Srinivas observed that 'important as the secular criteria are, ritual superiority has an independent existence and power of its own'.[4] He added that on secular criteria alone, a Brahmin may occupy a very low position, but he is still a Brahmin and as such entitled to respect in the context of ritual and pollution. In this work, I am using the category 'dominant caste' not entirely in the sense that Srinivas uses it; it is mainly to indicate the dominating power of the castes, which are usually mentioned as 'upper castes'.

Dumont made a distinction between power and status, in which the former is dominance in the realm of the political, and the latter, in the domain of the spiritual. He further noted that:

> ... the extension of the term 'dominance' to the religious level seems even less defensible than the extension of 'status' to the non-religious level. Whereas on the present view it is absolutely necessary to distinguish clearly, in the very terminology, between these two levels, we have noted that in certain conditions power scrumptiously becomes the equal of status.[5]

For Dumont, while spiritual aspects were important, he categorized that domain separately from the realm of the political.[6] M. S. S. Pandian in his work on the non-Brahmin movement in Tamil Nadu pointed out that the domain of the spiritual always extended to the domain of politics and that, therefore, both should be considered as hybrid spaces.[7] The claim of ritual purity by Brahmins, for example, was extended to the claims of their dominance in the public spaces. In this chapter, I attempt to situate such claims and the transformations in these claims of dominance in the context of the emergence and dissemination of colonial knowledge in the second half of the nineteenth century. Both the concept of the material versus spiritual domains and the concept of hybridity are insufficient to explain the transformations that took place in the nature of claims of dominance during the colonial period. While it is true that there were always multiple factors that made a caste dominant, there was always a central aspect around which the claims of superiority were made, although that too changed historically. I use two categories, the order of acharam and the order of knowledge, to mark these transformations. I will explain these categories in detail in the later part of this chapter, but shall note here that an order of knowledge that emerged in the colonial condition gradually replaced the order of acharam, and this change played a critical role in the transformations of the claims of caste dominance. In this conceptualization, neither acharam nor knowledge is located in the divided domains of the material and the spiritual.

In the nineteenth century, before an order of knowledge was established, it was in the name of acharam that the Nampoothiris of Kerala claimed their higher status over other communities. While acharam can be understood as the performance of ritual actions, it was also the customary law that ordered the action of all caste communities. All actions of Nampoothiris in their daily practices were ordered in reference to acharam. The Nampoothiri community's entry into the colonial order of knowledge in the 1920s transformed not only the concept of ritual, tradition, wealth, and politics—that is, altogether, acharam as it was practised in the nineteenth century—but also the daily life practices of the community or caste practices in general.

Nicholas Dirks argued that it was in the process of colonial knowledge production that 'caste has been constituted as the principal modality of Indian society'.[8] While he makes significantly different arguments from the earlier sociological and anthropological scholarship on caste, Dirks's definition of the concept of 'political' is a limited one. Throughout his analysis, it is the activities of kings, rulers, and political and social leaders like Gandhi, Periyar, and Ambedkar that constitute the realm of politics. In other words, for Dirks, politics is situated in the 'public', which is as defined within the colonial notion of divided spheres of public and private. His definition pays little attention to a large sphere of activities where the native communities contested, negotiated, or adapted to the colonial construction of caste. This is important considering the fact that both in the colonial and post-colonial period, caste is reproduced both through everyday life and public activities around caste. This is not to say that Dirks's arguments about the construction of caste in the realm of the political is invalid; rather, I want to extend his analysis by showing the importance of considering the activities of both public and private realms simultaneously. The concept of acharam helps us to understand the politics of claims of dominance, without dividing it into the domains of public and private.

Acharam and Daily Lives of Nampoothiris

From our analysis of the practices of Nampoothiris in Keralam, it becomes clear that until the context of the reform activities in the 1920s, their economic activities were part of the wider ritualistic practice, and conversely, their daily rituals were political as well as economic. I use the category 'acharam' in order to overcome the separation of the activities in the domains of public and private and to explain both the claims of superiority and the modes of domination. The anthropological studies in the 1960s and after, which explored the practices of the Nampoothiri community of Keralam, have noted the uniqueness of the practices compared to the Brahmin communities in other parts of India. At the same time, most of these studies consider the Vedas or other Sanskrit texts as the source and reference point for the practices of the Nampoothiris as elsewhere.[9] For example, Marjatta Parpola, who conducted a lengthy and detailed ethnographic study of a Nampoothiri family, began her analysis by placing *Shankara Smruti* (supposedly a fourteenth-century Sanskrit text) as the reference point from which she explored the changes taking place in the daily practices of Nampoothiris in the twentieth century.[10] Parpola's work could be considered an example of the scholarship in Indological tradition in which Vedic texts were always considered the central source to understand the brahmanical practices. Joan P. Mencher, moving away from the textual interpretational method, analysed the various aspects of the Nampoothiri community by using data from her fieldwork in the early 1960s. Her analysis situated the Nampoothiri practices in the wider context of ecology, land relations, and kinship systems.[11] Frits Staal, whose study focused on the actual practices of brahmanical rites, has convincingly argued that neither were these rites purely religious nor did the practitioners intend any specific meaning to the *mantra*s recited in these rituals.[12] He explained:

> A widespread assumption about ritual is that it consists in symbolic activities which refer to something else. It is characteristic of a ritual performance, however, that it is self-contained and self-absorbed. The performers are totally immersed in the proper execution of their complex tasks.... Their primary concern, if not obsession, is with rules.[13]

While Staal's analysis helps us to understand ritual as a practice and action, his focus is limited to rites, and hence, the idea of ritual is explored only in that context. In my analysis, I use the category 'acharam', which could be roughly translated as ritual, as a more overarching term, which includes all kinds of daily activities of the Nampoothiri life. The discussion of 64 *anacharam*s (unique acharams, supposedly prescribed in *Shankara Smruti* specifically for Kerala Brahmins) in the Nampoothiri reform literature points towards the importance given to acharam as a guiding principle. Here, acharam included a set of actions and normative principles which determined individual actions in the spheres of economic, religious, social, and political life. Acharam should be understood in the context of similar terms which were used to mention the rules of daily life practices. For example, terms like *mamool* and *keezhkkade* referred to precedence and rules formed from the earlier practices. Hence, in the following analysis, acharam should be understood as an umbrella term which refers to both the prescriptions and the practices of Nampoothiri life-world. In short, acharam determined the daily life of Nampoothiris in the nineteenth century and enabled them to maintain their claims of superiority over other caste groups. I call this situation of domination attained through the forces of acharam as the *order of acharam*.

In a nineteenth-century Nampoothiri household, every activity in the daily life was a ritual, or acharam. In his three-volume memoirs, Kanippayyoor Shankaran

Nampoothirippad has recorded detailed descriptions of daily life in a Nampoothiri household. A Nampoothiri man had to wake up from the bed looking eastwards. After a short prayer, he had to take a bath, which was a long ritual. There are very specific rules regarding how to dip inside the water, how to dry oneself, and what to wear after the bath. He had to then proceed either to a temple or to worship the gods inside the house. This took at least two to three hours, after which he ate his first meal. Eating, like other activities, was also a ritual guided by the principles of pollution and purity. After the meals, he engaged in conversation with the fellow Nampoothiri men in the house, with the *karyasthan* (manager of farming activities) or with the guests. There were strict guidelines regarding the varied use of language in conversations depending on the caste, age, and gender status of the individuals engaged in the conversation. In the evening, he had to bathe with a different set of rituals, and after an early meal, he went to sleep after short prayers.[14]

For a Nampoothiri girl or woman, the day started before sunrise. She had to take a bath before sunrise, which itself was an elaborate ritual, and do prayers and *puja*s for *netumangalyam* (long married life), which would take more than two hours. After that, she had to cook food with other women in the house, which should be ready by ten in the morning. She could eat only after the men and the children finished their meals. Between this meal and the preparation for the evening puja, they read *Bhagavatha* or some other puranic texts or prepared materials for the evening puja. By around five, she would begin the evening prayers, and immediately after that, the preparation of evening food. Men usually ate at about eight in the evening, followed by the women. After the meal, she had to clean the kitchen and the place where the deity was placed, where the Nair servants were not allowed to enter. Before sleeping, she had to recite some prayers for keeping evils and bad dreams away. In short, every action—waking up, taking bath, prayers, cooking, eating, washing vessels, taking rest, wearing, washing clothes, or engaging in conversation—is conducted in a predetermined and ritualistic manner controlled by the rules of pollution and purity.[15]

J. Devika, in her analysis of reform narratives of the dominant caste communities in Kerala in the early twentieth century, noted that 'within the *illam* [the Nampoothiri household] the relations between men and women and their everyday routines were carefully delineated'. She further added that Nampoothiri women 'were subjected to a strict and Spartan sartorial code, and as with almost everything else, even bedecking the body was subjugated to ritual purposes'.[16] Devika also noted that while the 'everyday life in illam was organised in a highly complex set of rules of conduct upholding various hierarchies', 'the very structure of regulation itself permitted potentially subversive spaces'.[17] Hence, the point is not whether every individual followed the norms of acharam but that it was through the principles of acharam that Nampoothiris decided whether an act is normal or subversive.

By the end of the nineteenth century, new social forces emerged in the context of accelerated interactions of the dominant castes in the region with the colonial institutions of knowledge production. This interaction engendered many forms of challenges to the order of acharam. The rest of this chapter explores the tensions between the dominating order of acharam and an emerging order of knowledge, and Nampoothiri attempts at maintaining the order of acharam against these new challenges in the early decades of the twentieth century. By focusing on acharam as a source of domination, the chapter interrupts the supposedly long historical role of knowledge in brahmanical power and situates the power–knowledge entanglement in specific historical contexts. By analysing the daily life practice of Nampoothiris in the late nineteenth and the early twentieth centuries, the chapter traces how the Nampoothiris redefined acharam in the context of increasing intervention of knowledge in daily life. It also maps the effects of this redefinition of acharam on jati and gender practices in this period.

The Challenges to the Order of Acharam

The last decades of the nineteenth century witnessed dramatic changes in the caste practices of jatis like Nair, Ezhava, and Pulaya in the Malayalam-speaking region, Keralam, which comprised the princely states of Thiruvithamkoor and Kochi and the British-ruled district of Malabar. In Malabar, Nairs began challenging the order of acharam based on their newly acquired status within the colonial administrative apparatuses. By the end of the nineteenth century, a number of individuals from the Nair jati, who were trained in various colonial educational institutions, attained positions of power, such as revenue administrators, magistrates, and police officers. Their participation in the colonial practices produced new ideas of individuality and new norms and values regarding social life.[18] These ideas, which were predominantly influenced by colonial discourses, were not commensurable with the existing order of acharam imposed by Nampoothiris and of which they were a part. The interaction of Nairs with colonial discourses produced new notions of family and morality based on the bio-logic of colonial knowledge. Nairs, under the leadership of educated individuals, started revaluating and questioning the existing norms and values, especially regarding the special conjugal practices Nair women had with Nampoothiri men.

In the period of interest, in a Nampoothiri illam, only the elder son married from within the caste. The younger brothers practised a particular kind of conjugal relation—which was known as *sambandham*—with women from the dominant castes, including Nairs. Children born in these relations did not belong to the Nampoothiri caste but to that of their mothers.[19] The women or children in the sambandham relation did not have any right to the property of their 'husband' or father. Nairs followed a matrilineal system and property was transferred through the lineage of women. Nair women generally practised serial monogamous relations with dominant-caste men, including Nampoothiris. Theoretically, a Nair woman could suspend one such relation and begin a new one on her own. Typically, however, the suspension of a conjugal relation was more complicated. But the idea of chastity was not a factor in these decisions.

The colonizers and missionaries considered this matrilineal system unhealthy, uncivilized, and immoral.[20] English-educated Nair men in the late nineteenth century attempted to reform this lineage system through various channels, including legal enactment. They demanded that Nair women should 'properly' marry from within the caste and follow patrilineal monogamous conjugal relations. They influenced the British administration successfully to pass the Malabar Nair Marriage Reform Bill of 1896 in the Madras Legislative Assembly.[21] The bill envisaged to make sambandham a legal marriage so that the wife and children in the marriage would have the right to the property of the husband. Nampoothiris considered this as a challenge to their economic power and threat to acharam. In the first decade of the twentieth century, Nampoothiri community leaders started propaganda against this act through articles and memorandums.

The second challenge to the order of acharam originated from the British government's attempts to reform the land revenue system in the last quarter of the nineteenth century. From its inception in Malabar in the late eighteenth century, British rule granted full ownership of the land to the *janmis* (landlords). Their objective was to create manageable and defined land authorities from which they could collect tax, which was the major portion of their revenue. This destroyed the age-old arrangement between the janmis and the *kutiyans* (tenants), which was also an exploitative system.[22] Now, the janmis were able to evict a tenant more easily and to pressurize kutiyans to pay ever-increasing rents. The tenants, especially the Muslim tenants, protested this in different ways from the beginning of the nineteenth century. Low-level officers of the British government warned that this might lead to serious riots and rebellion. Once the situation became alarming, in 1887, the government appointed a commission headed by William Logan. Logan, in his report, suggested important reforms, including the prohibition of large-scale evictions of the tenants by the janmis. Though the government did not implement his suggestions, in 1897, a more diluted bill was introduced in the Madras assembly. The Malabar Janmi–Kutiyan Bill of 1897 aimed to rationalize the renting of land.[23] It suggested certain restrictions in the rights of janmis to transfer tenancy from one person to another. However, the Bill did not intend to change the absolute right of janmis or their right to choose the tenant; its only objective was to rationalize the process. Still, Nampoothiri janmis considered even these minor changes in the land tenancy system a major threat to their rights over the land.

The debate around these Bills within the assembly and the propaganda for and against the Bills outside it created anxiety and tension among the Nampoothiri janmis. They reasoned that English education and the *parishkaram* (reforms) that accompanied it were the roots of the problem. A few Nampoothiris who were closely following the debates of various reforms in the first decade of the twentieth century occasionally wrote articles in contemporary Malayalam journals and newspapers. In an article in 1903, Narayanan Nampoothiri reminded the Nairs and the British government that 'there are certain things that are more valuable than knowledge and parishkaram for a society'.[24] He claimed that it was traditional values that protected the culture of the country from time immemorial. According to him, knowledge of the universe was a result of 'good practices', not the cause or basis for a good life.[25] P. K. Nampoothiri argued that both the Bills in the legislative assembly reflected the 'new ideas of the educated class and their total disrespect to the age-old acharams'. He warned that the Bills, if enacted, would create 'social disorder and chaos' among the 'upper castes'.[26] Despite the protests by the Nampoothiris, the Madras Legislative Assembly passed the Janmi–Kutiyan Bill in 1906.

The passage of the Janmi–Kutiyan Bill gave a clear message to Nampoothiris that occasional articles in journals or a few meetings of interested parties were not enough to overcome the challenges they were facing in that period. It was in this context that Nampoothiris formed a community organization, the Yoga Kshema Sabha (YKS), in 1908. Later, this organization would be a platform for radical demands of reform within the community. At its formative period, however, the major objective of the organization was the protection of the order of acharam and the maintenance of dominance in the social world.

The Yoga Kshema Sabha (YKS) and the Protection of Acharam

In its initial years, conservative janmis in the community controlled the YKS. In this period, the objective of the YKS was not to widen the base or to mobilize each community member. Rather, the *sabha* (an organized group) was a body of a few elites who imagined their interests to be the interest of the community.[27] The resolution passed in the first meeting of the YKS stated that 'no member of the sabha should utilise the platform of the same to speak, decide or act against acharam and the customary traditions of Nampoothiris'.[28] M. R. Bhattathirippad remembered that until the seventh annual conference in 1915, the sabha did not take any positive action regarding English education, women's education, sambandham, or dress reform.[29]

Even though the main objective of the YKS was to protect the community from the invasion of colonial knowledge, colonial governing practices directly inspired the modalities of the activities of the organization. They adopted techniques like writing articles, submitting memorandums to the government, and finally constituting a formal organization, all of which were forms of colonial governance. At the same time, the adoption of these techniques did not prevent them from opposing colonial intervention through knowledge. As we saw in the article of Narayanan Nampoothiri, the main targets of the YKS were English education and *parishkaram*, which would destroy traditional values and morals.

In community reform attempts among Nairs, Ezhavas, and Pulayas, education was one of the central objectives. The reformers from these caste groups considered knowledge as the light that would remove the darkness of ignorance in which the community was supposedly immersed. Knowledge became the measure of welfare within the community. The reform leaders in these communities regarded education as the sole means through which one can attain knowledge. The YKS considered knowledge as a threat to what they considered more important aspects of human life, such as values and morals based on acharam. The first and the prime objective of the YKS was to overcome the threats to acharams from various social forces. In the first decade of the twentieth century, Nampoothiris recognized that without certain changes in the jati practices, it would be difficult to maintain their dominance in society. Thus, the YKS at this period attempted to incorporate the new social situation into the order of acharam with minor changes and adjustments. In this attempt, for the first time, Nampoothiris had to define acharam and then try to widen its scope and range of application, both in opposition to and in relation to colonial practices of knowledge.

In the nineteenth-century practice of acharam, representation of acharam was not a technique that was separate from the daily practice of acharam. In other words, the practice of acharam and the discourse about acharam were inseparable, similar to the case of *asharippani* as we saw in Chapter 1. In order to communicate with a new audience—colonizers and English-educated natives—

it was necessary to use representative strategies based on writing and, hence, to separate the elements of representation from daily life practices. In this situation, Nampoothiri authors started defining acharam according to the contemporary needs and requirements. Most of these authors followed a strategy of defining Nampoothiri acharam as a practice that has been protecting the life-world of not only Nampoothiris but also that of all other caste groups who were part of the network of caste hierarchy. They argued that Nampoothiris through their daily life rituals protected the whole society from sins and evils. Hence, according to them, it was important to not change these daily life activities in the name of education or employment.

According to Nagam Ayya, a non-Malayali Brahmin officer from Thiruvithamkoor who wrote the first manual of the princely state, the Nampoothiri community gravitated towards acharam through strictly followed daily rituals. Every action was a ritual, and it was the proper performance of these ritualistic actions that constituted the jati. The moment one broke a rule, it affected not only the person or the Nampoothiri jati but also the whole order of things in the jati world.[30] Several Nampoothiri authors echoed Nagam Ayya's opinion and defined acharam as a force that extended beyond the Nampoothiri world. For example, Krishnan Nampoothiri claimed that different jatis have different kinds of responsibilities towards society. The responsibility of the Nampoothiri jati was 'the performance of rituals and the maintenance of acharam that are necessary to keep the whole human world happy and peaceful'.[31] Even a single person's activity that violates the code of acharam could invite a number of sins and create different kinds of difficulties in daily life. According to the author, Nampoothiris responsibly performed the rituals in proper ways without hesitating to expel even powerful persons from the community who deviated from the rules of acharam. 'The superiority of the Nampoothiri jati was commonly approved for the [aforementioned] reason.'[32]

This claim was important, especially because, in the nineteenth century, Nampoothiris had only indirect control over the daily life of other jatis, and even if they wanted, they could not directly intervene in it in any substantive manner because of the issue of untouchability. For example, in the first decade of the nineteenth century, Francis Buchanan observed that each caste was 'a world of its own' and the internal rules 'were different for each caste'.[33] In 1890, Edgar Thurston noted that, as far as the daily practices of other castes were concerned, 'the power of Brahmins is limited'.[34] This did not mean that the brahmanical domination was less violent or exploitative at this period; it meant only that the strategy of domination in the nineteenth century was different from that of the early twentieth century. In the former period, brahmanical domination acted as an external force that restricted and bounded the daily life of other castes; but within the boundary, these caste groups conducted their daily life with different internal rules and customs.

To reiterate, in the first decades of the twentieth century, Nampoothiris claimed that acharam could be protected only through their proper performance of rituals in their daily life. In order to understand this claim, we have to explore how Nampoothiris at this time represented the relation between acharam and their activities of daily life. In the introduction of his autobiography, Kanippayyoor Shankaran Nampoothirippad wrote:

> It is very easy to write my biography. I took a bath in the morning and had a coffee; had lunch and another coffee in the evening; had supper and slept. I did all these according to acharam. Thus, one day's history is complete. Now, if I change the date and write 'ditto', it is the next day's history. I am sixty-eight now. If I write all the dates in this period and write 'ditto', my biography is complete.[35]

Nampoothirippad's description underscored the aspect of repetition of the performance of acharam, which was the most important characteristic of Nampoothiri daily life. Even though the author himself was not completely against colonial education, he believed that the performance of acharam in daily life was 'the basis of all good values such as simplicity, peace and bodily health of Nampoothiri men', which was incommensurable with the 'modern practices'.[36] A champion of reform and an activist of the Indian National Congress, Mozhikunnath Brahmadathan Nampoothirippad has noted that in the beginning of the twentieth century, 'conservatism appeared with a new vigour, which was the final leap of the fire before it was put down'. According to him, at this period, Nampoothiris began 'performing acharam more rigorously than before to protect themselves from the storm of reform which had already started showing its strength'.[37]

In its initial years, the leaders of the YKS argued that colonial education and the reforms accompanying it were totally antithetical to the rules of acharam. The first and foremost point of their objection was regarding the rule of untouchability. The conservative leaders defined acharam based on the notions of purity and pollution. According to this concept, objects, human beings, and actions were either pure or polluted. Nampoothiris could not touch anyone outside the caste without being polluted. The degree of impurity depended on the caste of the individual: the lower the position of the caste, the higher was the impurity. Hence, it was impossible for Nampoothiris to attend a school without violating the rules of acharam, where all the objects (pen, paper, and so on) and several human beings (subaltern-caste people) were polluting. The conservative section of Nampoothiris argued at this period that the threat of being polluted was one of their reasons for not participating in colonial educational institutions.

By the second decade of the twentieth century, a new group of individuals from within the community began questioning the conservative leaders of the community. These individuals did not challenge the order of acharam as such; their attempt was to incorporate education within the order of acharam. They argued that Nampoothiris could and should redesign the daily life of a Nampoothiri boy so that he could attend school and keep himself pure. V. Keshavan Bhattathirippad suggested that 'not eating at school and taking a bath after school before entering the illam' was sufficient to keep a Nampoothiri boy unpolluted.[38] At this period, this was a minority voice, which did not have much influence among community members. The conservative authors in this period argued that colonial education would not only interrupt daily life during the educational years but would also introduce changes in future daily life. In an article describing the objective of Nampoothiri life, Parameswaran Nampoothiri argued that 'if a Nampoothiri boy learns modern knowledge instead of the Veda recital, he might get a job in the government. And if everyone in the community follows this, Nampoothiris might gain some wealth in the form of money, but they will be equal to the caste of untouchables in their culture'.[39] According to the author, the status of a Nampoothiri who does not follow the acharam is equal to a 'lower-caste' person. Several other articles in various journals criticized English education for the values and norms that this education imposed on individuals. In an article in 1912, K. Neelakantan Moosathu explained English education as a 'training which compels students to think only about the material success in this world, not about the importance of the otherworldly life'. According to the author, both the institution of modern knowledge and the content of that knowledge were polluted. 'The modern knowledge promoted the value of money but not the value of culture.'[40]

The YKS meetings regularly passed resolutions that juxtaposed acharam and English education as antithetical and incommensurable. A resolution passed by a subunit of YKS in 1915 stated that the major three challenges the community faced were (*a*) the increasing ignorance of traditional spiritual practices, (*b*) the economic dependency due to the reforms that were modelled on the West and based on English education, and (*c*) the changes in the objectives in life due to the imitation of unadvisable Western models. The resolution added:

> In the present time, gaining English education has become a fashion which encourages individuals to breach acharam in all possible ways. But Nampoothiris should be very careful in their method of attaining education. If we want to protect the wellbeing of Nampoothiris, we should protect our acharams and traditions.[41]

The resolution did not completely reject the idea of education but warned that Nampoothiris should give preference to maintaining acharam over gaining education. The juxtaposing of education in opposition to acharam made acharam more than a daily practice of rituals; it attained a new role as the protector of the well-being of the Nampoothiri jati.

Tradition, Traditional Knowledge, and Acharam

The new status of acharam had certain connections with the colonial discourse of traditional knowledge. As we discussed in the Introduction, within the colonial hierarchical series of knowledge, traditional knowledge had a lower status than modern knowledge. At the same time, within traditional knowledge, the brahmanical tradition was superior to the traditions such as artisanal practices. The orientalists depicted the textual tradition of Brahmins as a prequel to the modern forms of knowledge.[42] Nampoothiris utilized this depiction of tradition to underscore the importance of acharam in protecting the values that led the whole society towards well-being. While Nampoothiris utilized the higher status attributed in the colonial discourse to their tradition, at this period, they did not necessarily connect acharam with knowledge, as they would in the period of reform in the 1920s.

In the first two decades of the twentieth century, Nampoothiris articulated acharam more as tradition than as traditional knowledge. This was because, within the dominant discourse, knowledge, modern or traditional, was already connected on the one hand to writing, and on the other, to institutional education. Acharam as understood by Nampoothiris in this period was related to neither writing nor institutional learning; it was learned and practised through the daily life activities. In other words, the colonial depictions of brahmanical tradition and Nampoothiri interpretations of this colonial representation were not the same.

One author claimed that 'the Western scholars themselves have proved that the brahmanical traditions kept our society intact and efficient'. According to this author, those who ignore this scholarly understanding were 'imitating the white men like monkeys, without knowing the meanings or values of our own tradition'. He further argued that Nampoothiris should teach the young generation how to practically perform acharam more rigorously and effectively. If they knew the importance of acharam, they would not 'chase the vulgar fashions of Western tradition'.[43] However, even while quoting the point of view of Western scholars, the author did not argue for an education based on Sanskrit texts. Learning the performance of acharam was more important than learning the language and texts. Another author of this period reminded the importance of the practice of acharam by comparing it with swimming. He wrote:

When one is in water, there is no use of the knowledge of swimming taught by an elder or an expert, unless one oneself cannot swim. If every Nampoothiri boy studies Sanskrit and the Veda, he would not get the time to conduct family life and rituals of daily life. We should leave that [the learning of texts] to a few who are seriously dedicated to that purpose.[44]

The conservatives in this period actively prevented the members of the community from joining educational institutions in the name of protecting acharam. It was, however, more difficult for them to insulate themselves from some of the other 'polluted' objects and practices that emerged through increasing colonial governmental activities in the region. In such situations, they evaluated each object or event based on notions of purity and impurity and then incorporated or excluded them according to the new interpretation of acharam.[45] According to N. P. Nampoothiri, Nampoothiris 'were never afraid of changes, but they were cautious on deciding what elements they should accept and what they should reject'.[46] For example, paper in itself was considered a polluted object, but printed books were partially pure. N. P. Nampoothiri further explained that

... if paper was considered polluted earlier, now everyone reads *Ramayanam* or *Mahabharatham* in the printed form and doesn't have to take a bath after touching a book. Still, nobody takes the books inside the shrines or near the deities. Factory tiles when they first appeared were considered polluted, but now, they are widely used even in some temples.[47]

We can observe here that whenever a new material emerged, Nampoothiris determined its status according to acharam. Although the author attributed certain permanence to acharams, it is obvious that acharams were also changing in this process. However, the fundamental objective of the community leaders in the first two decades of the nineteenth century was not to change but to maintain the acharam, unlike in the reform actions in the 1920s.

The example of restaurants that emerged at this period further demonstrates the aforementioned point. In the late nineteenth century, when the first restaurants came up, Nampoothiri elders strongly prohibited their family members from eating here. As the transportation facilities increased with the introduction of buses and trains, while long-distance travel became more frequent, the prohibitions on eating created many difficulties for Nampoothiris in these travels. Slowly, many Nampoothiris started to eat at restaurants but only at 'Brahmanal hotels'.[48] Tamil Brahmins usually ran these hotels, where they made special arrangements for Nampoothiris. The restaurant owners arranged special spaces for Brahmins where non-Brahmins were not admitted. These restaurants offered food cooked and served by Brahmins, accompanied with the rituals as in a Nampoothiri home. Most of these hotels carried the sign 'Pure Brahmanal Hotel' on the name board. The menu was also different from the hotels run by non-Brahmins. Nampoothiri elders justified this new practice with the logic that a Nampoothiri would be already polluted on the journey and he should have to take bath before entering the illam. Hence, eating the food prepared by a Brahmin at the hotel would not further pollute the person.[49]

The bus journey was another event that Nampoothiris had to negotiate at this period. Outside their illam, Nampoothiri women were not allowed to show any part of their body in public and they always carried a cadjan umbrella when they went out of the house to cover themselves. This umbrella was not foldable and had a long handle. It was very difficult to take this inside the bus. To solve this problem, the bus operators provided seats with curtains inside the bus. When Nampoothiri women entered the bus, they would first cover their face with the same cloth (purdah) that already covered the rest of their body. Once they were seated, the umbrella would be passed to them from outside the bus. While the women held the umbrella's handle, its dome would remain outside the window. Thus, while the curtains would block the view from inside, the umbrella would do so from outside.[50]

Nampoothiris attempted to order the newly emerging public spaces according to the jati rules based on acharam. For this purpose, in the early decades of the twentieth century, Nampoothiris often interpreted acharam in new ways to include the emerging objects and practices. At this period, while attempting to incorporate new objects and events, they preserved most of their practices from the earlier century. It is important to explain how, even in the early twentieth century, acharam continued to order the daily life of Nampoothiris according to the principles of purity and pollution.

As mentioned earlier, acharam derived its rules from the notion of purity and pollution, which could be essential or relative. In the nineteenth-century practice of acharam, Nampoothiris treated some objects and people as essentially polluted. For example, they considered certain trees, some animals, and all 'lower-caste' people to be always polluted and untouchable. Any pure material could become polluted through the association of polluted objects or according to their spatial positions. Flowers or sandal paste used for different types of *puja* (ritual worship) were pure before the use but were impure when they were lying down near the deity after the use. If a Nampoothiri touched any of these, he had to wash his hands; otherwise he himself and whatever objects he had touched after touching the polluted object and before washing the hand would become polluted.

Rice in its uncooked form, even though touched by many subordinated-caste people in the process of its preparation, was not polluted. Once the Nair maid-servant washes it and hands it over to the Nampoothiri woman for cooking, it should not be touched again by a non-Nampoothiri person. But then, the cooked rice also had certain impurity. Every time one touched the vessel that contains the cooked rice, one had to wash the hand. If they gave a portion of the rice from the vessel to anyone outside the jati, the remaining portion had automatically become impure and could not be used by Nampoothiris.[51]

Nampoothiris preserved these rules of acharam from the nineteenth century even up to the early decades of the twentieth century, including the rules regarding the social obligation of other jatis towards them. The practices based on the rules of social obligation of other jatis provided the required material and ritualistic resources for a Nampoothiri household. Veluthedath Nairs (the washer caste) washed clothes in boiled water, in which a tiny amount of ash was dissolved to make the cloth 'pure'. These clothes were necessary for Nampoothiris when they observed pollution on certain occasions like death, birth, and menstruation. On these occasions, after the purification ritual, they had to take a bath and wear the pure cloth supplied by the Veluthedath Nair. Usually, if a non-Nampoothiri person had touched any cloth, it would have become polluted. But the cloth supplied by the Veluthedathu Nair would not become polluted even if other subaltern-caste people touched it before the use.[52]

This shows that, in the order of acharam, the objects' internal qualities were not a concern. Its position in space and its association with other objects, including human beings, determined the 'temporary essence' of the object. The question of what constituted an object was not enunciable in this order. Often, even the locus of the travel of an object was less important than its position at a particular time. Thus, through acharam, Nampoothiris controlled the circulation and exchange of material objects, and this helped them in exploiting the labour and material resources of other caste groups for their benefit.

As in the nineteenth century, the rules of purity and pollution controlled even the use of language in the daily life in the early years of the twentieth century. Nampoothiris used a very different vocabulary from other castes to articulate objects and actions. A person carried the mark of his or her jati in the language he or she spoke. Kanippayyoor provided a table of words used by Nampoothiris along with its 'translation' in the language used by the people from other castes. For example, the non-Nampoothiri person should add a prefix *pazham* (from the word *pazhaya*, which means old, rotten, or polluted, and so on) to mention all of his or her possessions, including body parts, when talking to a Nampoothiri.

He or she would say *pazha-manas* to refer to his or her *manas* (mind), *pazham-kanji* for kanji (rice porridge), and so on.[53] On the other hand, the objects when possessed by Nampoothiris carried a prefix of *thiru* or *palli*, both of which denoted their pure, blessed, or superior status. Thus, while the manas was pazha-manas in the case of oppressed castes, it was *thiru-manas* in the case of Nampoothiris.

Through the ritualistic practice of language, acharam determined the qualities of an object according to its possessors. The moment it was transferred from a subordinated caste person to Nampoothiris or vice versa, an object was transformed not only in name but also in its quality. This shows that, in this period, within the Nampoothiri world (and the world they come in contact with), it was acharam that determined the very ontological status of objects. In other words, Nampoothiris understood the world through the performance of acharam, and this performance constituted their knowledge of objects and actions.

The Disconnect between Knowledge and Acharam

Understanding acharam as an action leads us to an important conclusion regarding the relation between Nampoothiris and knowledge practices. The scholarship on caste and brahmanical ideology in India understood acharam as a practice based on the prescriptions of the Vedas and other Sanskrit texts.[54] This interpretation was clearly a continuation of colonial understanding of written text as the only valid form of knowledge. In the present, the major difference of the scholarship from the colonial version is that the former have begun to include oral traditions as well in the field of knowledge. In both cases, the Sanskritic textual tradition was understood as the base of the brahmanical world. I argue that it was the practice of acharam, not knowledge, in Vedic texts that constituted the Nampoothiri understanding of the world. The discursive practices that Nampoothiris engaged with in this period had no association with knowledge as it was conceptualized in colonial discourses. These practices were part of the practices of acharam and were not related to the production of knowledge. In order to demonstrate this argument, we have to explore how Nampoothiris used the Vedas in their daily life in the early decades of the twentieth century.

The learning of Veda recital was an important part of the life of Nampoothiri men; women did not learn the Vedas. In the pre-colonial period, there were two major centres of Veda learning in Keralam: one in Thrissur, which was sponsored by the Raja of Kochi, and another in Thirunavaya, sponsored by the Samoothiri Raja of Kozhikode. After the British took over of the administration of Malabar, the Thirunavaya centre declined because of the lack of sponsorship. The Thrissur centre, which was known as Brahmaswam Matam, continued to prosper under the Kochi *rajas* (kings or princes), and at the time of our interest, it provided residential learning facilities for all Nampoothiris who wished to learn the Vedas.

Nampoothiri boys began Veda learning after the sacred thread ceremony, which was a ritual that would start the process of transformation of a boy into a Nampoothiri. Depending on the *gothra*[55] one belonged to, each learned one of the *Rigveda*, the *Yajurveda*, or the *Samaveda*. This was usually conducted between the ages of ten and twelve. The one who taught the Veda recital was the *othikkan*.[56] In the early twentieth century, to learn Vedic recital, Nampoothiri boys from Malabar either joined the Brahmaswam Matam at Thrissur or stayed at their respective othikkan's house for the whole period of learning. Memorizing the verses in a totally unfamiliar language was not an easy task. The recital of these verses with the proper movement of head and hand added to the difficulty, and many Nampoothiris remembered this as the worst period in their life. As most of the boys struggled to learn the recital properly, the teachers used severe punishment tactics, such as slapping and even hitting the boys' heads on the wall.[57] In most of the cases, the othikkans who taught the Vedas were 'illiterate' and they themselves had no knowledge of the meaning of these verses. The most important part of learning was to memorize hundreds of verses and the corresponding body gestures that accompanied the recitation of these verses. The boys learned how to *perform* the recital, not the *knowledge* that the Vedas supposedly carried. For example, the prescriptions of the Vedas on brahmanical duties were never a subject matter of study in the aforementioned process of learning. Even though recital of some of these verses were part of the daily rituals in later life, the boys soon forgot a major part of what they learned during the study, as it was never used in their daily life.

Mapping the debate around the oral and written traditions, C. J. Fuller, in agreement with Jonathan Parry's observations on the defective learning of the Vedas in the oral tradition, confirmed that the 'situation is undoubtedly widespread in India, so that for every Brahmin who knows his texts accurately, there are many others who are just winging it'.[58] However, even when recognizing the performative aspects of Veda learning, Fuller and others tend to consider the Brahmins responsible for the transfer of Vedic *knowledge*. Parry's concern that 'the authenticity of knowledge transferred purely by oral means can no longer be automatically accepted as axiomatic',[59] comes from a premise that if Brahmins were reciting the Vedas properly, it could be considered as authentic knowledge. This assumption clearly stems from the orientalist notions of traditional knowledge.

In a parallel history, by the end of the nineteenth century, the Vedas attained a new status through colonial orientalist scholarship. This scholarship considered the Vedas as the only authentic texts which provided the principles of the brahmanical practices in India.[60] Emerging disciplines like history reinforced the status of the Vedas as the source of traditional knowledge in India. There were two assumptions behind this conclusion. The first was that all human practices could be divided into discursive and non-discursive practices, and the second was that discursive practices constituted knowledge. In other words, for the colonialists, knowledge existed only in the form of language. In this conceptualization, language—and knowledge too—was always a representation of external reality.

In the period of our discussion, Nampoothiris' relation with language did not match with the aforementioned assumptions. Most Nampoothiri boys and girls were initiated in language learning at the age of four or five, which also was a ritual. Over a period, many of them learned to write and read Malayalam and to do basic arithmetic. Teachers used *puranic* texts and prayers during this process. By this time, several publishers had started publishing printed texts of *purana*s and *ithihasa*s, and they sold these books through salesmen who travelled from house to house.[61] The reading of these books became another ritual of the daily life of Nampoothiris, especially of women in the early twentieth century. Again, most readers were unaware about the meaning of the verses, and even when they understood the meaning, their focus was on the recital itself. The objective of the reading was to attain *punyam* (blessings) or *sukritham* (welfare of the family) through the recital of the stories of gods. The girls had to discontinue their study once they attained puberty or even before that. The boys also had to stop the initial stage of learning once they became Nampoothiris though the sacred thread ceremony, after which they would start learning the Vedas either at the aforementioned centres or under individual instructors. They never used their writing skills again in their life.[62]

Here, the use of language was a performance, an embodied action similar to many other actions such as prostrating before the deity or offering flowers to the deities. Even the correct pronunciation was not a major concern, and this would become a contentious subject later in the debate within the reform movement when meaning became an important issue. At this period, the function of reading texts was purely ritualistic. In short, even within the colonial definitions of knowledge, the discursive practices of Nampoothiris in the early twentieth century did not carry or engage with knowledge, traditional, or otherwise. Nampoothiris themselves did not consider their discursive activity a practice of knowledge. Rather, these activities were part of ritual performances that helped maintain the order of acharam.

The attempt of Nampoothiris to keep acharam as a performance is interesting, especially in comparison with the other elite caste groups' reaction to the changing understanding of texts and traditional knowledge in the same period. It is important to note that in early twentieth-century Malabar, most of the experts of traditional knowledge such as astrology or *vydyam* (medicinal practice) were from castes like Moosathu who were Brahmins but who were considered having lesser status by Nampoothiris, or from the Ampalavasi (literally, one who resides near the temple) jatis, or the non-Nampoothiri elite castes who were not socially powerful as Nampoothiris or even Nairs.[63] These experts taught their disciples Sanskrit, astrology, and medicine in a system known as Gurukula Sampradayam. In this tradition, students resided at their guru's house and learned language, astrology, or medicine, all of which were interconnected. In this traditional system, a guru transferred knowledge to disciples not through texts but through practices. For example, in the case of vydyam, there were standard Sanskrit texts that students had to learn. They used these texts mainly to memorize certain methods or some properties of medicinal plants and the human body. The major focus was on the practical activities like preparing medicine, determining the condition of the patient from bodily symptoms, and applying the medicine in proper ways. Along with this practical work, the guru would teach the corresponding verses in the text, mostly to memorize the methods. By the end of the nineteenth century, as discussed before, texts in general and Sanskrit texts in particular attained a special status in relation to traditional knowledge. This resulted in new forms of knowing, which differed from the earlier practices and created new spaces of learning and teaching.

The story of the learning centre at Pattambi run by Punnassery Nampy in the early years of the twentieth century is a good example for how some communities incorporated colonial concepts into their traditional practices. Punnassery Nampy, who was from a Moosathu family, was an expert in Sanskrit language, astrology, and medicine, who learned his profession from various teachers in a traditional manner. One of Nampy's famous disciples, K. V. Moosathu, in his memoir described Nampy as the first 'modern traditional vydya [healer], who had deep knowledge in traditional methods but who was eager to modernise the tradition'.[64] In 1898, Nampy started Saraswathodyothini, a school for teaching Sanskrit. The curriculum in this school underscored the importance of Sanskrit texts and the possible new interpretation of the verses in the texts of medicine according to new situations. Moosathu remembered that 'unlike other scholars, Nampy began his teaching of vydyam from texts'.[65] Nampy installed a printing press and started a publishing firm, Vijnanachinthamani, at his home and published numerous translations of Sanskrit texts to 'propagate the valuable knowledge among common people'.[66] The influence of the colonial concept that texts in the form of printed books could carry knowledge and hence could be used for the transfer of knowledge, was evident in Nampy's reform attempts. However, what is important for our purpose is to notice that most of the narrative on Punnassery Nampy considered him an exception at his time and many influential Nampoothiri landlords were sceptical about his initiatives.

The example of P. S. Variyar shows another instance of appropriation of colonial knowledge into traditional practices. P. S. Variyar was an expert of Ayurveda, which was a traditional medicinal practice followed mainly by the dominant castes. Variyar developed a pedagogy for teaching Ayurveda completely based on Sanskrit texts. In later years, he established an institute, modelled on colonial educational institutions, where texts became the central source of teaching. At this institute, in the first two years, students learned only Sanskrit and texts on Ayurveda. Only after the second year, they were allowed to practice vydyam.[67]

In this period, Nampoothiris in general, unlike the Ampalavasi castes, were not eager to engage either in the new colonial educational institutions or in the learning centres such as the aforementioned ones. Most of the students in the such centres were from the Ampalavasi or Nair castes; a very few Nampoothiri students joined these centres of learning. The community leaders in this period were sceptical about reforms based on colonial methodologies of production of knowledge. They justified this by juxtaposing knowledge against acharam and by making acharam the defining activity of jati.

To reiterate, making acharam central to the definition of jati in the early twentieth century was a reaction to the challenges Nampoothiris faced from both outside and within the jati. In the previous chapter, we saw that Asharis, in reaction to colonial intervention, centre-staged asharippani as the organizing category of their jati. It would be worthwhile to compare the Ashari and Nampoothiri reactions in this period to understand the similarities and differences in the performance of acharam and asharippani and their positions in relation to the colonial production of knowledge. In the early decades of the twentieth century, both the Asharis and the Nampoothiris of Malabar saw colonial practices as a threat to the customs and traditions of their respective jatis. Both refused to be part of the hierarchical series constructed in the colonial production of knowledge. Nampoothiris, however, had the advantage of already being the dominant caste and being positioned at the top among natives in this series of knowledge.[68] They still believed that to maintain their dominance in society, it was more strategic to protect the order of acharam than to participate in the production of knowledge. This was because acharam was not just an internal matter of Nampoothiris, but also a process of bringing other jatis into the order. Asharippani, on the other hand, as a trade and as a discursive category, acted strictly within the jati Ashari. It was the bounded nature of asharippani within *desham* and jati that the Asharis underscored in their attempt to avoid colonial intrusions into their practice. Unlike asharippani, acharam externally determined the principles of hierarchy of the jatis, and hence, it was active not only within the jati but also in the social spaces outside the jati. Acharam worked as an external force on the other jatis, especially in the moments of inter-jati communications.

Each jati had special obligations towards specific Nampoothiri families in their desham. The men and women from other castes conducted a number of physical jobs for Nampoothiri illam to satisfy all the material needs of the household. They served Nampoothiris in different capacities on the occasions of birth, death, birthdays, puberty, menstrual periods, auspicious days, and so on. As mentioned earlier, Veluthedathu Nairs provided the pure clothes for all these occasions. Vilakathila Nair did the job of the hairdresser. Asharis did the maintenance of the houses. People from the Cheruma or Pulaya and Nair castes did all the agriculture work in the field and karyasthans (managers) from the Nair or Ambalavasi (temple-dwelling) castes supervized the agriculture production. The people from the subordinated castes brought all agriculture produce to the house of the Nampoothiri janmi. Paddy was de-husked and made rice by Nair women. The men and women from the Ampalavasi castes prepared materials for rituals.[69] Nampoothiris appropriated these obligations, which were economic and ritualistic, through acharam. Hence, when they projected acharam as the central factor of their jati practice, they were attempting to maintain the hierarchical caste order, which provided them the economic and social resource for domination.

Acharam and Gender Differentiation

The redefinition of acharam produced corresponding effects on the Nampoothiri practices of gender; acharam became a central category in the new process of gender differentiation as well. Even in the nineteenth century, acharam was part of the patriarchal practices of the Nampoothiris. These patriarchal customs institutionalized gender difference through the practice of acharam. For example, in the seventh month of pregnancy, Nampoothiri couples performed a particular ritual called *pumsavanam* so that the baby would be a boy. If it was a girl, they repeated this ritual until a boy was born. There were elaborate rituals after the birth of a baby boy, especially for the first boy who later becomes the *moos* (the head of the family). Most of these rituals could not be performed for a girl child. Boys wore golden ornaments, but girls were allowed only copper or bronze. Just before puberty, girls started wearing a *mundu* (a white plain waist cloth) in a special way as the adults did. From then onwards, her life was strictly dedicated to ritualistic performance and household work. She had to learn *nedikkal* (the ritualistic offerings to gods, done by women inside the house on a daily basis) and she was introduced to cooking at a very early age. In the Nampoothiri illam, women lived in the inner part of the house, and hence, they were known as *antharjanam*, which literally means a person of the inside. Acharam did not allow them to appear before any male person other than their father, husband, or son.[70] As mentioned earlier, when they went out of the house, they had to wear a purdah and carry a cadjan umbrella to cover their body. Kanippayyoor has observed that these rituals not only discriminated against women but also created a sense of inferiority from the time of childhood so that it was naturalized.[71]

Scholars have already shown the nature of discrimination and exploitation of the women in a Nampoothiri illam. Our purpose is not to re-establish that the Nampoothiri jati in the early twentieth century practised patriarchy. The focus here is on the increased importance of acharam in Nampoothiri self-understanding of gender differentiation in the early twentieth century. If in the nineteenth century, customs and rituals were a 'natural' part of the Nampoothiri life-world, by the beginning of the new century, the community elders believed that in order to protect acharam, they would have to forcefully impose acharam on every individual of the community. They started overemphasizing the practices of control through traditional methods like *smarthavicharam* and *bhrashtu* (ritualistic exclusion from the jati).

Smarthavicharam was a complex ritual of legal intervention to investigate the allegation of sexual infidelity among Nampoothiri women. If there was a 'convincing' case, the elder of the desham would decide to hold a smarthavicharam. The raja would appoint a *smarthan*, who was the inquisitor and judge of the whole process. They kept the accused woman in a secluded room outside the main structure of the illam, where she could contact only a servant woman. From then onwards, she was addressed as sathanam ('a thing' in a derogatory sense). After gathering evidence from the accused woman and the servants, if smarthan confirmed that the woman had sinned, he would declare bhrashtu for the accused woman along with the man or men she named as her partners in the sin.[72] In the nineteenth century, the Nampoothiris invoked this form of punishment in exceptional situations. In the first decades of the twentieth century, however, as community leaders resumed stringent policing of sexuality based on acharam, they started using smarthavicharam on a regular basis. According to Mozhikunnath Brahmadathan Nampoothirippad, a greater number of smarthavicharam and bhrashtu happened in the first two decades of the twentieth century than might have happened in the whole nineteenth century.[73]

In the process of gender differentiation based on acharam, notions of masculinity and femininity had very little relevance. Within the household, the moos (the eldest son, as called moos by other Nampoothiris) was the controlling authority who was in charge of the economic and ritualistic activities. As mentioned earlier, only the eldest son was allowed to marry within the jati. Ideally, he took over the charge of the family after his father and would become the head of the family. His authority was based on his gender and age. But this authority did not give him any additional manliness, and conversely, masculinity was not a necessary quality of an efficient moos. For example, Nampoothiris did not consider an individually weak moos less manly or more womanly. However, if he were not following the acharams correctly, they would consider him a lesser Nampoothiri. This was true not only in the case of moos but also for all the male members of the community.

K. P. K. Nampoothiri's story is revealing in this sense. He was one of the few persons from the community who gained higher education in the second decade of the twentieth century. When he joined the Madras University, it was a totally new world for him. The difference he felt was not just about city life, the weather, or the food. Whenever he began a conversation with other students or when he was just walking towards them, he saw a veiled laughter on their faces. Later, it was his friend Bhaskaran Nair, who was one year senior to him, who saved him from this agony. He told Nampoothiri that his classmates were thinking that he did not have enough manliness in his manners. He was confused what this manliness meant. Nobody in the illam had told him about this before. There, the focus was on whether one was doing the ritual performances properly or not. So, he started physical exercises with Bhaskaran Nair, who was also a football player. He changed his 'manners' in a year and did not face any further difficulties in this regard. The most interesting part of the story is that when he came back to the illam, he was afraid or shy about his new bodily manners. But nobody at the illam even noticed this; the elders in the house were more worried about the degree of pollution he carried because of his non-Nampoothiri life during his study at Madras.[74]

Bodily behaviour was not a measure to evaluate the manliness of a Nampoothiri man. N. P. Nampoothiri wrote in 1919 that 'in public spaces, Nampoothiri men invite attention for their dress and appearance. Most of the people consider their appearance comic or sometimes even pathetic. They, however, never care about their appearance or what others say about that. In a public space, they will be focusing more on keeping the prescribed distance from people from lower-caste communities'.[75] N. P. Nampoothiri justified this behaviour because he thought that 'the quality of a Brahman is not in his appearance but in the properness of his action in protecting *Brahmanyam* [Brahman-ness]'.[76]

Once the reform movement in the 1920s and 1930s started reordering the community based on self-knowledge, the process of gender identification also transformed accordingly. The performance of gendered roles became directly linked to education and self-knowledge. Devika argued that in the reform period, '[s]elf knowledge was to specify the ground of the reformist activity, identify its key players, target and goals'[77] In the pre-reform period, however, it was more important to perform gendered rituals in order to be a Nampoothiri man or woman. In this performance, the idea of masculinity or femininity was not a factor because there was no concept of inherent bodily qualities of being a man or a woman. The body, especially the woman's body, was marked at different occasions like birth, puberty, pregnancy, and so on, but was not at the centre of the gender differentiation process. As Devika explained, 'even bedecking was more a ritual process'.[78] In short:

Inside and outside,
Everywhere,
The polluted and the untouchable,
Subordinated by their Karma.
I am the one to lead,
For I preserve purity,
Guard the world with my purity,
Not knowledge, but *acharam* is my refuge
Without erring from my *charya*
I guard *acharam*,
And I guard the world.[79]

In the early twentieth century, asharippani and acharam constituted Ashari and Nampoothiri jati rules, respectively, through embodied action. While Nampoothiris practised acharam in order to extend their control over other jatis, Asharis used asharippani as a technique to seclude themselves inside their jati and to prevent intrusion from colonial practices. Both Nampoothiris and Asharis juxtaposed the corresponding central organizing categories of jati (that is, acharam and asharippani) against the colonial category of knowledge.

By the 1920s, equipped with the colonial concepts of knowledge, the young generation of Nampoothiris began challenging the order of acharam from within. It became impossible for the conservative section of the community leadership to protect acharam from various internal and external social forces. The next chapter analyses this process of transformation or translation of the order of acharam into an order of knowledge, the process which is generally understood in the scholarship as the Nampoothiri reform movement.

Notes

1. For example, see George Birdwood, *The Industrial Arts of India* (London: Chapman and Hall Ltd, 1884); Max Müller, *A History of Ancient Sanskrit Literature* (London: Williams and Norgate, 1860); William Jones, *The Works of Sir William Jones* (London: Robinson, 1801).
2. B. R. Ambedkar, *Annihilation of Caste* (New Delhi: Samyak Prakashan, 2013).
3. M. N. Srinivas, 'The Social System of a Mysore Village', in *Village India*, ed. Mckinn Marriot, 1–35 (Chicago: University of Chicago Press, 1955), 18.
4. M. N. Srinivas, *Social Change in Modern India* (Berkeley: University of California Press, 1968), 13.
5. Luis Dumont, *Homo Hierarchicus: The Caste System and Its Implications* (Delhi: Oxford University Press, 2009), 392.
6. C. J. Fuller, following Andre Beteille, characterizes Dumont's view as 'book view' in opposition to 'field view'. He argues that 'for the analysis of caste, however, the book view has become increasingly impedimental because if focuses attention on continuities with the past and the scriptural tradition at the expense of the discontinuities that are becoming proportionately more salient'. C. J. Fuller, 'Introduction: Caste Today', in *Caste Today*, ed. C. J. Fuller, 1–31 (Delhi: Oxford University Press, 1996), 5. See also A. Beteille, *Society and Politics in India: Essays in Comparative Perspective* (London, Athlone Press, 1991).
7. M. S. S. Pandian, *Brahmin and Non-Brahmin: Genealogies of Tamil Political Present* (New Delhi: Permanent Black, 2007).
8. Nicholas Dirks, *Caste of Mind: Colonialism and Making of Modern India* (New Delhi: Permanent Black, 2003), 8.
9. Scholars, especially from the West, studied Nampoothiri ritual practices based on the Eurocentric idea of religion. They considered acharam as a spiritual activity practised with an objective of attaining salvation and a better afterlife. For studies based on these notions, see Genevieve Lemercinier, *Religion and Ideology in Kerala* (New Delhi: D. K. Agencies, 1984); Bardwell L. Smith (ed.), *Religion and Social Conflict in South Asia* (Leiden: E. J. Brill, 1976).
10. Marjatta Parpola, *Kerala Brahmins in Transition: A Study of a Namputiri Family* (Helsinki: Finnish Oriental Society, 2000).

11. Joan P. Mencher, 'Namboodiri Brahmins: An Analysis of a Traditional Elite in Kerala', *Journal of Asian and African Studies* 1, no. 3 (1966): 183–196. See also Joan P. Mencher and Helen Goldberg, 'Kinship and Marriage Regulations among the Namboodiri Brahmans of Kerala', *Man* 2, no. 1(1967): 87–106.

12. Frits Staal, *Rituals and Mantras: Rules without Meaning* (New York: Peter Lang Publishing, 1990).

13. Staal, *Rituals and Mantras*, 115.

14. Kanippayyoor Shankaran Nampoothirippad, *Ente Smaranakal* (My Memories) (Kunnamkulam: Panchangam Pusthakasala, 1964).

15. Nampoothirippad, *Ente Smaranakal*.

16. J. Devika, *En-Gendering Individuals: The Language of Re-forming in Early Twentieth Century Keralam* (Hyderabad: Orient Longman, 2007), 122.

17. Devika, *En-gendering Individuals*, 125.

18. Robin Jeffry studied the transformation of Nair social power and the changes in the caste practices in the context of colonial interventions and modernization in Thiruvithamkoor. See Robin Jeffrey, *The Decline of Nair Dominance: Society and Politics in Travancore, 1847–1908* (New Delhi: Manohar, 1994). G. Arunima's study on the matrilineal practice of the Nairs of Malabar may be the first systematic scholarly work on the transitions of Nair social life in Malabar in the colonial period. She analysed the interaction of different values and social norms in the context of colonialism and how Nair reform leaders, influenced by colonial discourse, began considering matriliny as an immoral practice. See G. Arunima, *There Comes Papa: Colonialism and the Transformation of Matriliny in Kerala, Malabar, c. 1850–1940* (Hyderabad: Orient Longman, 2003).

19. There is difference of opinion among historians regarding the emergence of sambandham relations. Some consider this as a compromise arrived between Nairs and Nampoothiris in order to keep the family property undivided and thus benefiting both communities. But for others, the system began when Nampoothiris, who were immigrants from the North, inserted themselves into the age-old matrilineal system of Nairs somewhat forcefully after attaining dominance in the social order. For the first view, see, E. M. S. Nampoothirippad, *Keralam Malayalikalute Mathrubhumi* (Keralam: The Motherland of Malayalis) (Thiruvananthapuram: Chintha Publishers, 1984 [1946]). For the latter view, see Elamkulam Kunjan Pillai, *Kerala Charithram* (The History of Keralam)(Kottayam: National Book Stall, 1961). Whichever may be the case, this system as it was practised in the late nineteenth and the early twentieth centuries in Keralam was unique. The couples who entered into a sambandham relation did not live in the same house. The Nampoothiris who had sambandham with Nair women would arrive at the Nair house in the evening and leave the house in the morning. They would not eat at their wives' houses. Their children were not allowed to touch their fathers because they belonged to the mothers' castes.

20. Arunima, *There Comes Papa*.

21. The Malabar Nair Marriage Bill of 1896 was the result of the recommendations of the Malabar Marriage Commission set up by the Madras government in 1891. Chandu Menon, one of the members of the commission, strongly condemned the Nampoothiris for their exploitation of Nair women through sambandham and underscored the right of Nairs to institutional legal marriage. See the *Report of Malabar Marriage Commission*, Madras Legislative Records, 1891, 26. The actual Act that was passed in 1896 did not include all the recommendations of the commission but legalized sambandham as marriage. For a detailed discussion of the Act, see, C. J. Fuller, *Nairs Today* (Cambridge: Cambridge University Press, 1976).

22. Most historians assume that the system of land tax was first introduced in Keralam by Tipu Sultan. The British followed his taxation system but installed the Nampoothiri and Nair janmis as the sole proprietors of the land. Earlier, for all practical purposes, the tenants had the right over the land, though technically, the janmis were the owners of the land. For an analysis of the changes in the land ownership system during the British rule, see K. N. Panikkar, 'Land Control, Ideology and Reform: A Study of the Changes in the Family Organisation and Marriage Systems in Kerala', *Indian Historical Review* 4, no. 1 (July 1977): 30–46.

23. For a detailed discussion of tenancy acts in Malabar, see, V. V. Kunhikrishnan, *The Tenancy Legislation in Malabar, 1870–1970: A Historical Analysis* (New Delhi: Northern Book Centre, 1993).

24. Narayanan Nampoothiri, 'Acharavum Parishkaravum (Acharam and Reform)', *Yuvadeepthi* 2, no. 3 (March 1903): 27–35, 34.

25. Nampoothiri, 'Acharavum Parishkaravum', 35.

26. P. K. Nampoothiri, 'Janmi–Kutiyan Billum Achara Vyvasthakalum (The Janmi–Kutiyan Bill and the Order of Acharam)', *Malayala Manorama*, 12 October 1904.

27. The discussions of the initial meetings of the YKS were centred on the question of the tenancy act and its possible implications for the janmis. For the details of the activities of the YKS in its initial years, see I. V. Babu, *Keraleeya Navothanavum Nampoothirimarum* (The Enlightenment of Kerala and Nampoothiris) (Kottayam: Sahithya Pravarthaka Sahakarana Sangham, 2001).

28. Quoted in M. R. Bhattathiripad, 'Kal Noottantinullil (In a Quarter Century)', *Mathrubhumi* (Special Issue), 1936, 33–37, 34.

29. Bhattathiripad, 'Kal Noottantinullil'.

30. Nagam Ayya, *The Travancore State Manual* (Thiruvananthapuram: Government Press, 1874).

31. Krishnan Nampoothiri, 'Nampoothirimarum Jati Dharmavum (Nampoothiris and Jati Responsibilities)', *Kerala Pathrika* 3, no. 12 (December 1905): 3–5, 3.

32. Nampoothiri, 'Nampoothirimarum Jati Dharmavum'.

33. Francis Buchanan, *A Report on the Native Customs of South India* (London: Abe Scot Publishing Company, 1812), 86.

34. Edgar Thurston, 'Notes on the Hindus of Madras', *Journal of Madras Museum* 2, no. 13 (1890): 20–27, 23.

35. Kanippayyoor gave several insights into the daily practice of the Nampoothiris in his three-volume memoir. In the introduction, he makes interesting connections between memory and history. He claims that he is writing these memoirs in order to record certain practices which no longer exist and which would be soon erased even from memory. For him, history writing is a struggle against forgetting, because through writing, memory becomes immortal. See the preface in Nampoothirippad, *Ente Smaranakal*.

36. Nampoothirippad, *Ente Smaranakal*, 78.

37. Mozhikunnathu Brahmadathan Nampoothirippad, *Khilafat Smaranakal* (Memories of Khilafat) (Kozhikode: Mathrubhumi Books, 2006), 141–143.

38. V. Keshavan Bhattathirippad, 'Vidyabhyasavum Achara Samrakshanavum (Education and the Protection of Acharam)', *Kerala Pathrika*, no. 5 (May 1909): 21–25, 22.

39. Parameshwaran Nampoothiri, 'Vinasha Kale (In the Period of Destruction)', *Prabhatham*, March 23, 1911.

40. K. Neelakantan Moosathu, 'English Vidyabhyasa Bhramam (The Desire for English Education)', *Kerala Pathrika* 5, no. 8 (March 1912): 20–23, 21.

41. The memorandum submitted to the YKS by the Kottakkal unit (Kottakkal, 1917).

42. Edgar Thurston, who was a colonial officer and anthropologist in his analysis of castes, considered Brahmins as a ritual community who possessed the knowledge of the Vedas from time immemorial. See Edgar Thurston, *Castes and Tribes of Southern India*, vol. 1 (Madras: Government Press, 1909). A continuation of this thought can be seen in the nationalist and communist historians. For a nationalist version of this argument, see L. A. Anantha Krishnan Iyer, *Castes of Cochin* (Kochi: Government Press, 1934). For a Marxist interpretation of the same argument, see Namboodiripad, *Keralam Malayalikalute Mathrubhumi*. Scholars who have raised strong criticisms against brahmanical ideology have also ironically assumed that in the precolonial period, Brahmins controlled all forms of theoretical knowledge. See P. K. Balakrishnan, *Jativyvasthayum Keralacharithram* (The Caste System and Kerala History) (Kottayam: D. C. Books, 2003).

43. P. Anujan Bhattathirippad, *Puthiya Noottandu* (The New Century) (Kozhikode: Kalpadruma Publishers, 1913), 22–23.

44. K. V. Nampoothiri, 'Nampoothirimarum Vidyabhyasavum (Nampoothiris and Education)', *Sahithya Chandrika* 1, no. 4 (April 1914): 30–35, 32.

45. Most of the literature on caste practices generalized this brahmanical principle of pollution and purity as an organizing principle for the caste system. See G. S. Ghurye, *Caste and Race in India* (London: Routledge, 1932); Dumont, *Homo Hierarchicus*; M. N. Srinivas, *Social Change in Modern India* (Hyderabad: Orient Longman, 1996); Dipankar Gupta, *Interrogating Caste: Understanding*

Hierarchy and Difference in Indian Society (New Delhi: Penguin, 2000). I argue that the principle of purity and pollution as the defining category of caste practices was applicable only to the Brahmin castes and that each caste had its own specific organizing principle.

46. N. P. Nampoothiri, 'Nampoothiri Acharangalute Innathe Avastha (The Present Condition of Nampoothiri Acharams)', *Bhasha Poshini* 9, no. 8 (September 1919): 25–41, 27.

47. N. P. Nampoothiri, 'Nampoothiri Acharangalute Innathe Avastha', 30.

48. Tamil Brahmins who ran restaurants invented the term 'Brahmanal Hotel' to attract the elite-caste population in general and Brahmins in particular. Many such restaurants have now become chain restaurants with branches in various metro cities of the world. For a description of such restaurants in the early twentieth century, see Nampoothirippad, *Ente Smaranakal*, 71.

49. Nampoothiri, 'Acharavum Parishkaravum', 27–35.

50. For a description of buses and bus journeys in Malabar in the first quarter of the twentieth century, see V. K. Menon, *Smaranakal* (Memoirs) (Ottappalam: Sudarshanam Publications, 1954), 67–72.

51. For a description of the acharams of Nampoothiris connected to cooking and dining, see P. Bhaskaranunni, *Keralam Irupatham Noottantinte Arambhathil* (Keralam in the Beginning of the Twentieth Century) (Thrissur: Kerala Sahithya Academy, 2005), 172–173.

52. Bhaskaranunni, *Keralam Irupatham Noottantinte Arambhathil*, 129.

53. Nampoothirippad, *Ente Smaranakal*, 252–257.

54. See note 3.

55. Gothra is subdivision within the Brahmin jati, based on specific claimed lineage to one of the seven sages. Each gothra is an exogamous group.

56. Each family was associated to an othikkan who not only oversaw the rituals in the family on special occasions like weddings or funerals but also taught the boys in the family the Veda recital.

57. Mozhikunnath Brahmadathan Nampoothirippad remembered that his othikkan was very short-tempered and he once pushed Nampoothirippad down some steps, who then fell to the ground floor. Nampoothirippad, *Khilafat Smaranakal*, 3.

58. C. J. Fuller, 'Orality, Literacy and Memorisation: Priestly Education in Contemporary South India', *Modern Asian Studies* 35, no. 1 (February 2001): 1–31, 2.

59. Jonathan Parry, 'The Brahmanical Tradition and the Technology of the Intellect', in *Reason and Morality*, ed. Joanna Overing, 198–222 (London: Tavistock, 1985), 207.

60. William Jones, the founder of the Asiatic Society, the German orientalist scholar Max Muller, colonial officers like George Birdwood and E. B. Havell, and so on, were some of the pioneers of orientalist scholarship in the late eighteenth and the nineteenth centuries. Following the Western conceptualization of Latin

as the scholarly language, this scholarship positioned Sanskrit as the language of knowledge in India. For an analysis of the changing status of Sanskrit, see Sheldon Pollock, *The Language of the Gods in the World of Men* (Berkeley: University of California Press, 2006).

61. In the early years of the Malayalam book industry, the most popular subject was dominant-caste mythological stories based on the Ramayana or the Mahabharata. For a history of printing in Keralam, see K. M. Govi, *Adimudranam: Bharathathilum Malayalathilum* (The First Printing: In Bharatham and Malayalam) (Thrissur: Kerala Sahithya Academy, 1998).

62. V. T. Bhattathirippad, *Veetiyute Sampoorna Krithikal* (Complete Works of V. T.) (Kottayam: D. C. Books, 1997), 159–168.

63. For a detailed description of Ambalavasi life in Malabar in the first half of the twentieth century, see K. V. Moosathu, *Kazhinja Kalangal* (The Bygone Days) (Thrissur: Vidyavijayam Printers, 1963).

64. Moosathu, *Kazhinja Kalangal*, 78.

65. Moosathu, *Kazhinja Kalangal*, 80.

66. Moosathu, *Kazhinja Kalangal*, 80.

67. K. N. Panikkar argued that the process of Sanskritization of indigenous medicinal practices was part of the elitist nationalist attempt of maintaining their hegemony during the freedom movement in India. See K. N. Panikkar, *Culture, Ideology, Hegemony: Intellectuals and Social Consciousness in Colonial India* (London: Anthem Press, 1995), 153–158.

68. For an explanation of the concept of hierarchical series of knowledge, see the Introduction.

69. Bhaskaranunni, *Keralam Irupatham Noottantinte Arambhathil*, 178.

70. Nampoothirippad, *Ente Smaranakal*, 134–137.

71. Nampoothirippad, *Ente Smaranakal*, 91.

72. For a detailed description of smarthavicharam, see A. M. N. Chakyar, *Avasanathe Smarthavicharam* (The Last Smarthavicharam), trans. K. K. Shankaran Nampoothiri (Thiruvananthapuram: Cultural Publication Division, Kerala Government, 2001).

73. Nampoothirippad, *Khilafat Smaranakal*, 73.

74. K. P. K Nampoothiri, *Madrasile Jeevitham* (Life in Madras) (Calicut: Mathrubhumi Publishers, 1972).

75. N. P. Nampoothiri, 'Nampoothiri Acharangalute Innathe Avastha', 34.

76. Nampoothiri, 'Nampoothiri Acharangalute Innathe Avastha', 34.

77. Devika, *En-gendering Individuals*, 131.

78. Devika, *En-gendering Individuals*, 122.

79. Translated by Bindu Menon.

4

Nampoothiris and the Order of Knowledge

As mentioned in Chapter 3, by the 1920s, the Nampoothiri world of *acharam* faced serious challenges from both inside and outside this world. The order based on acharam became incapable of incorporating new and emerging social relations and concepts based on colonial forms of knowledge. This resulted in organized attempts in the leadership of the Yoga Kshema Sabha (YKS) to reform and to reconstitute the community based on new principles. Analysing the reform literature and scholarly debate on the Nampoothiri reform movement of the 1920s and 1930s, this chapter argues that Nampoothiris entered the order of knowledge through the reform movement, which incorporated the prominent elements of acharam that resulted in a colonial–brahmanical system of knowledge production. The chapter details the process of confrontation and mutual incorporation of these two orders and explains the elements of Nampoothiri life in the order of knowledge.

The concept of the order of knowledge explains less an ordered structure than the process where objects, human beings, and their actions were evaluated, indexed, transformed, or excluded with reference to their relation to knowledge. Knowledge attained such importance in the Nampoothiri life that even the conservatives in the community began justifying the importance of acharam based on its relation to knowledge. The order of knowledge also denotes a condition of domination in which various social forces created hierarchical series by assigning indices to objects and actions with reference to knowledge. The order of knowledge incorporated acharam into its fold by reinterpreting the ritualistic practices of Nampoothiris. Contemporary debates within the reform writers actively produced what they considered a scientific interpretation of acharam. This interpretation made some of the old practices superstitious or inhuman. The acharams in the daily life of Nampoothiris did not transform radically in this period, but acharam was no longer the reference point for these actions.

Nampoothiri reformers attempted to reorganize their *jati*, where acharam was the central organizing force, into *samudayam* (community) in which knowledge was the pivotal point around which new social relations were imagined. These attempts introduced a process of engendering individuals in which each man and woman required knowledge to be a member of the reformed community.[1] This knowledge included self-knowledge, a new bio-logic of gender, a nationalistic history (of the community, religion, and nation), and a new cosmology based on scientific explanation. This new knowledge introduced a new process of gender differentiation based on the biology of the body, which may be called bio-logic. In this bio-logic, the earlier entwinement of gender and caste was untwined, and gender became a part of nature, and caste, a part of culture. The concepts of purity and impurity continued to inform the process of understanding the nature of objects in circulation, but many objects that were considered impure earlier now became pure. This chapter traces the changing relation of the Nampoothiris to the social world as they entered the order of knowledge.

The Nampoothiri Yuvajana Sangham and the Emergence of the Order of Knowledge

By the second decade of the twentieth century, new social forces, especially the reform movements among other lower castes, ignited panic, discontent, and, moreover, a desire for change among the young members of the Nampoothiri community. The active involvement of young members in the YKS turned the organization in new directions. The reformists and the conservatives attempted to influence the community through public meetings, journal articles, and face-to-face conversations. In 1916, the YKS initiated the publishing of a daily, *Yogakshemam*. Initially, *Yogakshemam* was under the control of the conservatives, and they used this as a platform to raise their criticism against the reformists. The influence of the reformists within the organization, however, gradually increased in the period between 1915 and 1920.

In the eighth annual conference of the YKS held at Vellinezhi in April 1916, the major debate was around English education. In the conference, one of the young members introduced a resolution that strongly called for members to join educational institutions and learn English, which was 'the language of new civilisation, knowledge and progress'.[2] The conservatives argued that 'English is a language of people who indulge in material pleasures and of those who totally disregard the spiritual aspects of human life'.[3] While the conference passed the resolution only with a thin majority, the debate gave a clear sign that the subjects of knowledge and education would be the major field of contestation in the future activities of the YKS. Even though a majority of the conference, through voting, disapproved the position of the conservatives, the latter continued their propaganda against English education among the community members. They formed another group, Nivarini (the remedy), to create awareness about the importance of acharams for the well-being of the community. Towards this, they organized meetings of community members and published some articles in journals. However, these efforts did not last long, and within two years, the group became defunct.[4]

By this period, the young generation who entered colonial educational institutions started interacting with the colonial idea of knowledge. This interaction created a new imagination of the status of the Nampoothiri community in relation to knowledge. This imagination depicted the community as one engulfed by the darkness of ignorance and the community members as individuals facing severe internal crisis. The young leaders of the reform movement considered education as the first and the most important step in overcoming this crisis. The entry of Nampoothiris into education was a slow, gradual, and contested process. In the beginning, even those who argued for English education did not consider it proper for a Nampoothiri boy or girl to sit along with the students from other jatis. In other words, the reformists at this period did not outright reject the relevance of the practices of acharam. Their attempt was to make acharam and knowledge commensurable and co-habitable. Kuroor Unni Nampoothirippad, who was one of the most respected leaders of the reformist group, reminded young and enthusiastic members that while criticizing the conservative position, they should not disrespect elders or the acharams in general. In 1916, he wrote:

> Our criticism is against certain acharams which are standing in the way of the progress of the community, especially those which are preventing Nampoothiris from attaining modern education. This should not lead us to abandon all other acharams, without which we will not be Nampoothiris.[5]

Nampoothirippad further argued that modern education in Britain had not prevented the British from following Christianity. Rather, modern knowledge helped them in propagating their religion. Similarly, educated young Nampoothiris would provide the community a better image and status in front of outsiders.[6]

The major question for the reformists in this period was how to implement their plan for education without completely abandoning acharams, especially that of untouchability. In public schools, Nampoothiri boys would have to sit with other 'lower-caste' people, which would make them polluted. If they were polluted especially by certain 'lower-caste' students, they would have to undergo different rituals, which may have extended for more than a day. Even though a few individuals from the reformist section argued that the community should privilege education even at the cost of acharam, for the majority of reformists in this period, that was not an acceptable solution. This debate brought out the idea of Nampoothiri Vidyalayam (a special school for Nampoothiris) where Nampoothiris could attain modern education and at the same time keep their acharams, especially the acharam of untouchability, intact. The first Nampoothiri Vidyalayam was established in 1918 in Edakkuni, under the management of the Raja of Kochi, and was later moved to Thrissur. Within two years, the community established four more Vidyalayams in various places in Kochi Rajyam with the help of the Raja.[7] In Nampoothiri Vidyalayams, all the teachers were from dominant castes but were not necessarily Nampoothiris. Hence, coming back from the school, the students had to bathe before entering their home or hostel where they resided. The subjects taught in these schools included Malayalam, Sanskrit, history, science, and mathematics. The management provided residential facilities for students who came from distant places. Even though the Raja was the patron of these schools, the Nampoothiris in the locality had to raise funds for the daily expenses of the schools and hostels. From the beginning, the Nampoothiri Vidyalayams faced a number of difficulties, including severe financial problems and low attendance. At this period, the rich among the community did not feel any need to financially support these schools. Most of the community members were also not eager to send their children to any kind of school.[8] Still, the few who studied in these schools later became the leaders of the YKS. The schools continued to exist at least in a nominal way, until they were taken over by the government in the 1950s or were closed in the same period.

The activities of the reformists made knowledge a debatable category within the community. Acharam still dominated the organization of Nampoothiri daily life, but at least one section of the community established communication and connection with the order of knowledge. The reformist criticism shook the unquestionable status of acharam and created a possibility that certain acharams could be changed or even excluded from daily life. The passing of a resolution by the YKS in 1917 condemning the *vadhyar* (teacher and manager) of Thrissur Brahmaswam Matam was such an instance where acharam was questioned by the community members.

The vadhyar was both the manager of the Brahmaswam Matam and a figure of authority regarding acharam. His words were final in cases of disputes and confusion regarding ritualistic practices. Technically, the Thrissur Yogam—which was a committee of important Nampoothiri families in the locality—owned the matam, but for all practical purposes, the vadhyar was the actual authority.

In 1916, the residents of the matam complained to the Yogam and the Raja of Kochi that the current vadhyar was highly authoritarian and corrupt. The Yogam conducted an inquiry and found that the allegations were correct, and eventually, the vadhyar resigned from the position. In 1917, the same vadhyar unilaterally took over the administration of the matam and re-established his position. Kuroor Unni Nampoothirippad took the initiative of the campaign against the vadhyar and presented the case in front of the Raja of Kochi. The Raja did not take any steps against the vadhyar, as he considered it the responsibility of the Thrissur Yogam to act on the matter. The annual conference of the YKS in 1917 condemned the vadhyar and appealed to the Thrissur Yogam to take immediate action against him. The Yogam, pointing out the unanimous resolution in the YKS conference, removed the vadhyar from the position and took over the administration of the matam. M. R. Bhattathirippad remembered this as the first instance where the community members successfully challenged one of the sacred authorities of acharam, whose position was so far unquestionable. Bhattathirippad concluded that this was made possible mainly because of the awareness of the educated young Nampoothiris 'who depended on their own knowledge and wisdom instead of following the elders without any question or doubt'.[9] The campaigns of the reformists and the debates within the community in the years between 1915 and 1920 brought the order of acharam and the order of knowledge in contesting positions in different arenas of daily life of the community.

In 1920, in a meeting conducted at Thripoonithara, the young members of the community formed an association, the Nampoothiri Yuvajana Sangham (Nampoothiri Youth Wing [NYS]). The stated objective of the NYS was to propagate the ideals of the Yoga Kshema Sabha and create awareness among members regarding the importance of education. The clear reason for forming such an organization, besides to use it as an independent platform, was to challenge the conservative leaders of the YKS partially from within.[10] The NYS took the initiative to publish a new journal, *Unni Nampoothiri* The Young Nampoothiri), which became an important medium in the reformists' struggle against the conservatives. The formation of the NYS inaugurated a new face of reform, where the inclination towards knowledge became clearer and stronger.

By the third decade of the century, the discourse of knowledge versus ignorance significantly influenced the process of imagining the community. The NYS gradually moved into a firmer position regarding the question of education and acharam. They now strongly urged community members to join public schools even though that may be a violation of acharam. They described the community as one immersed in darkness and pointed out that only education could bring light into the community. The young reform leaders urged the members of the community to be equipped for new occupations, new family practices, and, in general, a new way of life. They emphasized that education was the first and foremost step for the beginning of this new life. This was the second stage where the order of acharam began losing its tight control over community members and the order of knowledge appeared in the horizon of the self-imagination of the community.

The debate around the Nampoothiri Family Regulation Committee formed by the Kochi government demonstrated the increasing influence of knowledge over acharam. In 1923, the Kochi government formed a committee to study the possibility of introducing new family laws for Nampoothiris. During this period, all the three legislative assemblies in the Malayalam-speaking region were considering Nampoothiri family regulation bills for legalization. The committee report clearly suggested that the community could progress only based on knowledge. The report pointed out that 'the true and permanent wellbeing of the community does not depend upon the promulgation of royal legislation'. According to the members of the community, 'It is education and knowledge of the individual that create the strong base of any community.' The report concluded that 'the community will be truly blessed only when such knowledgeable and open-minded individuals become numerous'.[11] The report showed that knowledge had become the measure of evaluating the existing condition and the imagined future of the community. The community began evaluating each action and value based on their respective relation and position in the future order of knowledge. At the same time, in particular instances, there was no consensus even among the reformists regarding what they understood as knowledge; it had multiple connotations and different hierarchical levels.

At the basic level, knowledge meant the capacity to write and read Malayalam. This was the necessary condition for any individual to be a member of the (imagined) reformed community.[12] In other words, the formation of this new community was dependent on the degree of the dissemination of literacy among Nampoothiris. Krishan Bhattathirippad wrote in 1925:

> In those days, the majority of Nampoothiris considered only the members of their family and their relatives as 'our people'. Even after the formation of the Yoga Kshema Sabha, only the active leaders believed that all Nampoothiris are 'our people'. Nampoothiris became familiar with the idea of *samudayam* [community] and the idea that all Nampoothiris are 'our people', only after they started reading about the common problems of Nampoothiris in *Yogakshemam, Magalodayam* and *Unni Nampoothiri*.[13]

Kanippayyoor Shankaran Nampoothirippad mentioned that while the famous *smarthavicharam* (ritualistic exclusion from the jati) of Kuriyedathu Thathri in 1903 invoked serious discussion among other dominant-caste communities, Nampoothiris did not take it as an issue that would affect them in any manner.[14] According to Kanippayyor, this was because the Nampoothiris did not read any newspapers or magazines, and hence they were not aware of this issue.[15] Kanippayyoor's point was that Nampoothiris were not a samudayam at that point because they were not a reading community. It was the knowledge of reading or writing that predicated the formation of a samudayam.

Knowledge at the next level was related to occupation. The colonial governing practices mapped the hierarchy of occupation in the colonial bureaucracy to a hierarchy of knowledge; each occupation required a certain degree of knowledge attained through institutional learning. The reform discourse of Nampoothiris, in interaction with this colonial idea, produced a certain kind of relation between knowledge and occupation—precisely, the idea that occupations are someway related to knowledge itself emerged in this interaction.[16] Until the third decade of the twentieth century, the majority of Nampoothiris engaged in only two 'occupations'. Usually, in each family, one (male) person engaged in the management of the landed properties and issues related to rent and other returns. If the family was poor, men worked as priests in temples. In both cases, authority or efficiency in these jobs was not in any way related to the possession of institutional knowledge. By the 1920s, Nampoothiris started recognizing that the other 'upper-caste' people, especially the Nairs, who started entering into the new occupations that colonialism produced, had managed to improve their status individually and as a community. In a meeting of *janmi*s (landlords), in 1926, M. V. Nampoothiri warned the Nampoothiri janmis that they have to seriously assess the status of Nampoothiris in society. Explaining the history of the Janmi–Kutiyan Bill in the Madras and Kochi assemblies, he argued that 'it was not just a defeat of our demands. It was a defeat of ignorance in the hand of knowledge'. The members of those castes 'which promoted English education from the very early days have now reached at critical decision making posts in administration and have gained respect among the common people'. He reminded that the passing of the Bill showed how other communities moved upwards in their status.[17] On the one hand, the community recognized that for the progress and well-being of the community in the future, it was necessary to join in the new occupations in colonial institutions. On the other hand, as M. V. Nampoothiri has argued, it was clear that even to protect the existing occupation, the presence of knowledgeable individuals was a necessary factor. It was evident that *janmitham* (landlordism) alone could not protect the economic or social status of the community any longer. This was the background in which the discussion about entering into new occupations began within the community. This debate attempted to historicize the relation between occupation and knowledge.

The conservative section of the community attempted to create a historical relation between the traditional occupation of Nampoothiris and knowledge. Vadakkumkoor Rajaraja Varma rejected the argument that the occupations in which Nampoothiris were involved had no relation to any kind of knowledge.[18] He argued that the only occupation that Nampoothiris (he was talking only about Nampoothiri men) engaged in was related to learning or teaching of the Vedas, which were the ultimate form of knowledge. He insisted that all Nampoothiris should learn the Vedas, teach the Vedas, and practise the acharams according to the Vedas, as Veda teaching was the traditional occupation of Nampoothiris. Further, Varma claimed that the Vedas were very much connected to knowledge; the present crisis, according to him, was that nobody actually learned the Vedas even though everybody could recite them from memory. The young leaders of the reform movement who argued for English education challenged this argument and observed that Nampoothiris were not engaged in any occupation. K. M. Anujan wrote that 'the only occupations Nampoothiris engaged in were eating and procreation'. According to him, the crisis the Nampoothiri community faced was 'a welcome sign, so that the community will try to overcome the crisis by marching towards the daylight of knowledge at least because of the selfish need for survival'.[19] Thus, it was through the connection between occupation and knowledge or ignorance that these authors explained the conditions of the community in the present and in the future.

Knowledge at its highest level was expert knowledge. However, there was no consensus on what exactly expert knowledge was. One section argued that the practice of astrology, *vydyam* (medicine), and debates of grammar and logic based on Sanskrit texts were forms of expert knowledge, similar to the modern disciplines in science. The related claim was that the Nampoothiris as a community had been the possessors of this knowledge from time immemorial. Further, they agreed that science was a form of expert knowledge, but as a morally corrupt enterprise, it was totally unsuitable to Indian culture. For example, T. N. Thirumulppad argued that scientists are experts in finding solutions to the material world, but the Vedas provide knowledge for success in the material and spiritual life not only in this world but also in other worlds. According to him, Western societies were clear examples of immoral civilizations, where the desire for material gain has overpowered the respect for human values. Thirumulppad argued that it would be disastrous for the community to renounce the great tradition of Sanskrit knowledge and to embrace an alien culture in the name of science.[20]

Another section approved the importance of science but considered traditional knowledge important as well. They argued that while science was the basis of expert knowledge, traditional Sanskrit knowledge also was scientific. Numerous articles in *Mangalodayam* and *Unni Nampoothiri* raised this claim, explaining various developments in the emerging disciplines such as Physics, Economics, and History according to the principles of Hindu *shasthra*s (sciences). M. R. K. C.'s[21] article on wireless technology concluded as follows:

> We, Hindus, have a lot to learn from this technology of the Westerners. It is through the medium called ether that we bring gods to earth or send our request to them. Since we have separate manthras [verses] for each God, each of them must be receiving without failure, the 'telephonies' sent to them by the Hindus. This is the same principle based on which the Vedanthis [the experts of the Vedas] form the concept of Nada Brahma [the universe of sound] and the Yoga experts conduct yoga practice controlling the five senses.[22]

M. R. K. C.'s comparison underscored two important points. According to the author, the basic principles of Hindu knowledge and modern science were the same, and the new technologies were just an application of these principles in new ways. The second point was that Hindus were equal, if not superior, to Westerners in expert knowledge. The only difference was on emphasis: Hindus focused on using expert knowledge in the field of spirituality and Westerners used it for material success. M. R. K. C. believed that the development in science was not antagonistic to the Hindu shasthras; rather, scientific principles proved the facticity of traditional knowledge. Hence, according to him, Nampoothiris should learn science and use it to revive the traditional knowledge to its conjectural superior status in the past.

A third section believed that traditional practices were superstitions and only scientific practices could produce knowledge. They demanded total abandonment of acharam and imagined a new daily life based on scientific principles. P. K. Raman Nampoothiri described contemporary Nampoothiri life as 'unhealthy, immoral and uncivilised'. He ridiculed the claim that acharam was scientific or rational. 'If Nampoothiris take bath twice a day, it is not because of concerns for hygiene, but just the fear of being out-casted otherwise.' According to him, the Vedas were suitable as guiding principles at a certain point in human history, but in the contemporary world, only science could provide these guidelines.[23]

Reconstituting Acharam in the Order of Knowledge

Through the discourses on knowledge and ignorance, the Nampoothiri community entered into the order of knowledge, though there was no consensus on what constituted knowledge or ignorance. The order of knowledge was simultaneously a force that produced new hierarchical stratifications and an explanatory system that gave new meanings to the elements of the everyday practices of the community. The community was imagined as a network of 'knowledgeable' individuals, in which the status of the individual was related to his knowledge. Acharam was still a central part of the daily life, but now, knowledge mediated the meaning and methods of understanding acharam. In other words, the community recognized that even to protect their acharam, knowledge attained through modern education was necessary and important. For example, K. N.[24], one of the important leaders of the YKS, argued that between the two objectives of the YKS, namely promoting education and the formalization of acharam, education was a fundamental requirement and the latter would follow naturally if the community achieved the former. He introduced plans of formalizing acharam through compiling a dictionary and coding the rituals in a uniform manner. He reminded that in order to achieve this, the community needed members who were educated and who were *aware* of the Nampoothiri acharams.[25] K. N. considered the reform of acharam a derivative of the education of members of the community. K. N. further observed that even the issue of *kutumba* (family) regulation depended on the issue of education. As mentioned earlier, the younger brothers in a family were not allowed to marry within the community. The leaders of the NYS considered this as one of the major moral and cultural issues that made the Nampoothiri a comical figure in front of other communities. They strongly demanded that all Nampoothiri men should marry within the community. K. N. argued that this could be achieved only if each individual has their own occupation and income. For obtaining the newly emerged occupations, an educational qualification was necessary. Hence, he concluded, the process of reforming acharam was completely dependent on the issue of education.[26]

P. K. Bhattathiri concocted another relation between education and the progress of the community. If K. N. considered Sanskrit education as a thing of the past and unsuitable for the present times, Bhattathiri argued that both Sanskrit and English education are necessary for the welfare of the community. He advised the young generation not to neglect the acharams while participating in colonial educational institutions because if they completely exclude acharams from their daily life, Nampoothiris would no longer be Nampoothiris.

At the same time, Bhattathiri reminded that education should be considered 'not as a practice opposed to acharams but as a way to reform and preserve acharams'.[27] The speech by A. K. T. K. M. Valiya Narayanan Nampoothirippad at the 15th annual conference of the YKS, in 1925 at Vykom, reflected the anxieties of the community regarding the proper method of education at that period. He criticized the older generation for their attitude of neglect in the matter of education. According to him, 'Those who are interested in protecting acharam should look into the present status of acharam among other communities.' He observed that 'the educated public thinks that acharam is a superstition, because in the present situation, it has become a comical act losing all its intended meaning, deviating from the original objectives'. He reminded that it was the duty of Nampoothiris to prove that acharam was a scientific practice, which allows an individual to lead a simple, nature-friendly, and hygienic life. In order to prove this, all individuals of the community should be empowered with scientific knowledge through education. An educated individual would continue to perform acharam but in a scientific manner.[28] Rajaraja Varma's article is an example of another position different from both of the aforementioned arguments, but again, one which considered education as the measure of the welfare of the community. Varma argued that it was impossible to bring the East and the West together, as they are fundamentally different in all aspects. He observed that the origin of the present crisis of the community was the disjuncture between the Nampoothiri daily life and Vedic principles. According to Varma, 'If Nampoothiris start learning the Veda again in a proper way, they will become respected individuals in the society. If they were to learn English, they will end up in government jobs like sweepers and lower-grade clerks in the government offices.'[29]

Bhattathiri, Varma, and K. N. took very different positions regarding the method of education that was proper for the community. All of them, however, underlined that education was a crucial factor in the future well-being of the community. They all considered ignorance as a major reason for contemporary problems faced by the community. This position was very different from earlier debates on education, as discussed in the previous chapter. The discussion of the community reform in the first two decades of the twentieth century considered education only as an additive factor for the progress of the community. The idea that the community was immersed in ignorance did not appear in the discussion at this period. In its initial years, the YKS considered protecting janmitham and acharam through social and political interventions as its major objective. Once the notion of knowledge versus ignorance gained prominence in the reform discourse, education became a measure of the status of the individual and the community.

By the 1930s, the meaning of education narrowed down to the practice of education in colonial institutions. All other forms of education became a deviation from this normal and normalized form, and the former could be expressed only with adjectives such as traditional, practical, and so on. As in colonial conceptualizations, the difference between discursive and non-discursive activities became crucial in the practices that emerged through the reform movement. In this conceptualization, the production of knowledge was a discursive activity, and the resulting knowledge could exist only in a written form. The higher status given to discursive activities helped Nampoothiris to justify their domination with a new claim that historically, they were the 'jati of knowledge'. This also compelled them to enter into colonial educational institutions in order to maintain their higher status in the order of knowledge, because it became the only accepted way of attaining knowledge.

Nampoothiris as Hindus: A Nationalist Concept of Jati

The entry into the order of knowledge transformed the Nampoothiri understanding of jati, gender, and acharam. The immediate signs of this transformation were the use of universal categories such as Hindu religion, history, nation, and so on in the debate around reformation. In the world of acharam, the conceptual categories were inseparably connected to the practices of daily-life world. We saw in the previous chapter that Nampoothiris at that period understood jati and gender in the localized space of their specific acharams. By the 1930s, Nampoothiris began locating themselves in the space of Hindu religion, nation, and history.

In various Malayalam magazines, newspapers, and journals, the writings on or by Nampoothiris in the first two decades of the twentieth century hardly mentioned Hindus or even religion. The articles that appeared in the context of the Malabar rebellion in 1921, where some Nampoothiri janmis were killed at the hands of Muslim rebels, discussed the event either as an altercation between Muslims and Nampoothiris or as a struggle between janmis and *kutiyans* (between landlords and serfs). It was rarely mentioned as a Hindu–Muslim issue even though Islam was already considered a religion with essential characteristics.[30] P. N. Bhattathirippad described the rebellion as an act of 'ignorant and arrogant Muslim kutiyans against Nampoothiri janmis who were affectionate and benevolent'.[31] P. Narayana Menon, a leader of the Indian National Congress in Malabar, saw the riots as 'a rebellion against imperialism, which later became a riot against Nampoothiri Janmis'.[32] Mozhikunnath Brahmadathan Nampoothirippad, who was arrested by the British police for his alleged support for the Muslim rebels, later in his memoirs described the rebellion as one 'which began with respectable intentions but which was later turned against Nampoothiris, misguided by the fanatical Muslim leaders'.[33] Even when attributing a religious nature to Muslims, Nampoothirippad did not align it against Hindus but Nampoothiris.

In the early writings of reform leaders of the Pulaya, Ezhava, and Nair castes, the issue of jati was rarely conflated with the issue of Hindu religion. This was not because the category 'Hindu' was not known to the authors of these articles. By the second half of the nineteenth century, the English-educated native historians have started using the term 'Hindu religion'. Padmanabha Menon's *Travancore Manual* published in 1864 had mentioned the Thiruvithamkoor Rajyam as a Hindu Rajyam.[34] Still, this idea was rarely circulated among the general population, especially among the illiterate Nampoothiri community. By the early twentieth century, colonially educated dominant-caste individuals started 'recognizing' themselves not just as Ezhavas, Nayars, or Nampoothiris but as Hindus too. Even then, for the majority of the members of these communities, though Hindu may be a familiar category, it was not a group that they belonged to. They primarily identified with jati, and the inter-jati relation was never considered as a relation within Hindus.[35]

In the context of creating a history of individual jatis, the reform journals introduced the categories of 'Hindu' and 'religion' among Nampoothiris. Historians widely used orientalist texts which mentioned Hindu as a religion and Sanskrit as its language. For example, the article by K. V. Moosathu cited orientalist scholars Max Müller and William Jones to argue that 'among *Hindus*, Nampoothiri men were assigned the responsibility of keeping the Vedic knowledge alive through generations [emphasis added]'.[36] V. R. Nampoothiri used the words 'Hindu' and 'Brahmin' as interchangeable, and his *History of the Hindu Religion* is a justification of brahmanical domination over other jatis.[37] Similarly, K. Raman Ilayathu, who considered the contemporary practices of Nampoothiris archaic and immoral, situated these customs as part of the Hindu religion and its *varna* principles.[38] In other words, both the orthodox and reformist positions started using the categories of 'Hindu' and 'religion' as historical facts. The reform discourse familiarized the notions of Hindu and religion (which was also a new category) among the educated Nampoothiris community and disseminated further among other members of the community through speeches, plays, and songs. In 1930, for the first time in the history of the YKS, in its annual conference, the presidential address portrayed the issues of Nampoothiris as the issues of Hindus.[39] The reformers, using the colonial oriental scholarship, created a historical essence for the category 'Hindu', and the meaning of this category became increasingly stabilized within the community.

The colonial and the missionary discourses depicted Christianity as the only rational religion and all other religions as irrational and uncivilized.[40] The reform historians had to challenge this concept in order to establish the historical existence of a religion for Hindus based on rational principles. K. V. Raghavan Nair's article 'Scientificity of Religion' is an interesting example in this regard, which attempted to prove the scientificity of the Vedic tradition of the Hindu religion. The author was not a Nampoothiri, but the magazine *Unni Nampoothiri* gave a prominent space to this article because it established a connection between scientific knowledge and the tradition of the Vedas, which was considered a brahmanical tradition. Nair began his article by stating that 'the present time in which we live is known as *vijnyana yugam* [the millennium of knowledge]'. The West has connected knowledge with progress, and it has changed the life of the human beings in the whole world. Scientists could not only explain the laws of nature and society but they have also developed the scientific method of practising art, dressing, cooking, and eating. According to Nair, the secret behind the success of science was that it has produced one single general law to explain all the phenomena in the universe.

Nair further analysed the basic principles of different religions such as Christianity, Islam, and Zoroastrianism and argued that since all these religions propagated dualism of good and bad, they could not explain the world by one general principle, and hence, these religions were not scientific religions. But the Hindu religious principle, which was based on non-dualism of Vedanta philosophy, explained the world with one general law, and hence, it was the only scientific religion. Nair provided a historical reason as well for the Hindu religion being the one and only scientific religion. All other religions were established by prophets who had magical or extra-human power. But the Aryans formed the Hindu religion through experiments in real life, as is done in scientific practice. Before the West invented modern scientific principles, the Hindus had the knowledge of evolution, a theory of the atom, and they were familiar with many other scientific laws.[41] Nair's argument expressed the general view of the educated dominant castes at the time. Several articles in *Unni Nampoothiri*, *Mangalodayam*, and *Vidya Vinodini* shared similar views regarding the Hindu religion.[42] It was in this comparison between modern science and the dominant-caste practices that a concept of Hindu religion emerged for the first time among the dominant castes in Keralam. Although the words 'Hindu' and 'religion' were not expressed for the first time in this period, these debates reinforced the concept of identity based on religion and also filled that identity with a historical essence. Further, the primary identification of 'individual' was still with the jati-turned-samudayam, but the samudayam itself was now part of the larger entity called religion.

The assimilation of jatis into the fold of Hindu religion was a contested process. In the order of acharam, Nampoothiris never had to justify their dominance verbally and rationally. Thus, up to the early twentieth century, the various jati practices of Nampoothiris in the daily life naturalized and reproduced their dominance. Note that at this time, the other jatis experienced the domination of Nampoothiris as an external force which restricted and bounded them within the limits of their own jatis. However, the brahmanical ideology, in general, did not determine the internal configuration of the non-brahmanical jatis, especially their belief systems and ritualistic practices. But by the 1930s, as jatis started to transform into communities and as rituals and other practices were explained based on scientific principles, the newly emerged brahmanical notions of acharams and the daily practice of rituals became the reference point for other jatis as well.

In the transformation from jati to samudayam and to a religious community, reading and writing were crucial activities of imagining the new communities. Hindu religion and samudayam were imagined communities where individual members shared a common imagination through reading and writing. In other words, unlike in the earlier jati order, where Brahmins dominated other jatis through localized daily practice, in the new situation, knowledge became an essential factor for the imagination and reproduction of community identities. Although scholars recognized the importance of education and knowledge in the reform process and community formation, most of them imagined an already existing community that was the target of reform.[43] However, the community itself was a result of the development of a reading–writing group through the reform movements. It is also important to emphasize the difference between jati hierarchy based on acharam and the new hierarchies based on knowledge.

This will be clearer when we look closely into the ways in which Nampoothiris attempted to position themselves in the emerging Hindu religion. It was already evident that jati-based acharam was incommensurable with the emerging notion of the Hindu religion where different jatis share a common past. The oppressed-caste reform movements had already challenged the concepts of untouchability and caste-based labour exploitation. Only by making these caste practices an exception in the notion of Hindu religion could the reformers justify a shared common past. The demand for dismantling the hierarchical relations of jatis by establishing horizontal relationships was already prominent in the political arena. Hence, the imagination of communities as a part of a religion required reorganization of the existing jati hierarchy. This resulted in two simultaneous processes: first was the emergence of an idea of *savarna* jatis (literal meaning of which is 'with colour' but intended as a jati within the varna system), which comprised the jatis from Nampoothiris to Nair in the jati hierarchy, as a group distinct from the *avarna* jatis (literally, 'without colour' but a category for jatis outside the varna system), which included Ezhavas to further 'lower-castes' such as Pulayas. The second process was the transformation of jatis based on separate internal principles into samudayams based on a common principle of knowledge.

From Hierarchy to Dichotomy: Savarnas and Avarnas

The concept of savarna and avarna emerged in the context of textual interpretation of history and religion. In the second quarter of the twentieth century, educated individuals from the dominant caste started writing the history of jatis based on a notion of a Hindu religion and *chathurvarnya* principles as laid out in the Vedas. These histories introduced the distinction between savarna and avarna jatis based on 'scientific' explanations of practices of different jatis.[44] According to these histories, at the origin, the chathurvarnya system was only division of labour and all varnas had equal status. In a later period, when Brahmins started dominating the social and political domains, they interpreted the chathurvarnya principle as a hierarchy of jatis in which Brahmins were on the top. These histories described the hierarchical ordering of jati as an aberration in the historical process, which could be and should be rectified in the present. For dominant-caste jati historians, the concept of savarna and avarna became the principle of reorganization of jatis.[45]

Academic historians of caste, while keeping their differences regarding the basic principle of the caste system, agree that varna principles were not followed in the actual practice of caste anywhere in India.[46] In the case of Keralam, the actual regrouping of castes as savarna and avarna did not follow the chathurvarnya distinction. But the point is that the production of historical knowledge referring to chathurvarnya created an impression of the historical existence of a Hindu religion in which all jatis shared a common past. This history was necessary for the dominant-caste historians to project a common present and future for savarna jatis based on a shared common past.

The grouping of dominant-caste jatis as savarna reduced the degree of hierarchy in the relations within these caste communities, though the differences between them were not totally obliterated. The claim of association of communities with knowledge—either in the past as in the case of Nampoothiris or in the present as in the case of Nairs—helped savarna communities to claim superiority over the avarna communities, which were portrayed as ignorant groups. In other words, the order of knowledge challenged the hierarchical order of jatis but did not produce horizontal relations or equality between all jatis. Therefore, the dominance of savarna jatis over avarna jatis continued in this order, with the justification based not on acharams but on knowledge.

By the 1930s, Nampoothiris, especially educated young men, started co-dining with other savarna men, an act which would have resulted in expulsion from the jati in the previous decade. They also began to ignore the acharam of untouchability among savarna jatis. The scientific explanations of hygiene justified these new customs. V. K. Raja explained the new formations based on the 'new knowledge of universal laws of nature, which state that every action has its own reaction'.[47] For Raja, this meant that the future of a person was not determined by birth but by his actions; the actions in this world should be the basis in which people form groups.

> Nampoothiris, Rajas, the Ambalavasis, and Nairs now dine together because they are all vegetarians. They are educated and hence share common views about this world and society. The new grouping of savarna jatis is based on a new awareness about healthy ways of living. The jatis which are yet to reach this awareness are naturally excluded from this grouping.[48]

It is not surprising that Raja did not make any reference to the fact that traditionally, Nairs were not vegetarians. In this period, the idea of vegetarianism was spreading among some sections of Nairs, and it was strictly followed in situations of co-dining. The savarna castes developed certain shared spaces through measures like hygiene or education adopted from colonial discourse and excluded avarna castes from these spaces. The more important point is that this exclusion was justified not on the basis of customs but on scientific principles. Of course, avarnas challenged this kind of exclusion, especially in public spaces, but they also used the rationale of hygiene and knowledge to establish their claim.[49]

Jati continued its presence in the order of knowledge but in new forms and modes. As explained earlier in the chapter, jati in its earlier form was incommensurable with the emerging order of knowledge. The reform leaders of different jatis imagined samudayam as the future form of identification and association. Education was a common constitutive factor for all samudayams because samudayam in the first instance was imagined as a network of knowledgeable individuals. In this sense, samudayam was constituted very differently from the constitution of jati. In the latter case, each jati had its own constitutive factors: for Asharis, it was asharippani, and for Nampoothiris, it was acharam, and so on, as we saw in the previous chapters. It is important to note that dominant-caste reform leaders did not consider education as a project to transcend the difference between jatis; rather, they imagined it as a process through which the internal elements of jati could be reconstituted so that jati would transform into samudayam. The reform leaders attributed for each jati a historical relation with knowledge and constructed a hierarchical order of samudayams in the present based on this relation in the past. The reform movement of Nampoothiris attempted to put their community on the top of the hierarchical series of knowledge through a claim of their assumed relation with knowledge in the past.

This may seem a difficult task considering the contemporary colonial claim of knowledge as universal and independent of human subjectivities. As we saw in the Introduction, in actual practice, the universals in colonial discourse were arrangements of elements with incremental differences in series, and these series were hierarchical with dichotomous elements at each end of a series. For example, knowledge was considered a universal category, but not all types of knowledges were equal. In the hierarchical series of knowledge, Western scientific knowledge was on the top and practical knowledge of the artisans of the East was at the bottom, the latter being almost equal to ignorance. The Nampoothiri reform leaders focused on inserting themselves in the series of knowledge by actively producing a history of the community and its relation to knowledge. In other words, in the reconstitution of jati based on acharam into samudayam based on knowledge, history was one of the most important elements that determined the processes of this redefinition.

Historical knowledge was critical in the formation of samudayams, as samudayam was imagined as both historical and as a continuation of jati. Influenced by colonial ideas of caste, the early reformers described jati as natural and unchanging. However, by the third decade of the twentieth century, the Nampoothiri reform narratives began emphasizing change rather than continuation in the history of jati practice. These inquiries resulted in an exploration of the origin of jati, and a variety of 'origin stories' started appearing in magazines and newspapers. Among those of Nampoothiri samudayam, two specific origin stories became dominant. The first one was the myth of Parasurama, who was a *rishi* (sage) and who had thrown an axe from the mountains of the Western Ghats to the Arabian Sea to recover the land from the sea, which became known as Keralam. He invited sixty-four Brahmin families from the northern part of India to settle in this newly recovered land and gave each one a village and the full authority to administer the land. This story attributed a historical justification for janmitham, through a description of an originary moment in the history when Nampoothiris became the landlords. It should be noted that this story was always quoted as a myth but as one which had a certain connection with the actual history of the region; in other words, it was a glorified version of an actual event in the past.

For example, M. N. Nampoothiri explained that while the Parasurama story might not be factual, it was created based on actual events. According to him, in the ancient period, one of the ruling rajas invited Nampoothiris to Keralam because they were experts of astrology, which was a science necessary for the development of agriculture. The king gave them the full authority to administrate the land, which later transformed into full-fledged janmitham.[50] For Ramanatha Iyer, the Parasurama story was a proof that Nampoothiris were the community which developed agriculture by recovering land from water. According to him, for lack of evidence, one cannot say whether the rulers invited Nampoothiris to Keralam or they came on their own. But it was evident from the Parasurama story that 'their authority over the land had centuries-long history and they were known for their knowledge even in distant lands'.[51]

The second story was about Shankaracharya, a philosopher sage who established the *advaita* (non-dual) philosophy. He was born in a Nampoothiri family, and even as a child, he showed his aptitude towards the Vedas and other Sanskrit texts. He accepted sainthood in his teenage and then developed the advaita school of philosophy, which challenged the Buddhist philosophy that was dominant in that period. He travelled widely and established four *math*s (a kind of monastery) at four different places to teach and propagate his philosophy. *Shankara Smriti*, a Sanskrit work, which coded the sixty-four acharams of Nampoothiris, was supposedly written by Shankaracharya.[52]

These two stories became a mandatory element in most of the histories of Keralam written in the first half of the twentieth century.[53] The adaptation of these stories into the history of Keralam indicates the way in which the dominant castes selectively constructed a past as the pre-history of the samudayam. One of the main objectives of this history writing was to connect the Nampoothiri jati with knowledge. In all these histories, which claimed a golden past of Nampoothiris, Shankaracharya was a prominent figure as a scholar-philosopher. The reference to Shankaracharya created an impressionistic connection of Nampoothiris with knowledge. By this time, colonial oriental scholarship had already established Sanskrit texts as the source of the great traditional knowledge of India. Now, making a connection with this traditional knowledge helped Nampoothiris to claim an admirable position in the hierarchical series of knowledge. For example, in the article mentioned earlier, K. N. coined the phrase 'English Saraswathi' (Saraswathi is the goddess of learning) in order to position English education in a continuum with the history of learning of Nampoothiris. He wrote that the golden heritage of the past was 'only the first chapter of the world history'. His argument was that 'in the present, English is the goddess of education, but she is the daughter or granddaughter of the Sanskrit Saraswathi'.[54]

However, this brings up the question: If Nampoothiri as a jati was already associated with knowledge from ancient time onwards, what was the necessity of the reform of jati into samudayam? The reform leaders justified this necessity with a reason associated with another attribute of knowledge, which is *meaning*.[55] The (lack of) connection between the use of language and its meaning became a subject of historical inquiry for reformers. This was in context of the colonial depiction of language as a medium of representation, where language supposedly had a one-to-one connection through meaning with the external world that it represented. Consequently, the Nampoothiri reformers constructed a history in which the present disjuncture between the use of a language and the knowledge of that language was articulated as a problem. According to this history, once Brahmins became dominant in the society of the ancient period, they started mechanically repeating the acharams without learning and teaching their meanings. Hence, in the present world of Nampoothiris, the individual who performed acharams did not know the actual objectives and purposes behind the acharams. The loss of the meaning of acharams was the crucial point of departure from the great tradition of knowledge. N. P. Bhattathirippad explained:

> The famous Sanskrit verse says that 'word and meaning are inseparable like Parvathy and Parameswara'. But Nampoothiris who chant the Vedas without learning the meaning have separated Parvathy from Parameswara. Without Parameswara, Parvathi is just another woman. Only when words are combined with the respective meanings, knowledge is produced. Parrots can speak but can never have knowledge, because they don't know the meaning of the words they speak.[56]

The question of meaning was a major debating point in the community reform process. While differing on the method of explanation, both the orthodox and reformist positions accepted that the reformed samudayam could accept into its fold only those acharams which have some meaning that could be proved through scientific explanations. This resulted in increased attempts in interpreting the meaning of acharams based on scientific principles. Many authors interpreted the acharams related to bathing based on scientific principles of hygiene, those related to eating and cooking with the scientific explanations of the body and health, and so on.[57] As we have seen, the transformation of jatis into samudayams and the process of the reinforcement of the order of knowledge were intermingled processes. The reform literature that we analysed, however, gives us only ideal forms of expectations, objectives, and visions of future; these were not directly reflected in practice. Still, there were real effects and changes in practice which were, of course, different from the ideal forms.

The Nampoothiri daily life underwent significant changes in the process of transformation of jati into samudayam. Many community members now considered the practice of eating in a restaurant run by people belonging to the savarna caste or eating with the members of other savarna jatis in their home acceptable. The practice of untouchability also transformed in new ways as an increasing number of members enrolled in schools and joined in occupations in government or private offices. K. P. Rama Variyar in his memoirs described these changes through a description of the daily life of one Narayanan Nampoothiri, who was working as a teacher in a government school. On a normal day, Narayanan Nampoothiri, like his conservative father, would wake up early in the morning, take a bath with all the rituals, and do *puja* (ritual worship) according to the acharams. Although his father usually finished these pujas in four to five hours and Narayan Nampoothiri took only an hour, no important part of the ritual was excluded. He would eat breakfast and then go to the school, which was a half-an-hour walk away. Narayanan Nampoothiri wore a *mundu* (a white plain cloth that is wrapped around the waist, covering up to the ankle) and a shirt, like all other teachers in his school did. His hairstyle was also not different from the others.

At school, most of the teachers were from various dominant castes except one Ezhava teacher and one Muslim teacher. According to Variyar, Narayanan Nampoothiri had friendly relations with these two teachers, but never ate with them or went into their house, not because of their jati or religion but because they were meat eaters. He would come back from the school and directly go to the pond to take a bath; he would enter the house only after that. In the evening, he did all the acharams as his father did, but ate dinner a little later than his father did. In short, at home, he continued his daily rituals as the earlier generation did, whereas outside the home, he was now less a Nampoothiri and more of the general savarna.[58]

This description of Narayanan Nampoothiri's daily life in the 1940s, by Variyar, demonstrated that the major transformation that took place was in the practice of jati in public spaces; in private, the Nampoothiris maintained jati acharams as before, though in an abridged version. We should note that the divide between the public and the private might not have been as sharp as Variyar depicted it, but the concept of this division was already evident in the social life of Nampoothiris. In private, the concept of jati-based acharams still loomed over daily life, though these were interpreted in new ways based on scientific knowledge. In public, the distinction between savarna and avarna samudayams became more important than the difference between jatis. In short, the order of knowledge emerged not by completely displacing the order of acharam but by reconstituting some of the elements of acharam.

The practice of purity and pollution continued to determine the status of materials inside the *illam* (Nampoothiri household). For example, Nampoothiri women started wearing a blouse, but they removed it when they were doing the *nedikkal* (a ritual worship) because it was considered impure for such an occasion. The clothes would become polluted once they were worn while travelling outside the house. The women continued to strictly follow the pollution rituals related to menstruation and childbirth. But a majority of them stopped wearing the *khosha* (a cloth that covers from head to toe) or taking cadjan umbrellas when they travelled outside. Nampoothiri women continued to follow the rules of purity related to cooking, eating, and serving, with minor modifications.[59] Reform in the domain of acharams was more a discursive activity—of explaining the acharams on a scientific basis—than changing the performance of acharam altogether in daily life. In other words, the transformation process mainly involved giving new meaning to existing actions so that people experienced the same actions in new ways.

Gender and the Order of Knowledge

As jati became an 'inappropriate' element in the order of knowledge, the forces of gender that were entwined with jati forces began enforcing their own separate axis in new ways and forms. We have already seen that the colonial production of knowledge was inherently a gendered process based on the bio-logic of bodies. Interaction of Nampoothiri reform with this bio-logic produced a new kind of engendering process of individuals. If the space one resided in and the rituals one performed constructed man and woman differently in the order of acharam, bio-logic determined this construction in the order of knowledge. The reform discourse attributed natural, essential, and mutually exclusive characteristics to these bio-logically constructed binary bodies, that is, man and woman. In this order, it was necessary to train each individual in developing inherent natural characteristics of their genders and to suppress any other unnatural traits one may attain from outside. As gender became a central issue of reformation, *antharjanam* (the Nampoothiri woman) became a central figure in the initiatives of the YKS in the 1930s.

The process of transformation from jati to samudayam passed through the prism of gender, and each element in the emerging samudayam carried a mark of gender as a sign of identification. Some early works on gender have mapped this process as a spatial division into public and private, which corresponds to the sexual division of male and female.[60] All the actions in the public were designated to men, and the realm of women was private. Lately, scholars have pointed out the problem of a neat division between public and private spaces.[61] Taking the case of Nampoothiris as an example, we can see that the process of gender differentiation was not just a process of restriction of women into private spaces. The reform discourse assigned each object, action, and concept, both in the public and private realms, as a natural correspondent of either one of the sexes. The gendering process in the public could be best explained in the case of education.

The Nampoothiri reform discourse took education as one of the important domains of reform. Each element in the series called 'education' could be mapped onto a corresponding element in the series of 'gender'. The early debates on education, where general education was the subject, focused only on the education of Nampoothiri men. N. Damodaran Nampoothiri wrote in 1920 that 'the time has not yet arrived when one can think about Nampoothiri girls attending schools'. He argued that 'this is not because Nampoothiris as a samudayam has not progressed as did Nairs, whose girls are attending schools in large numbers'. His reasoning for this was that Nampoothiris were still 'considering only two types of education: one for the sake of knowledge and the other for new occupations'. According to Damodaran Nampoothiri, both these types of education corresponded to men.[62]

Even in the late 1920s, when women's education became one of the major agendas of the YKS, it was clear that women's education should be 'special education'. A commission was set up in 1926 by the YKS to chart out the programme of educating women. The report of this commission suggested that the Nampoothiri girls from the age of six to twelve years should be educated, but it is not proper to send them to public schools. If in a certain region, there were several illams, one had to be selected as the centre for the education, where girls from the neighbouring illams could gather. Otherwise, girls should be taught at their own illams.[63] The commission recommended that a special curriculum should be developed to focus on training girls in 'womanly duties'. The subjects mentioned in the report included music and arts, embroidery and stitching, scientific ways of child-rearing, and healthy ways of preparing food.[64]

The reformist group in the YKS argued that the commission failed to understand the aspirations of the oppressed Nampoothiri women, and it was time to bring women on par with men in all spheres of life. Criticizing the report, Narayanan Bhattathirippad pointed out that the commission was still trying to seclude women in special education centres, and this was totally against the emerging spirit of freedom in society. According to him, Nampoothiri girls should be allowed to participate in public life by joining *suitable* jobs.[65] Bhattathirippad's argument sounded like a call for total equality for men and women in all domains of life. As we continue to read Bhattathirippad's criticism, we come to know that the new space he suggested for women was an already gendered space. He mentioned that 'the scientific understanding regarding the jobs in which women can be occupied without hindering their biological nature and womanly instincts' would help to chart out a program to 'liberate the Nampoothiri women from their centuries-long sufferings'.[66] In short, Nampoothiri women should seek jobs but only those jobs which were womanly occupations.

The debate over newly emerged occupations attempted to mark each occupation on the basis of gender. Nursing and teaching corresponded to the motherly nature of women. Dancing, music, and paintings were also proper for women because 'they corresponded to the light and emotive nature of their heart'.[67] The jobs that involved authority were 'naturally' not suitable for women. Even Nampoothiri men, who were supposedly not manly enough compared to Nairs, 'need proper training to bring out the *veeram* [valour] sleeping inside every man, in order to appear as a person who can assert his authority'.[68] M. R. K. C. invoked the case of the West, where some reformed women had taken manly jobs, as an example of moral degradation and where the laws of nature have been violated. Quoting the article by Eleanor Glin in the magazine *Pear Science*, M. R. K. C. explained the possibility of dividing actions, spaces, and values on a sexual basis.[69] Similarly, Kanippayyoor attempted to mark the gender of each ritual that the Nampoothiris performed and to explain the reasons why women were not allowed to perform most rituals.

In 1929, V. T. Bhattathirippad published *Rajani Rangam* (The Stage of Night), a collection of four short stories, which for the first time in Malayalam literature shone light over the dark inner world of antharjanams into public view. M. R. Bhattathirippad pointed out that the book came in a period where 'writers were not allowed to see Nampoothiri women even in their imagination'. *Rajani Rangam* was just the beginning of the career of V. T. Bhattathirippad, who continued to write plays, novels, and articles focusing on the issues of antharjanams.

The annual conference of the YKS in 1930 witnessed dramatic scenes of radical reforms, which challenged the precedents and customs based on acharam. In this conference, Mrs Manazhy, a woman leader of the YKS, came out of the veil in public—a first in the history of Nampoothiri women. The young members staged a satirical play, *Adukkalayilninnu Arangathekku* (From the Kitchen to the Centre Stage), written by V. T. Bhattathirippad. In the beginning of the play, the female audience were seated with curtains separating them from the male audience. When the play was over, the young members in the audience removed the curtain, and the female audience, though covered by veil, shared the space with the male audience.[70] Within the next two years, several antharjanams got rid of their veil in public, and several Nampoothiri girls joined Nampoothiri Vidyalayams, while a few even joined public schools.[71] In 1932, Parvathy Nenminimangalam became the first female member of a legislative assembly from the Nampoothiri community. Her speech in the Kochi assembly helped to present before the legislators the pathetic conditions of antharjanams on the basis of first-hand experience. Her contribution was crucial in the passage of the Nampoothiri family reform bill.[72]

It is important to note that the radicalism regarding the YKS and the NYS was conditional and limited in many domains. Scholars have explained the gendering aspects of the reform movement, which transformed an earlier form of patriarchy associated with jati into a new patriarchy based on engendered individuals and the heterosexual nuclear family. J. Devika argued that it is not enough to understand the 'problems' of women under patriarchy because this presupposes that the category 'woman' was always available as a subject of inquiry. She highlighted 'the discursive conditions and practices under which it became possible to speak of such categories as "Men" and "Women"'. [73]

We saw in Chapter 3 that in the pre-reform period, the gender differentiation was performed through gendered actions. As the idea of nature with definite fixed rules was not part of this process, these gendered actions were not considered 'natural' or 'unnatural'. Through the interaction with colonial knowledge, the concept of nature became a key element in all forms of knowledge.[74] In this conceptualization, the difference between man and women was natural and biological. The 'naturalization' of gender as the binary of man and woman produced a new kind of enunciability. Now, for the reform leaders, women became an independent subject matter of inquiry. It was now possible to ask questions like 'What was the status of women in the ancient Hindu period?' 'What is the condition of women inside an illam?', and so on. Women were now supposed to have a biology and a history. In the earlier gender differentiation process, sexual identification was just the preliminary step of gender differentiation; the actions that individuals performed in daily life assigned the gender for individuals. Now, gender was somehow reduced to sex and the life of the individual could be defined based on the sex. In other words, actions were the criteria for gender identification earlier, and hence, those who performed manly or womanly actions were males and females, respectively. In the transformed samudayam, sex determined the gender of all actions. This meant that manly and womanly acts were those actions that were proper to the male sex and the female sex respectively, rather than vice versa.

In his discussion about proper female behaviour, Elavoor Krishnan Nampoothiri explained the fundamental nature of sexual difference. According to him, modern science and traditional Indian knowledge agreed that for all living beings, the difference between 'male' and 'female' were natural and fundamental. 'God gave human beings special wisdom to maintain the laws of this nature in their culture.' At a certain period in history, men stopped asking the question 'What actions were proper for a man and for a woman, which would enhance the inherent properties of each sex?' Nampoothiri men started treating women not as the other sex but as another species. According to him, 'It is the duty of the reformers to educate each sex about the actions proper to their biology.'[75]

If Krishnan Nampoothiri used the biological explanation of gender difference to emphasize the importance of women's education, Kanippayyoor used the same bio-logic in his argument against *stree samajam*s (women associations). He argued that 'women's biological properties do not allow them to be equal to men, and hence, men and women can never mutually exchange the actions they are supposed to perform'. While the actions performed by women should be equally respected, 'a samajam which demands equality of men and women are acting against the fundamental laws of nature'. According to Kanippayoor, only male members should form associations and only they must lead the women out of their oppression and miseries.[76]

The process of gender differentiation based on sex produced its own effects on other hierarchical orders in the Nampoothiri world. Like any other difference articulated in the colonial discourse, man and woman were not just different; they were also unequally positioned in different series. For example, the Nampoothiri reformers put men along with expert knowledge, which was at the top of the series of knowledge. Reform itself was considered a domain of men, where women could participate at non-decision-making levels. In short, man, was the general, the universal, or the highest element in any series of the universal, and woman was just an instance of this universal. The general history of Hindu religion was the history of acts of male saints, kings, and philosophers. The Vedas, which were considered the ultimate base of knowledge, were also a domain of men. The reformers who championed women's education and respectability did not invoke female saints and philosophers like Gargi, Mythreyi, or Lopamudra in the general history; rather, they argued that the male saints *allowed these* women scholars to acquire knowledge.[77]

Once woman became a biological category, it was possible to trace a continuum of biological women independent of jati in the form of history. This does not mean that the reform discourse placed the category of woman totally outside the domain of jati. Rather, it produced new alignments such as savarna women who could have common characteristics and a shared past. J. Devika explained that by the 1930s, in the writings of female authors, '"women" often appear as a distinct collective that is supposed to have interests and problems, sometime opinions, specific to them, beyond consideration of caste and class'.[78] Still, the common interests and opinions these authors described as 'women's issues' were almost always the issues of dominant-caste women. Though there were exceptions, the majority of women who took initiative to form women's associations and who wrote articles, stories, and poems were from savarna communities such as Nairs or Nampoothiris. Hence, it would be more correct to say that although the aspect of gender became an independent category of analysis, it was included in the hierarchical differentiation of savarna and avarna.

There are many elements that were crucial in the formation of the order of knowledge. If education was the crucial constitutive force in the emergence of the order of knowledge, sex and samudayam were the axes through which this order was deployed. Many elements of the earlier order continued their presence in this new order. In other words, the order of knowledge challenged the hierarchical jati system only to create a different form of hierarchy based on savarna–avarna difference. The order of knowledge, which emerged in the colonial period, continued its dominance in the post-colonial period in India. The dominant-caste elites who became the rulers of the nation incorporated several elements of colonial governing practices into the practices of the newly formed nation-state. Among these practices, the production of knowledge was the most important activity that was adopted from the colonialists, with the least changes in method, form, and content. This continuity was vivid in the practices of the institutions of knowledge production such as colleges and universities, which continued with minor organizational restructuring. The major difference in the post-colonial period was that the nationalists baptized the same colonial–brahmanical knowledge as 'modern knowledge'. To conclude the arguments in this chapter:

In the vast sea of ignorance,
Knowledge is our light.
We, the guardians of knowledge,
From time immemorial,
Acharam is our knowledge,
We lead with knowledge,
Without losing our lead hand,
We keep the knowledge,
And we must lead the world.[79]

In the 1950s and 1960s in Keralam, the associations that were formed as part of the reform movements of various caste communities in the early decades of the century became part of the governmental political process in the state. These associations diverted their focus from internal life in the private—which was earlier the major domain of reform activity—to the public, where a proper share in education and government jobs was the central agenda. Compared to other community organizations like the Sree Narayana Dharma Paripalana Yogam (SNDP) of Ezhavas or the Nair Service Society (NSS) of Nairs, the YKS was not very active or effective in the post-independent Keralam. This meant neither that the post-independent governments marginalized Nampoothiris nor that their domination as savarnas became less influential. Instead, with a new authenticity and power, savarna ideology became an integral part of the nationalist identity and culture. In the domain of knowledge production, especially in the discipline of history, savarna nationalist ideology dominated by assimilating the differences within the nation into its fold and by erasing other practices and ideas. The next chapter analyses, how in such a context of savarna domination in the field of production of knowledge, Asharis initiated reforms, and how in this process, they incorporated the elements of the order of knowledge into their practices of knowing.

Notes

1. For an analysis of the issues of gender and subject formation in the context of dominant-caste reform in Keralam, see J. Devika, *En-gendering Individuals: The Language of Re-forming in Early Twentieth Century Keralam* (Hyderabad: Orient Longman, 2007).
2. K. P. Nampoothiri, 'The Report of the Annual Conference', *Mangalodayam* 22, no. 11 (November 1916): 19–22.
3. Nampoothiri, 'The Report of the Annual Conference', 20.
4. For the explanations of the conservative position and for a description of the Nivarini group, see, E. T. Divakaran Moos, 'Achara Vicharam (Thoughts on Acharam)', *Malayala Manorama*, 19 June 1917.

5. Kuroor Unni Nampoothirippad, 'Nampoothiri Yuvajanangalude Katama (The Duty of Nampoothiri Youth)', *Mangalodayam* 22, no. 9 (September 1916): 30–34.

6. Nampoothirippad, 'Nampoothiri Yuvajanangalude Katama', 33.

7. Sree Rama Varma, the Raja of Kochi (1901–1917), was considered a progressive person who implemented a number of administrative and legal reforms during his rule. He supported the idea of special educational institutions for Nampoothiris, suggested by the leaders of the YKS. The financial help he offered, however, was nominal, and the rich among the Nampoothiris were not interested in education at this period. Sree Kurur Raman Nampoothiri in his presidential address in the sixth annual conference of the YKS explained the various reasons for the failure of Nampoothiri Vidyalayams. See O. V. Nampoothirippad, 'The Presidential Address', *Unni Nampoothiri* 2, no. 7 (March 1917): 3–9.

8. O. V. Nampoothirippad, 'The Presidential Address'.

9. M. R. Bhattathirippad, 'Kal Noottantinullil (In a Quarter Century)', *Mathrubhumi* (Special Issue), 1936, 33–37, 34.

10. For the details of the objective of the NYS, see K. Krishnan Nampoothiri, 'Nampoothiri Yuvajan Sanghathinte Prvarthanodyesangal (The Objectives of the Nampoothiri Youth Wing)', *Unni Nampoothiri* 10, no. 11 (November 1924): 26–31.

11. *The Nampoothiri Family Regulation Committee Report and Draft Regulation* (Thrissur: Mangalodayam, 1925), 92–94.

12. The discussion of community as an imagined group by Benedict Anderson inaugurated a wide range of debates around different forms of community formation. The discussion here follows Anderson's idea of community as a group of individuals connected only as readers of the same text. See Benedict Anderson, *The Imagined Communities* (London: Verso, 2006 [1983]). For a criticism of Anderson, see Partha Chatterjee, *The Nation and Its Fragments: Colonial and Postcolonial Histories* (Princeton: Princeton University Press, 1993).

13. Krishnan Bhattathirippad, 'Nampoothiri Samudayam (Nampoothiri Community)', *Unni Nampoothiri* 10, no. 5 (May 1925): 21–23.

14. Kuriyedathu Thathri was accused of infidelity, and the Raja of Kochi ordered a smarthavicharam in 1903. During the inquisition, Thathri began giving evidence regarding the individuals who had sexual intercourse with her. As the inquisition progressed, she revealed names of many prominent and powerful individuals in society and gave evidence about sixty-four men, which included Nampoothiris, Nairs, and other elite-caste men, and, most importantly, her own father. It was said that the Raja ordered to stop the inquiry when she was about to reveal evidence against the brother of the Raja. Thathri and all the sixty-four men were expelled from their respective jatis. The incident has become a plot for several stories, novels, and a movie. For a novel based on the

incident, see Madampu Kunjikuttan, *Bhrashtu* (The Expulsion) (Kottayam: Sahithya Pravarthaka Sahakarana Sangham, 1991).

15. Kanippayyoor Shankaran Nampoothirippad, *Ente Smaranakal* (My Memories) (Kunnamkulam: Panchangam Pusthaasala, 1964), 56.

16. The orientalists who wrote about the caste system in India assigned an occupation for Brahmins: that of priests. In Keralam, only the poor among the Nampoothiris engaged in the 'occupation' of priests. And it is clear that different kinds of caste-based occupations carried different levels of power and authority, depending on the position of those castes in the hierarchy. The hierarchical levels of the new occupations produced by colonialism were directly linked to different levels of knowledge and educational qualification.

17. M. V. Nampoothiri, 'Janmithavum Vidyabhyasavum (Landlordism and Education)', *Yogkshemam*, 23 March 1926, 3.

18. V. Rajaraja Varma, 'Nampoothirimarum Vedabhyasavum (The Nampoothiris and the Veda Learning)', *Unni Nampoothiri* 7, no. 11 (November 1922): 6–10, 7.

19. K. M. Anujan, *Ormakalilute Oru Yathra* (A Journey through Memories) (Kozhikode: Jnyanavardhini, 1953), 58.

20. T. N. Thirumulppad, 'Mathangalum Vijnyanavum (Religions and Knowledge)', *Mathrubhumi*, 23 September 1929, 4.

21. Pen name; official name unknown.

22. M. R. K. C., 'Wireless Technology', *Unni Nampoothiri* 11, no 10 (October 1924): 130–134, 134.

23. P. K. Raman Nampoothiri, 'Pazhamakkarum Shasthravum (The Old and the Science),' *Vidya Vinodini* 3, no. 2 (March 1924): 22–25, 23.

24. Pen name; official name unknown.

25. The shift from the performance of acharam to the awareness of acharam shows a shift towards the order of knowledge. This was also a move where meaning became an important measure in legitimizing or delegitimizing an action. K. N., 'Nampoothirimarute Naveena Vidybhyasa Reethi (The Method of Modern Education of Nampoothiris)', *Unni Nampoothiri* 9, no. 12 (December 1922): 194–204.

26. K. N., 'Nampoothirimarute Naveena Vidybhyasa Reethi'. It should be noted that the initial agenda of the YKS was to protect janmitham and Nampoothiri domination in society. Here, while K. N. is not completely opposed to these agendas, he observed that in order to achieve these objectives in the changing world, education should be put as the first and primary agenda of the organization.

27. P. K. Bhattathiri, 'Nampoothirimarute Pouranikavum Naveenavumaya Vidyabhyasam (The Old and New Educational System of Nampoothiris)', *Unni Nampoothiri* 9, no. 3 (March 1923): 310–314.

28. A. K. T. K. M. Valiya Narayanan Nampoothirippad, 'The Presidential Address', *Unni Nampoothiri* 11, no. 12 (December 1925): 445–454.

29. Varma, 'Nampoothirimarum Vedabhyasavum'.
30. During the second half of the nineteenth century, there were several uprisings of Muslim tenants in Malabar against janmis and the ruling British government. Colonial reports described these rebellions as riots by illiterate Muslim fanatics. The 1921 rebellion was the most widespread armed struggle in this series, which was brutally suppressed by the British army. As Nampoothiris constituted the majority of the janmis in the localities where the struggle was intense, they were the main target of the attack by the rebels. Both contemporary writings and later academic writings have discussed whether the rebellion was a janmi–tenant issue or a religiously inspired struggle. But only in the later works were these rebellions described as a Hindu–Muslim communal riot. For a contemporary report on the Malabar rebellion in 1921 which describes it as a Muslim–Nampoothiri issue, see K. Madhavan Nair, 'Malabar Lahalakku Shesham (After the Malabar Riots)', *Mathrubhumi*, 25 October 1922. For a Marxist analysis of the rebellion, see K. N. Panikkar, *Against Lord and State: Religion and Peasant Uprising in Malabar 1836–1921* (Delhi: Oxford University Press, 1989).
31. P. N. Bhattathirippad, *Ormakurippukal* (Memoirs) (Kozhikode: P. K. Trust, 1923), 34.
32. P. Narayana Menon, 'Khilafathum Congressum (The Khilafat and the Congress)', *Mathrubhumi*, 21 June 1922, 5.
33. Mozhikunnathu Brahmadathan Nampoothirippad, *Khilafat Smaranakal* (Memories of Khilafat) (Kozhikode: Mathrubhumi Books, 2006), 27.
34. Padmanabha Menon, *The Travancore Manual* (Thiruvananthapuram: Government Press, 1864).
35. For a genealogy of the word 'Hindu', see Arvind Sharma, 'On Hindu, Hindustan, Hinduism and Hindutva', *Numan* 49, no. 1 (2002): 1–36.
36. K. V. Moosathu, 'Hindukkalute Pracheena Vijnyanam (The Ancient Knowledge of the Hindus)', *Arunodayam* 32, no. 5 (May 1931): 17–22.
37. V. R. Nampoothiri, *Hindu Mathathinte Charithram* (The History of the Hindu Religion) (Thrissur: Vidyodayam Publications, 1937).
38. K. Raman Ilayathu, 'Hindu Mathathinte Naveekaranavum Nampoothirimarum (The Reformation of the Hindu Religion and the Nampoothiris)', *Kerala Pathrika*, no. 5 (May 1931): 34–39.
39. Kaplingad Narayanan Nampoothiri, 'Adhyksha Prasangam (The Presidential Address)', *Bhasha Poshini* 20, no. 11 (November 1930): 27–33.
40. For missionary views on Christianity and Hinduism from the Malayalam-speaking region in the late nineteenth and the early twentieth centuries, see Samuel Mateer, *The Land of Charity: A Descriptive Account of Travancore and Its People* (New Delhi: Asian Educational Services, 1991 [1870]); and C. M. Agur, *Church History of Travancore* (New Delhi: Asian Educational Services, 1990 [1903]). For a scholarly analysis of the missionary narratives of Christianity and Hinduism, see Dick Kooiman, *Conversion and Social Equality in India: The London Missionary Society in South Travancore in the Nineteenth Century* (New Delhi: Manohar, 1989).

41. K. V. Raghavan Nair, 'Mathathinte Shasthreeyathvam (The Scientificity of Religion)', *Unni Nampoothiri* 10, no. 11 (November 1922): 69–79.

42. See Parasurama Iyer, 'Hindu Vishwasangalum Shasthravum (The Hindu Beliefs and Science)', *Mangalodayam* 6, no. 5 (May 1926): 81–90; N. K. Pisharody, 'Hindukkalaya Nammute Innathe Katama (The Responsibility of We Hindus Today)', *Vidya Vinodini* 9, no. 3 (October 1927): 41–47; M. R. K. K. C., 'Hindu Mathavum Veda Jnyanavum (The Hindu Religion and the Vedic Knowledge)', *Unni Nampoothiri* 14, no. 5 (May 1927): 211–218.

43. For example, T. H. P. Chentharasseri's various writings on reform leaders such as Ayyankali and Sree Kumara Guru Devan use the category 'samudayam' to refer to both the pre-reform jati and the reforming community. T. H. P. Chentharaseeri, *Ayyankali Nadathiya Swathanthrya Samarangal* (The Struggles for Independence Led by Ayyankali) (Kozhikode: Mathrubhumi, 1991); and T. H. P. Chentharaseeri, *Poykayil Sree Kumara Guru Devan* (Thiruvananthapuram: Navaodayam Publishers, 1981). Even the scholars who studied 'community formation' did not sufficiently demarcate between jati and samudayam in their analysis of the transformation of community identity. See G. A. Oddie, *Social Protest in India: British Protestant Missionaries and Social Reforms* (Delhi: Manohar, 1979); K. Saradamony, *Emergence of a Slave Caste Pulayas of Kerala* (Delhi: People's Publishing House, 1980); and Genevieve Lemercinier, *Religion and Ideology in Kerala* (New Delhi: D. K. Agencies, 1984).

44. See, for example, K. V. Sharma, *Varna Vyvasthayum Shasthravum* (The Varna System and Science) (Cochin: Pingala Printers, 1929); and O. M. Vasudevan Nampoothirippad, 'Chathurvarnyam: Chila Charithra Vasthuthakal (The Four-Varna System: Some Historical Facts)', *Unni Nampoothiri* 17, no. 11 (November 1933): 26–34.

45. M. Raman Nampoothirippad, *Jatikalude Utbhavavam Charithravum* (The Origin and the History of Castes), (Thalasseri: Kalpadrumam Publications, 1938); K. N. Nampeeshan, 'Aharareethiyum Jathiyum (The Eating Habits and Jati)', *Arunodayam* 12, no. 2 (May 1930): 28–34; P. N. Nair, 'Varnabhedavum Jathikalum (The Difference of Varna and Jatis)', *Mathrubhumi*, 21 June 1932.

46. M. N. Srinivas, *Social Change in Modern India* (Hyderabad: Orient Longman, 1996); Dipankar Gupta, *Social Stratification* (Delhi: Oxford University Press, 1992); Susan Bayly, *Caste, Society and Politics in India, from the Eighteenth Century to the Modern Age* (Cambridge: Cambridge University Press, 2001).

47. V. K. Raja, 'Acharangalum Shasthravum (The Acharams and Science)', *Mangalodayam* 11, no. 6 (June 1927): 35–41, 36.

48. Raja, 'Acharangalum Shasthravum', 39.

49. Sree Narayana Guru considered hygiene and education as the two major objectives of reform, and he articulated them as connected issues. He used contemporary Christian missionary notions of hygiene and knowledge as the two necessary conditions in each individual's journey to God. See Sree Narayana Guru and Muni Narayana Prasad, *Sree Narayana Guruvinte Sampoorna*

Krithikal (The Collected Works of Sree Narayana Guru) (Kottayam: DC Books, 2005).

50. M. N. Nampoothiri, 'Keralavum Nampoothirimarum (Keralam and the Nampoothiris)', *Arunodayam* 10, no. 6 (June 1928): 75–77, 76.

51. Ramanatha Iyer, *Keralathinte Adicharithram* (The Ancient History of Kerala) (Thrissur: Mangalodayam Publications, 1935).

52. For a detailed description of Shankaracharyar's life, see Ullor S. Parameshwara Ayyar, *Adi Shankaran* (Kottayam: National Book Trust, 1981).

53. It is interesting to note that almost all the colonial and elite-caste historians, including the Marxists, had included Parasurama myth as an introductory story when they wrote about the ancient history of Keralam. We can see this story in the colonial writings of Francis Buchanan and William Logan, in the twentieth-century histories written by Malayali historians such as Elamkulam Kunjan Pillai, E. M. S. Namboodiripad, and A. Sridhara Menon, and in the academic histories written in the late twentieth century such as by Robin Jeffrey and Maria Parpola. In short, we can conclude that it was history writing that converted a Nampoothiri myth into an origin story of Kerala history. See Francis Buchanan, *A Journey from Madras through the Countries of Mysore, Canara and Malabar* (London: Cadell & Davies, 1807); William Logan, *Malabar Manual* (Madras: Government Press, 1887); Elamkulam Kunjan Pillai, *Kerala Charithram* (The History of Kerala) (Kottayam: National Book Stall, 1961); E. M. S. Namboodiripad, *Keralam Malayalikalute Mathrubhumi* (Keralam: The Motherland of Malayalis) (Thiruvananthapuram: Chintha Publishers, 1984 [1946]); and A. Sridhara Menon, *A Survey of Kerala History* (Kottayam: Sahithya Pravarthaka Sahakarana Sangham, 1967).

54. K. N., 'Nampoothirimarute Naveena Vidybhyasa Reethi', 201.

55. The debate around the relation between word and meaning has dominated the whole discipline of linguistics. Our interest here is only to understand the way the idea of meaning was debated in non-scholarly circles and how it became important in the Nampoothiri reform discourse.

56. N. P. Bhattathirippad, *Matangi Varatha Kalam* (The Time Which Will Never Return) (Thrissur: Bharathi Printers, 1940).

57. See Raja, 'Acharangalum Shasthravum'; Nampeeshan, 'Aharareethiyum Jathiyum'.

58. K. P. Rama Variyar, *Pinnitta Vazhikaliloote* (Through the Treaded Paths) (Kottakkal: Keraleeyam Press, 1963), 73–88.

59. N. Madhavi Amma, 'Navothanathinu Shesham (After the Enlightenment)', *Mathrubhumi*, 20 October 1949, 4.

60. See Jean Bethke Elshtain, *Public Man, Private Woman: Woman in Social and Political Thought* (Princeton: Princeton University Press, 1981); Carol Pateman, *The Sexual Contract* (Cambridge, UK: Polity Press, 1988); and C. Katz and J. Monk, *Full Circles: Geographies of Women over the Life Course* (London and New York: Routledge, 1991).

61. See Susan B. Boyd, *Challenging the Public/Private Divide: Feminism, Law, and Public Policy* (Toronto: University of Toronto Press, 1997); Leela Fernandes, 'Beyond Public Spaces and Private Spheres: Gender, Family and Working-Class Politics in India', *Feminist Theory* 23, no. 3 (Autumn 1997): 525–547; Asma Afsaruddin (ed.), *Hermeneutics and Honor: Negotiating Female 'Public' Space in Islamic/ate Societies* (Cambridge, MA: Harvard University Press, 1999).

62. N. Damodaran Nampoothiri, 'Vidyabhyasam: Ventathum Ventathathum (The Education: Desirable and Undesirable)', *Mangalodayam* 24, no. 6 (June 1920): 88–93.

63. Narayanan Bhattathirippad, 'Sthree Vidyabhyasa Commissionte Report (The Report of the Women Education Commission)', *Unni Nampoothiri* 12, no. 4 (April 1928): 407–410.

64. N. Bhattathirippad, 'Stree Vidyabhyasa Commissionte Report'.

65. N. Bhattathirippad, 'Stree Vidyabhyasa Commissionte Report'.

66. N. Bhattathirippad, 'Stree Vidyabhyasa Commissionte Report', 409.

67. Kanippayyoor Shankaran Nampoothirippad, 'Sthree Samajam (Women's Association)', *Unni Nampoothiri* 10, no. 2 (January 1926): 279–289.

68. K. S. Nampoothirippad, 'Sthree Samajam', 285.

69. M. R. K. C., 'Prakrithi Virodham (Against the Nature)', *Unni Nampoothiri* 12, no. 2 (February 1927): 124–128.

70. M. R. Bhattathirippad, 'Kal Noottantinullil (In a Quarter Century)', *Mathrubhumi* (Special Issue), 1936, 33–37, 35.

71. Bhattathirippad, 'Kal Noottantinullil', 35.

72. For the full text of Parvathi Nenminimangalam's speech in the Kochi Assembly, see Parvathi Nenminimangalam, 'Nampoothiri Billum Parvathi Nenminimangalavum (The Nampoothiri Bill and Parvathi Nenminimangalam)', *Manorama*, 10 March 1932, 4.

73. Devika, *En-gendering Individuals*, 18.

74. For an analysis of the ways in which nature is conceptualized within modernity, see Bruno Latour, *We Have Never Been Modern* (Cambridge, MA: Harvard University Press, 1993).

75. Elavoor Krishnan Nampoothiri, 'Antharjanangalum Parishkaravum (The Antharjanams and Fashion)', *Unni Nampoothiri* 11, no. 7 (July 1927): 89–96.

76. K. S. Nampoothirippad, 'Sthree Samajam'.

77. See M. C. N. Nampoothiri, 'Rishimarum Vijnyanavum (The Sages and Knowledge)', *Yogkshemam*, no. 5, 13 May 1932, 2.

78. Devika, *En-gendering Individuals*, 175.

79. Translated by Bindu Menon.

5

Asharis and the Order of Knowledge

By the last quarter of the twentieth century, Asharis started interacting with the order of knowledge, and this interaction transformed Ashari practices. In Chapter 2, we saw that throughout the first half of the twentieth century, Asharis avoided entering the order of knowledge by maintaining *asharippani* as a practice of knowing. In the context of India's formal independence from colonial domination in 1947 and the subsequent nationalist takeover of the institutions of production of knowledge, Asharis faced new forms of intervention in their world of knowing. Analysing the changing relation between *jati* and asharippani in the second half of the twentieth century, this chapter demonstrates that Asharis in this period entered an overlapping world of production of knowledge and practices of knowing. If in the period between 1950 and 1970, the processes of transformation in the Ashari world were slow and indistinct, in the last two decades of the century, by contrast, they gained momentum and attained concrete forms. This chapter analyses the new social forces that produced the transformations in the Ashari world in the second half of the twentieth century and the important elements of the transformed Ashari world.

Soon after the formal declaration of the independent Indian Republic in 1950, the Government of India began reorganizing regional states based on language. Keralam was formed on 1 November 1956, by merging the supposedly Malayalam-speaking regions of Malabar, Kochi, and Thiruvithamkoor.[1] From this very moment, caste organizations had a central role in the democratic politics of the state. Even in the early twentieth century, caste-reform organizations had declared sharing and redistribution of resources among different caste communities as one of their main demands.[2] Still, the reform leaders in that period equally focused on the internal reform of daily life practices and on the introduction of new forms of marriage and family. After independence, these organizations became involved in electoral political processes and became the mediators between the caste community and the government. J. Devika, in her analysis of the role that caste played in the development of the Kerala Model, argues that the *savarna* caste domination in this model was assured by the left through a political strategy of 'secularized caste'.[3] The dominant castes protected their interest by actively controlling state policies and simultaneously making themselves invisible through governmental categories such as 'general category' in the context of reservation.[4] *Avarna* communities have also been actively taking part in politics, but largely by secularizing their agenda in such a way that their demands were restricted in the domain of the material, such as larger representation in modern forms of education and in government jobs.

In this period, every village had at least one lower primary school and the state government took initiatives to expand the network of educational institutions. Various caste organisations, especially the Nair Service Society (NSS) and the Sree Narayana Dharma Paripalana Yogam (SNDP), opened schools as part of their attempt to strengthen their respective communities' influence in the public domain.[5] The government and community organizations depicted illiteracy as a disease that had to be eradicated from society.

The physical presence of schools and the dominant discourse around the importance of education compelled parents to enrol their children in schools, even in the rural areas. Asharis were unable to completely resist this new social pressure. Many parents from the community enrolled their children in primary schools; however, as demonstrated through interviews in Chapter 2, they withdrew their children before they reached the tenth standard, which was the qualification for several lower-level government positions.[6] There were many reasons for Asharis still not actively associating with the education process initiated by the various governments in the post-colonial period. Shreedharan, who was one of the first few students who completed eighth standard at school from the Ashari community, reasoned that 'in the 1960s and 70s, Asharis, though considered as a lower caste, could still hold considerable respect in villages and had minimum job security'.[7] Hence, they did not seek any kind of major changes in their occupation or caste practices. According to Ramachandran Achari, in the period between 1960 and 1980, less than 1 per cent of the Asharis in Malabar completed high-school education and below 10 per cent completed primary-school education. He explained this as the 'continuing influence of traditional values and the socio-economic systems in the villages which help sustain the traditional values'.[8]

The contemporary technology of house construction was also a major reason for Asharis' reluctance to participate in the modern institutions of production of knowledge. Until the 1980s, most of the houses built had tiled roofs, which required elaborate wooden roof frames. The Ashari's role was critical in the construction of such houses. More importantly, the *moothashari* (chief carpenter) not only designed the whole house but also conducted the rituals of the construction. Ramachandran Achari noted that 'if we compare the 1920s and 1960s for the methods of house constructing and the role assigned to Asharis as the designers of the houses, we would not see any significant difference in these periods'.[9] In 1972, V. N. Menon observed that in most of the places in the Kozhikode district, it was very difficult 'to get hold of Asharis for minor works because they had sufficient major contracts within their villages'.[10] In short, until the 1980s, asharippani was a localized practice, and Asharis enjoyed certain respect within their *desham* as the authorities of architectural practices.

Economical and Technical Forces of Change

The oil boom in the early years of the 1970s intensified the industrialization process in West Asian countries, which created a large-scale demand for skilled and unskilled labourers. Indian labourers started migrating to the Arabian Gulf in the late 1970s, and by the end of the century, about three million Indian workers were labouring in various countries in this region. Nearly half of the Indian migrants were from Keralam (around one-and-a-half million), and, according to one approximation, they brought 550 million rupees per annum to Keralam.[11] Migration and remittance transformed the socio-economic scenario of Keralam; these changes consequently produced reverberations in the Ashari world as well. Migrants spent a large percentage of their income from the Gulf for housing, and by the late 1980s, building construction became one of the important domains of economic activity in Keralam.[12] For the Gulf migrants, the size and design of the new houses they constructed in their home village were directly a demonstration of their newly acquired social and economic status. They wanted to design their houses in 'modern' ways, the demand for which transformed the basic methods of house construction in Keralam. This transformation brought a corresponding change in the role of Asharis in construction work.

Most of the new houses built after the 1980s in Keralam used the technology of reinforced concrete (RC) for building the roof, instead of the old method of wooden frame and tiles. Concrete, which is a mixture of cement, sand, and crushed stone, was introduced in India during the British period. Until the 1970s, the use of RC—which is concrete strengthened with steel bars—was generally limited to public and commercial buildings.[13] By the middle of the twentieth century, the use of cement in construction works had transformed the method of building walls and floors. These changes, however, did not produce much impact in the methods of asharippani. On the other hand, the introduction of RC roofs affected Ashari practices in many ways. The change was not limited to the method of constructing the roof. The RC-roofed houses required different kinds of wall structures and basements from those of the tile-roofed houses. The RC technology also opened the possibility of radically changing the shape and measurement of the rooms and proportions of spaces for kitchens, bathrooms, and toilets. In Keralam in 1971, only 10 per cent of the houses had a modern kind of roofing; it had increased to 60 per cent in 1991.[14] As the majority of new houses constructed used new designs, formally qualified civil engineers took over the role of planners and designers from Asharis.

The new (amended) Municipal and Local Bodies Act of 1970 required that a plan approved by a civil engineer be submitted to get permission for the construction of each building.[15] However, this rule did not completely take over the authority of Asharis as the designers of houses. Until the 1990s, the moothashari designed and executed the construction; but, on paper, the owner had to get the plan, drawings, and estimates worked out and approved by a civil engineer for submission to the local authorities. In other words, in the 1970s and 1980s, the engineer's and Ashari's role in designing overlapped, and Asharis still controlled the actual execution of the construction. It is only in the 1990s that engineers established their overall control of the processes of planning and the construction of houses.

The aforementioned changes not only reduced the authority of Asharis over the practices of knowing in the field of house construction but also changed the very idea of knowledge within the community. Within the schema of the new order of knowledge, the expert was the one who produced objectified models and representations. Those who actually executed the work were practitioners whose capability was not knowledge but skills and techniques. The new RC technology removed the Asharis as a caste from their role as designers into that of workers, or from the role of experts to that of practitioners. The engineers trained in the new technology became the authority of architectural knowledge.

Asharis in the Order of Knowedge

The moothashari now, without any significant authority over the practices in his field, became a shadow of his earlier figure. However, he still maintained his authority in the field of ritual practices related to the construction of houses. In this new avatar, he was an expert in *thachu shasthram* (the traditional science of architecture), or, in other words, an authority of *traditional knowledge*, a category which was modern and colonial. Asharis, until then, never considered asharippani as *shasthram* (science), the category which was generally reserved for discursive knowledge. In asharippani, knowing was doing, and hence shasthras were not a reference point in this conceptualization. In the colonial period, many Sanskrit texts were rediscovered as traditional knowledge, and thachu shasthram was based on such texts. Scholars have noted that the practice of inventing traditions was important for the self-definitions of modernity in general and that of the nation-state in particular. Eric Hobsbawm observed that the invention of tradition was a response to 'novel situations which take the form of reference to old situations, or which establish their own past by quasi-obligatory repetition'. It is a result of 'the contrast between the constant change and innovation of the modern world and the attempt to structure at least some parts of social life within it as unchanging and invariant'.[16]

In the case of Asharis, until the 1980s, as seen so far, they were experts in the contemporary practices of house construction, and by the 1990s, they became the authorities of 'traditional knowledge'. In this new role, the moothashari had to prove both his knowledge in Sanskrit texts on thachu shasthram and his ability to understand and negotiate with the forces of the non-human world. In the role of a ritual practitioner, the moothashari still finalized the exact location of the house and the water-well in a plot, the direction of the front door, the area of the front yard, and so on, all according to thachu shasthram. Numerous publishers initiated the publication of old Sanskrit texts with introductions and interpretations by famous moothasaris.[17] In these introductions, they interpreted these texts as the base of asharippani, though we have seen that in the earlier period Asharis never used these texts as a reference for their actual practice. Knowledge in these Sanskrit verses became *the knowledge* of asharippani, and the capacity to execute practical work was measured in terms of skill and experience.

The invasion of new technology and its associated concepts into the field of construction reduced the status of Asharis in two ways. Further, one of the basic concepts in the order of knowledge was the notion of a divide between theory and practice.[18] Thus, this concept divided carpentry into a knowledge part and a practical part. The former included the capacity to create, learn, or reproduce textual or other forms of knowledge by treating it as an object. The latter involved bodily work, which required experience and skill. However, both these parts had a lower status compared to the technical knowledge of engineers. The dominant discourse depicted the knowledge part of carpentry as traditional knowledge, which had a lower position in the hierarchical series of knowledge compared to modern engineering knowledge. The second part, the practical work, had a lower status than *any* form of knowledge, including traditional knowledge. Therefore, although this gave the moothashari in his new role a higher status than an expert carpenter, even his status was never equal to that of the engineers.

It is important to note that the role of the moothashari as a ritual practitioner was not just a continuation of his earlier role in ritual activities. This 'traditional role' was very much a modern construct and only within that conceptual framework did this new role have any relevance. Earlier, it was not possible to separate the elements of work and rituals in asharippani, or, in other words, rituals were an integral part of asharippani as a practice of knowing. Now, the rituals became a negotiation with non-human forces, which may affect the residents of the houses if the houses were not properly built. Moreover, the rituals became a separate activity and were not part of the actual construction of the house. The moothasari's present role was to give advice and suggestions to satisfy the non-human forces related to construction work according to *vasthu shasthram*, which is now considered as 'knowledge of architecture' and which guides 'people to create spaces which harmonize with nature and with the universal forces'.[19]

While the moothashari became more or less a ritual figure, the status of other Asharis also changed in these circumstances. Before the phenomenon of Gulf migration, Asharis worked at the construction site as daily wage labourers. A large number of Ashari men migrated to the Gulf countries in the 1970s and 1980s, and then many returned by the 1990s.[20] The Gulf migration created a scarcity in the workforce in two ways. First, there was a reduction in the actual numbers of available working men. Second, although by the 1990s many of these Asharis working in the Gulf returned, they did not join the workforce of wage labourers.[21] Though there is no caste-based census on Gulf migration, various sample studies showed that most of the artisanal workers like Asharis and smiths who returned from the Gulf countries preferred to start their own small workshop units instead of working as daily wage labourers.[22] Working at construction sites always proceeded through trial-and-error methods, and each project was tailor-made according to the requirements of the customer. In the 1990s, as Asharis started working from shops which manufactured standardized products such as doors and windows, asharippani transformed into a different form of practice. In most of these shops, Asharis used new kinds of tools and machinery, and this in turn demanded different kinds of skill sets and capabilities, which they picked up.

Between the Practice of Knowing and the Production of Knowledge

The changing status of tools was an important factor in the changes of the Ashari practice of knowing. Scholars have noted that one of the important reasons for the loss of independence of artisans in the wake of industrialist production was the loss of control over the means of production.[23] In the case of Asharis, even though they were in control of their means of production, they were not able to maintain their authority over the knowledge practices related to construction work. Within the earlier form of asharippani, tools carried clear jati markers and were agents that could exert their own forces in asharippani. As discussed in Chapter 1, tools were not instrumental objects which could act only as directed by human beings. Tools, like human beings, had caste identity and agency.

In the workshops, the tools, especially the new ones like the lathe, were not specifically designed for carpentry. Unlike the old tools, the contents of which were enriched with stories and proverbs related to the Ashari jati, the new tools were commodities purchased from toolmakers. They were not caste-specific, and hence, the use of these tools moved carpentry practices beyond the jati boundaries. This was true for the measuring instruments as well. The intrusion of new technical knowledge in the construction field brought along with it new methods of measuring and calculation. The standardized measures like metre and degree partially replaced the subjective measures like finger, measure of eye, feet, and so on. Although colonialists had introduced these measures in the region as early as the second half of the nineteenth century, until the 1980s, Asharis did not incorporate these units into their practice.[24] In the new situation, where they had to work alongside engineers who were equipped with the colonial forms of knowledge and who had more authority in the field, Asharis began translating their calculations into these objectified measures. Measuring tapes in metres or feet replaced the *muzhakkol* (wooden scale with measures in fingers) and the *chartau* (measuring string), both of which had multiple symbolic dimensions in the Ashari practices.[25] As in the case of tools, the measuring instruments also lost their caste identity and pushed the Ashari practices beyond the jati order.

Similar to tools and measuring instruments, the work on wood, on which Asharis had the monopoly, was no longer a jati activity. By the 1980s, sawmills started taking over many activities on wood and Asharis depended on these mills for the initial processing of the wood. The sawmills took over the preliminary processes of cutting and planning the wood according to the requirements of Asharis. In this case, on the one hand, Asharis had to understand the techniques of operation in the sawmills so that they could give correct directions to the mill operator. On the other hand, as Asharis were neither experts nor practitioners of these techniques at the mill, they were not able to adapt this activity into the caste practices. The dependability of the mill owner and the personal relationship that Asharis had with him were crucial factors in getting quality wood pieces. If earlier the network of Ashari practices mainly included the objects and the individuals and their mutual relations within the jati community, in the present the network moved beyond the jati community by including many other objects, individuals, and relations. Asharippani, which was a process negotiated within the community, transformed into a network of activity that crossed the boundary of jati, and in this process, the community lost its exclusive monopoly in the practice of carpentry.

Another important factor that has changed within the Ashari practice was the spatial dimension of asharippani. Desham, which was the boundary condition of asharippani, lost its importance as the network of carpentry practices extended beyond desham. In the new form, space was no more a dimension of asharippani. We saw earlier that the particular weather, flora and fauna, or geography of a location were important factors in the Ashari ways of knowing. The location of the plot of land, the geological properties of the specific location, and the weather of a particular location were intrinsic elements in the Ashari practices. In the actual construction sites where carpentry works were executed earlier, weather was an important factor and the asharippani was seasonal work. However, in the case of RC-roofed houses, Asharis mainly produced windows, doors, and furniture, which they manufactured independent of the aforementioned factors of space. Moreover, as Asharis started working inside the shops, seasons did not have a significant effect on their work. The increased transportation facilities further reduced dependency on the locally available varieties of trees for wood. The increased mobility of carpenters gave them access to localities outside their desham.

Once Asharis shifted their location of work from the construction site to workshops, general carpentry work and artistic production became two separate activities. Earlier, it was not possible, and there was no need, to separate art and work in asharippani. In contrast, in the late-twentieth-century transformations of asharippani, artwork and general work became separate elements in asharippani. For the new-model houses, the carpentry work was limited to products like windows, doors, and furniture, which were generally made in a standardized format. Still, there was a demand for 'art-worked' windows, doors, or furniture as special features of a house. The customers in this case, however, considered artwork as a separate activity depending upon the creativity of the individual carpenter, and not based on the 'traditional' inheritance of the community. Asharis used new patterns and designs for these artworks, which were very different from the traditional patterns used in the earlier constructions. Like any other art, the individual Ashari became the author of his artwork, whereas earlier, the community was assigned the authorship.

The movement of asharippani outside the jati practices, however, does not indicate secularization or rationalization of Ashari work like some scholars had argued about the changes in the artisanal practices in the context of industrial development in the West.[26] Lately, historians have challenged the notion that the mechanization of production has totally disenchanted the world of work or has somehow secularized it. For example, analysing the case of Malaysian female factory workers, Aihwa Ong argued that the so-called scientific management principles deployed by the corporate factory owners incorporated the cultural aspects—including religion—as important factors in increasing the efficiency of the employees.[27] Susan George argued that technology was always a spiritual endeavour and that religion and technology in the capitalist world are mutually constitutive.[28] Following this scholarship, we can observe that the new relation between Asharis and the tools did not make Ashari practice either a secular or a rational practice.

To begin with, the new tools were soon incorporated into the symbolic dimensions not governed by jati rules but by a new spiritual dimension of religion. For example, in most of the workshops, the Hindu workers, irrespective of their jati, put sandalwood paste brought from the temples on the lathe before they started working. Some of the workers placed gods' and goddess' images on calendars, paintings, or prints. Unlike in the earlier caste-based production systems, the practices of spiritualizing the tools were not jati-specific but, rather, according to religious beliefs. Similarly, the new tools had not rationalized the methods of production as some scholars have argued.[29] Even in the new ways of production, it was difficult to separate logical and rational actions from intuitive and automatic bodily actions. For example, working on a lathe required certain kinds of hand skills, which were attained through experience. Similar to the earlier methods used in carpentry, hands have to 'think on their own' when one works on a lathe. The Ashari practice, despite incorporating the colonial–brahmanical notion of religion into their practice, did not follow the logic of the division of practices into secular and spiritual domains.

Until the 1980s, an Ashari's work began by selecting the appropriate tree for each purpose. For determining the quality of the wood, Asharis applied different senses, including taste, touch, and smell. In the new format, Asharis purchased wood pieces that were already cut and roughly shaped at mechanized sawmills. Here, Asharis could recognize the quality of the wood only during their work. The use of senses like taste and smell started disappearing from Ashari practices. The new generation of Asharis in the 1990s, who got their training in these workshops, mainly exerted the visual sense and, to a certain degree, the sense of touch. The visual sense was important not just because the appearance of the product now had a greater value in the market but also because the quality of wood purchased from sawmills had to be determined by the process of observation. Earlier, Asharis used the taste and smell of the tree leaves or trunk in order to determine the hardness or softness of the wood. Now, they had to completely depend on their visual sense to decide the quality of the wood they purchased. As a result, certain kinds of knowing methods disappeared from the Ashari practices.

Anthropologists who studied the sensual processes in non-Western cultures have argued that, in these cultures, proximate senses were very much part of the production of knowledge. A number of ethnographies have described how people used smell, taste, and touch for sensing and ordering the world around them.[30] However, Judith Okely noted that without the dining experiences she had in certain villages in France, she could not have understood the relevance of certain memories of old people from the village.[31] Okely added that the tasting experience was critical not only for the knowledge of the people she studied but also for her own anthropological inquiry of their knowledge. Okely's attempt was to critique the scholars who limited embodied knowledge to non-Western societies and written knowledge to the Western scholarship. While the anthropological scholarship mentioned here questioned the importance given to the visual and aural senses in Western scholarship, they did not challenge the Western notions of senses and sensory experience. Our objective here is not simply to understand the changes or comparative differences in the ways in which different cultures privileged different senses at different times. More important is the change that colonial knowledge introduced in the conceptualization of the process of sensing itself. Within the colonial concepts of knowledge, sensing was a subjective practice and not an element of objective knowledge. The sensing processes could, at most, be a part of the production process of knowledge, but not an element in the finished product. This did not mean that in the actual practice of science, subjective elements were not important. Historians and sociologists of science have observed that it is in the discourse on science—both by scientists themselves and by commentators of science—that objectivity became an intrinsic factor of scientific knowledge; in the actual production of knowledge, subjective elements still had a critical role.[32] These scholars identified the contradictions of discourse and practice as a central feature of modern institutions of production of knowledge.

The contradiction of discourse and practice was visible in the Ashari practices too, as they incorporated the elements of production of knowledge into asharippani. As mentioned earlier, the introduction of new production practices in asharippani in the 1990s changed the sensing practices of Asharis; the proximate senses of smelling and tasting were no longer part of asharippani. This does not mean that, in this transformation, Ashari practices became an objectified rational process. In all practical situations, asharippani remained an embodied practice because the processes of sensing and knowing were still inseparable. At the same time, in describing asharippani, Asharis began using the dichotomous categories of theory and practice, body and mind, or thinking and doing, all adopted from the colonial concept of knowledge.

Ravindran, a middle-aged Ashari who runs his own shop, equated the new situation with that of 'talking in multiple languages'.[33] He uses the new measuring instruments for work but uses the earlier proportions, measures, and calculations in practice. Ravindran explained:

> When I discuss the work with the engineer, I use the new terms and measures. When I supervise my young nephew, I use both the old and new terms. When I am working, my mind thinks in the same terms of calculations as my father taught me years before.[34]

Ravindran's example shows how Asharis utilized different registers of 'traditional' and 'modern' vocabulary in the context of asharippani at workshops. Asharis utilized scientific knowledge but by translating it into their language and method. For example, it was the engineers, using the new botanical knowledge, who selected specific wood for particular frames, but this knowledge did not directly control the understanding of Asharis regarding the way in which a wood piece might behave during the process of sawing. This does not mean that Asharis completely ignored the information supplied by the engineer regarding the quality of the wood. They assimilated both experiences into his practice and created new ways of knowing the qualities of wood.

Rajan, another Ashari in his forties, showed me several engineering design manuals and vernacular books on thachu shasthram, which he kept in the shop. He explained that he kept these books as a strategy to satisfy customers. According to him, the customers measured his capacity not just based on the quality of his product, but also by his displayed understanding of both modern scientific and traditional knowledge. Only by establishing a certain authority over both modern and traditional knowledge could he gain the respect of the customers. He mentioned that 'they [the customers] want to check what I *know* as well as what I *do*. Nowadays, in many instances, the former is more important than the latter'.[35] Asharis, in order to satisfy the customer of the present day, had to incorporate the ideas of knowledge as a written object and of written texts as the base of practical work. At the same time, the distinctive domains of discursive and non-discursive practices historically created by the colonial order of knowledge overlapped in asharippani. On the one hand, Rajan believed that in actual situations, asharippani was a practice beyond the definitions of knowledge as a written object. On the other hand, he accepted the dominant view that knowledge has a higher status than practical work. Thus, in his understanding of asharippani, Rajan incorporated these two contradictory views—one supporting the separation of discursive and non-discursive domains, and the other, the inseparability of these domains.

The 1980s and 1990s were socially and economically a challenging time for Asharis. As we observed, the new technology removed Asharis from their central role as the chief architects of house construction. The middle-aged and older Ashari men, who were not ready to adapt to the new technologies in the field, became partially or totally unemployed. Only a few—like Ravindran and Rajan—were successful in running carpentry workshops within their own village. Although the moothasaris still enjoyed some respect as ritual practitioners, this status did not provide them with enough economic gains to prosper or even survive.

One immediate response to the economic crisis was migration to towns and cities both within India and outside, which was mainly to the Gulf countries. In the 1980s, several Asharis moved into workshops and furniture production units in or near towns and cities. It was, however, not easy even for the younger generation to adapt to the new working conditions in these units and generally to the life in the cities. These units mostly paid Asharis based on piece rate, which was barely sufficient to survive in the cities.[36] Like in any other piece-rate system, in these units, the speed at which one could finish the work was the most important factor of economic success, which was completely antithetical to the earlier notion of asharippani. Further, in this system, as Ashari work was disconnected from the earlier jati network, Asharis found themselves disconnected from familiar spatial and temporal locations. In the manufacturing units and workshops, the social status of Asharis was similar to that of other workers like plumbers, electricians, or drivers, which the former considered as a downgrade.

The dilemma Asharis faced in the new mechanized production system was not one of deskilling, as some scholars have suggested, of artisanal practices in the context of mechanization. Historians of technology depicted the deskilling process as an outcome of modernization and industrialization. Most of these discussions focused on a teleological historical perspective based on modernist narratives of the transformation from artisanal production to industrial production.[37] These scholars considered skill an ahistorical category, which could be attributed to certain human capabilities across time and space. According to these scholars, only the degree of specific skill sets changes through time, and the definition of skill does not. This conception enables them to debate on deskilling and enskilling, with the concept of skill remaining the same before and after deskilling or enskilling. In the case of Asharis and many other artisanal castes, it is problematic to understand the changes in terms of deskilling or enskilling without re-evaluating the very category of 'skill'. We saw in Chapter 1 that the concept of skill itself emerged along with the notion of knowledge-as-object in the colonial condition. In the precolonial situation, as the bodily work was not considered separate from the act of the mind, the term 'skill' in its colonial sense was not relevant and so was not used to understand asharippani or any other artisanal practice. In other words, what industrialization triggered was not a process of deskilling, but the introduction of a new discourse of skill itself and a new way of understanding artisanal practices. It is only in the terms of this colonial history that we can discuss the question of deskilling.

There are two important difficulties in understanding the change of asharippani in the 1990s in terms of deskilling. First, even if we assume that Asharis were now executing the work designed by engineers, mere skill was not enough to turn a design into a product. For example, an engineer, using botanical knowledge, might suggest which specific tree should be used and in what dimensions it should be cut for a specific product. In a practical situation, however, an Ashari used his own method of calculation, testing, and reasoning, which too requires discursive, rational, and formal ways of thinking. In other words, the problem Asharis faced in the manufacturing units was not that they lost their traditional skill; rather, it was a predicament of disconnecting asharippani from the earlier network of jati and connecting it to a new network as practical work. In an article in 1992, V. Shanmukhan Achari noted:

> ... it is not correct to say that the young Asharis who migrated to the cities are less capable than the older generation. They are using their capabilities and skills in a different manner. The dilemma they face is whether they want to continue asharippani and perish or to engage in other works and give up their respectable position in the society.[38]

In the interviews I conducted, most of the young Asharis raised the same concern regarding the current disconnect between asharippani and the network based on jati. Divakaran, who is now in his late twenties and who is working in a distant city, explained that his present job in the furniture shop requires 'high bodily skill and capacity to adapt to machines. I am comfortable with the work as such. Still, there is no life in this; it is just a job'.[39] Asharis identified this crisis not as a problem of deskilling but as a question of self-identification in the new networks in which they found themselves. In its new format, asharippani was no longer the central organizing category of the jati Ashari. The disjuncture between jati and asharippani produced a vacuum in the practice of jati and self-identification practices.

The Vishwakarma Identity and the Nationalization of Caste

The crises Asharis faced in the 1980s were multi-dimensional. The Ashari self-understanding described the new situation as a loss of identity or their lack of commitment to their own jati. It was in the context of the aforementioned problem that the community initiated various forms of reform activities through a new community organization in the 1980s. While various organizations under the category of Vishwakarma[40] were present in Keralam from the 1940s, they were not very influential, and each organization was active comparatively for a short period of time. In the 1980s, the newly emerged Vishwakarma *sabha*s started negotiation with the state government in obtaining adequate shares in the governing process and in education. These organizations, however, took cultural reform as an equally important agenda, which was a response to the crisis in the practices of self-identification. Asharis were considered one of the five jatis included in the Vishwakarma tradition, and individuals from the Ashari community took major roles in the formation of these organizations.

The Kerala Vishwakarma Sabha, one of the major organizations, successfully mobilized members of the five jatis and led many agitations demanding reservations in government jobs and in other politically-appointed positions. In 1985, the state government, conceding to the demands of the Sabha, included the Vishwakarma jatis in the schedule of 'Other Backward Classes'. By the 1990s, the Sabha's membership reached around 27,000. In 1983, the Sabha initiated a publication named *Karmabhumi* (The Land of Work), which soon gained wide subscription among the community members. Started as a monthly, *Karmabhumi* soon became a bi-monthly in 1989 and a weekly in 1993. In 2000, the state government nominated the Sabha's state secretary as a member of the Public Service Commission, which was the body responsible for all government recruitments.[41] In short, within ten years, the Sabha made its presence visible in the domain of politics and successfully negotiated with the government on behalf of the Vishwakarma community.

Other than the activities in the realm of politics, the Sabha made significant attempts to improve the status of the community in a society where brahmanical values and concepts had already gained domination in social and cultural practices. The first step in this regard was to make the Vishwakarma identity part of the history of the nation, erasing the individual jati identity. In the case of Asharis, the crisis in the asharippani had already weakened their identification to jati, and hence, identifying with Vishwakarma was a timely opportunity to regain their lost respectability. It was in the shift from Ashari to Vishwakarma that History as a form of knowledge of the past intervened in the self-understanding of the community members. We already observed that, by the early twentieth century, through the processes of negotiations between jati communities and the colonial order of knowledge, history writing had become the dominant method of understanding the past. For all community-reform movements which intended to enter the order of knowledge, history writing became an unavoidable agenda for establishing and naturalizing the identity of the community. Therefore, individual and organized attempts to create a suitable past were always part of the activities of the community-reform movements.

The reform movements of the dominant-caste jatis such as Nairs and Nampoothiris in the late nineteenth and the early twentieth centuries used history writing as one of the major activities of reform. As seen in Chapter 4, the histories written as part of the reform activity created a Hindu past as the history of the nation, which justified the brahmanical traditions in the name of knowledge and superiority of values.[42] The leaders of the oppressed castes such as Ezhavas and Pulayas challenged this past with their own histories, in which the story of the nation was told as the story of invasion and domination of Brahmins over other cultures through a hierarchical jati system.[43]

The dominant-caste and the oppressed-caste histories opposed and challenged each other regarding the content, but both justified the importance of History as the knowledge of the past. The Brahmins justified this colonial form of understanding the past because it gave them the authority over traditional knowledge—the knowledges of the past—through which they justified their claims of superiority in the present.[44] The Ezhava and Pulaya reform leaders invested their hope in the self-description of colonial knowledge as 'modern', defined in opposition to the traditional. They imagined that entry into modern knowledge would help them challenge traditional brahmanical hierarchies. At the same time, all these histories following the colonial protocols of History considered the nation as the natural boundary of a particular culture, written text as the most convincing form of evidence, Sanskrit as the language of traditional knowledge, and science as a valid form of knowledge to which all other practices should refer.

Asharis, before the interaction with the practices of production of knowledge, invoked the past through their carpentry work and through storytelling and songs. These invocations of the past differed from History in its method, form, and content. The past in earlier Ashari practices was not completely detached from the present. For example, in the selection of the proper location for a house, Asharis considered the past of the particular space an important parameter. This past was not something that had already happened but a force that lingered over the present. A. B. Shivan explained that 'the moothashari observes the signals and learns who from the past are still residing in the location, what elements of the past are active in that space, and determines the proper place and design of the house'.[45] Kidangoor Raghavan Achari observed that 'the younger generation of Asharis considers that what happened yesterday is not important; they did not have the faculty to see the presence of the forces from the past'.[46] This was different from the idea of the alterity of the past from the present, which dominated in the history writing by Vishwakarma historians. The imagination of space in earlier Ashari constructions of the past was also different from the imagined spaces in new histories. Desham, not nation, was the genuine boundary condition in earlier stories of the past. As History became the dominant form of the knowledge of the past in the post-colonial situation, the earlier Ashari ways of invoking the past became local myth and folklore. The use of vernacular language, the absence of written texts, and the making of desham as the location combined to prevent the Ashari past from becoming the *history* of the community. It was in this situation that Vishwakarma sabhas turned to the Sanskrit tradition and began constructing a history of the Vishwakarmas, comprising five artisanal jatis in Keralam.

The idea of a group of five artisanal jatis was not completely new in the region. In the early literature in the Malayalam-speaking region, there were a number of mentions of Aynkammalar (a group of five hand-working castes). The colonial censuses of Malabar in the late nineteenth century categorized Asharis within the Aynkammalar. This was based on the local vernacular stories of Aynkammalar, which originated in a very different historical period. In the late nineteenth and the early twentieth centuries, these five jatis did not participate in any common jati practices—no two castes within the group intermarried, there were no common rituals, and common dining was not allowed. Aynkammalar was more a taxonomical category than an identity, and the varied rules of the individual jatis of the members determined their daily life. Still, through colonial categorization mediated by the brahmanical stories and myths, Aynkammalar became the vernacular equivalent of the category of artisan.

P. Bhaskaranunni observed that, in the context of colonial ethnographic practices, Brahmins as interlocutors imposed their ideas of caste into the colonial anthropological knowledge. 'The colonial writings in the nineteenth century, mediated by the Brahmins, determined the twentieth-century common sense regarding jati in Keralam.'[47] Within this colonial or brahmanical notion, the Aynkammalar story was a story of the local practice of jati, unlike the Sanskritized brahmanical stories which were 'national'.

In their attempt to write the history of the community, the Vishwakarma sabhas did not choose the local history of Aynkammalar; rather, they invoked the Sanskritized myth of Vishwakarma and presented this story as part of the history of the nation. In this history, God Vishwakarma originated as the founding figure of the community, and this history described the brahmanical tradition as a later manipulation of Hindu civilization. Vishwakarma, which means the creator of the universe, was a god with five faces. In the beginning of time, the five Brahmas, who were the gods of carpentry, goldsmithy, sculpture, blacksmithy, and coppersmithy, emerged from the five faces of Vishwakarma. These five Brahmas created the material world, which laid the foundation of human civilization. Many authors, mainly from the Ashari and Thattan (goldsmith) jatis, started to publish articles and books based on the Sanskrit *puranas* by interpreting the story of Vishwakarma as the originary moment in the history of the community.[48] This selection was important because through the assertion of Sanskritized history, the Vishwakarma communities claimed a higher status in the order of knowledge. In 1994, one of the articles in *Karmabhumi* articulated this claim as follows:

> All the great temples, forts, statues and other buildings are a representation of the knowledge of Vishwakarmans. But in the present, nobody recognises this as such. How do we make this historical fact known before the common public and the authorities? Only by establishing the connection between the Indian civilisation and Vishwakarma theories as explained in Sanskrit texts, can we prove the importance of our knowledge; and only by establishing the importance of our knowledge, can we regain the status of our community in the society.[49]

In Chapter 1, we saw that, in the first half of the twentieth century, in order to resist the interventions of the colonial knowledge, Asharis kept asharippani outside the purview of knowledge. Ashari representative practices were inseparable from asharippani, which included discursive and non-discursive elements. Even if we consider objects such as houses or sculptures as signs and hence related to language, the representative strategies of these objects were very different from oral or written representations like stories or songs.[50] In the changed circumstances in the 1980s, as contemporary society recognized knowledge only in the written form, the community had to establish its relation to written texts in order to claim a higher position in the order of knowledge. Knowledge, which was earlier a part of action, became a *representation* of actions and objects in the form of writing.

The Vishwakarma histories written in the last decades of the twentieth century had many similarities with the reform histories of other communities written in the early twentieth century. These Vishwakarma historians used the same narrative pattern in earlier reform histories, one that described a glorious past in a time immemorial and an invasion by a foreign culture which enforced the current subaltern position of the community.[51] At the same time, Vishwakarma histories differed in many ways from the early-twentieth-century community histories written by the reform leaders of both the dominant and oppressed castes.

The Nampoothiri reform movement in the 1930s redefined the daily practice of acharam according to the protocols of scientific knowledge. In this process, the reform movement produced a notion of continuity between traditional knowledge and scientific knowledge. The Ezhava and Pulaya reformers in the early twentieth century also spoke about a glorious past in a time immemorial, but they focused more on the necessity of breaking from their immediate past dominated by the Brahmins. The dominant colonial–brahmanical discourse had made these oppressed castes' contemporary practices, including their very occupation, impure or even culturally invalid. Thus, these reformers in the early twentieth century urged community members to move away from these traditional occupations to modern ones based on colonial education and scientific knowledge. The attempts of the major reform writers from the subaltern caste communities were not directed at establishing the historical importance of their traditional occupation. Rather, their focus was more on the need for reform in the current practices of the community members.

In the early twentieth century, Sree Narayana Guru, the spiritual leader and philosopher, firmly discouraged Ezhavas from participating in the traditional occupation of toddy-tapping. He directed community members to enroll in the colonial education institutions and participate in as many different government jobs as possible. Guru never attempted to analyse work as a spiritual concept. For him, knowledge was the more important concept. However, Guru's philosophical works did not attempt to create a history which would connect Ezhavas with knowledge in an immemorial past.[52] Similarly, the Pulaya reform leader Ayyankali focused on creating a rupture with the traditional Pulaya practices by urging the members of the community to discontinue the traditional occupation of agricultural labour. Even though the colonial–brahmanical discourse had not demonized agricultural labour as they did with toddy-tapping and leather work, it was still considered an impure work which supposedly did not require the application of mind or knowledge. For Ayyankali, the oppressed status of his community members was directly linked to the assumed impure nature of the traditional occupation.[53]

The Vishwakarma movement in the last decades of the twentieth century, on the other hand, attempted to create a continuity of their traditional occupation from the past to the present. The colonial–brahmanical mapping of traditional occupations of the five jatis within the Vishwakarma movement had not marked their occupations as impure or invalid. However, the occupations of these communities had a lower status compared to brahmanical knowledge. Hence, the objective of the Vishwakarma movement was not to create a break with the traditional occupation but to connect it with written traditions—that is, to connect it with traditional knowledge in the colonial sense.

Prajabodhanam (Enlightening the Subjects), written by Sree Karthika Peruman in 1998, shows how the Vishwakarma historians negotiated with the challenges mentioned previously as part of writing a national history of Vishwakarmas.[54] Peruman introduced his work as a product of 'factual experience'. According to him, 'A future with justice is impossible without the historical consciousness which has surpassed the test of fire of the past: the past which is an evolution of the material and spiritual history of Bharata.'[55] Peruman invoked historical consciousness as a necessary element in the imagination of future, and for him, it was a consciousness of the history of the nation, 'Bharata'.

In the first chapter of *Prajabodhanam*, Peruman compares the stories of the origin of the Universe as told by science and by the Vedas and puranas. To him, the similarity between the story of science and the origin story based on the Vishwakarma god makes the latter a fact or truth. Peruman asserted the validity of the Vishwakarma story by comparing it to the Big Bang theory in science.[56] This method was not different from that of the dominant-caste revivalist historians in the early twentieth century, who attempted to explain Sanskrit texts according to scientific principles. The difference of Peruman's text with the brahmanical interpretations becomes visible only when he discusses the story of the manipulation of the Vedas by the Brahmins. According to brahmanical interpretation, four was the important number in the Vedas and puranas. There were four faces for the creator Brahma, there were four Vedas, and human beings were classified into four varnas (colours). Peruman—quoting the same Vedas and puranas— argued that in the origin, it was not Brahma but the five-faced Vishwakarma who created the Universe. There were five Vedas, and there were five Vishwakarma sages who created the human civilization.[57] The details of his argument are not important for our purposes, but we underscore the difference between his explanation of the origin of the Universe and the brahmanical interpretation.

The word *karmam* (work) is the central organizing category of Peruman's text. By shifting the focus from the brahmanical concept of karma—the propelling force of all living beings—to the Vishwakarma concept of karmam, Peruman attempted to underline the divine and spiritual nature of work which created and sustained the universe. For Peruman, work was not just an action but a divine source, a force that was embedded in all objects and living beings. Peruman's attempt was to elevate the status of work from the position of bodily action to a concept which could explain all the phenomena in the universe, or, in other words, to relocate the category of work from the domain of practice to that of theory. Quoting *Vishwakarma Purana*, a Sanskrit text, Peruman explains that 'karmam is the expression of divine knowledge, which actualises in the world through five elements and perpetuates through the actions of the five Vishwakarma traditions'.[58]

A. B. Sivan, another scholar from the Vishwakarma group, also attempted to establish the theoretical nature of the Vishwakarma tradition. In his interpretation of the text *Vishwakarmeeyam*, published in 1999, he stated that 'the practices of Vishwakarma people are the continuation of the knowledge originated from Atharva Veda. It was the priestly traditions of Brahmins which created a distinction between the Vedic tradition and the Vishwakarma traditions'.[59] Similarly, another Vishwakarma author, Raghavan Achari, asserted that 'it was through the Vishwakarma people that the theorems of *Manushyalaya Chandrika* [a Sanskrit text on architecture], was handed over from one generation to another'.[60] In all these works, authors created a historic past—a past in which knowledge and Vishwakarma practices were inseparably aligned. These works also expressed concern over the negligence of theoretical knowledge by the young generation of the community. In an interview, Shanmukhan Ashari from Mundur expressed this explicitly:

> We Asharis always lament that society does not respect us anymore. How can we gain respect, if we are engaged only in such kind of work which can be easily replicated by a machine? My grandfather was very much respected even among Brahmins because he could explain every work based on theorems. The key is the knowledge and not the physical work; even animals which do not have any capacity to think can do work.[61]

In the Vishwakarma attempt to elevate the ascribed status of the community from that of practitioners to knowledgeable experts, the difference between theory and practice became reinforced, and work in its embodied form became degraded and devalued. The reform leaders attempted to position the Vishwakarma jatis as the communities of expert knowledge of manufacture. In the practical sense, this was a difficult task given the dominance of colonial–brahmanical knowledge, which was disseminated through wide networks of education institutions, art, literature, and electronic and print media. The attempt of various Vishwakarma sabhas, however, helped Vishwakarma communities claim a historical tradition similar to that of Brahmins and which was part of the history of the nation. In order to understand the effect of the Vishwakarma reform movement on the Ashari community, we have to explore the circulation of the reform discourse within and outside the community.

The reform discourse in the last two decades of the twentieth century had a significant impact on the younger generation within the Ashari community, especially on those who were still engaged in asharippani. Unlike the previous generation, they began learning Sanskrit verses and focused on the ritualistic practices assigned to Asharis during the construction work.[62] The availability of the printed copies of the old Sanskrit texts, which were now translated and interpreted in Malayalam, was one of the important factors that enabled this change. Even in their daily life practice besides work, many of these young Asharis started following the traditional rituals more strictly than the generation before. It is important to note that, unlike the early rituals, which were an integral part of asharippani, these rituals were less based on specific jati practices than on an understanding of common Hindu religious practice. The community leaders took initiatives to revive a number of Ashari temples, which were in a state of neglect for decades. Earlier, the Ashari temples had specific jati-based gods and goddesses and jati-based worship practices. These gods and goddesses were now renamed and transformed as part of the Hindu pantheon.[63] The worship rituals were also transformed based on the brahmanical model. Ironically, the new Ashari tradition, which emerged through opposition to the brahmanical ideology, became more brahmanical than it was in the pre-reform period. Through the reform processes, the Ashari rituals, which were originally integral to asharippani, formed their own domain, separating themselves from actual moments of work. In this situation, many of the Asharis who were now specialized in the ritual practices did not participate in the actual carpentry work; rather, they became the experts of the traditional knowledge of asharippani.

While carpentry moved beyond the perimeters of the Ashari jati, as explained earlier in this chapter, Asharis themselves moved into non-Ashari occupations in the last decades of the twentieth century. Many scholars who have studied aspects of the Gulf migration from Keralam have pointed out that the migrants in the

Gulf engaged in the kind of work in which they would never consider engaging in Keralam.[64] Many of the Asharis who migrated to the Gulf had to take up unskilled manual labour work, especially in their initial days of work abroad. When opportunities allowed, they worked as assistants in shopping malls and offices and in other jobs which did not require their traditional skills or capabilities. In contrast with the dominant Kerala migrant community, this engagement with non-Ashari occupations encouraged Asharis to venture into other occupations not only in the Gulf countries but also in Keralam. By the 1990s, the presence of Ashari men and women became visible in sectors like engineering, education, and agriculture, and in different kinds of service jobs in various government offices.[65]

The movement of asharippani beyond the jati boundaries and the involvement of individual Asharis outside the jati occupation redefined the earlier role of asharippani as the central organizing category of the jati Ashari. The practice of knowing of Asharis transformed significantly in the last three decades of the twentieth century. In Chapter 2, we observed how in the first half of the twentieth century, Asharis successfully ignored some and assimilated some other transformations taking place around them into the existing norms of their world without changing the basic principles of their practice of knowing. In the last decades of the twentieth century, asharippani itself transformed into new forms and methods, and this resulted in changes that were seminal to the Ashari practice of knowing. Asharippani moved from its earlier location of desham to the new location of nation. The Vishwakarma reform discourse attempted to connect asharippani to theoretical knowledge, a category which Asharis deliberately ignored earlier. The written texts—especially Sanskrit texts—became an important element in the practice of carpentry. Unlike in asharippani practised in the pre-reform period, where the discursive and non-discursive elements were entwined, in the new form, they functioned separately and independently. In the new form, asharippani became a hybrid activity located in the overlapping space of the production of knowledge and the practices of knowing. In short:

Once we crafted this world,
We slipped down
Into brahmin-laid traps.
Let us wake up from our sleep,
Once again, let us craft the world.[66]

In the current world, dominated by colonial–brahmanical epistemology and institutions of reproduction of this epistemology, Asharis struggle to locate themselves in multiple registers of self-identification. As practitioners, they refuse to consider themselves as workers with mere bodily skill. The thinking hand and the impressionistic practices of knowing prompt them to locate themselves between artist and worker. On the other hand, the colonial–brahmanical discourse of knowledge production and changing technological practices restrict their artistic creativities and reduce the autonomy they had on their practices of knowing. One section of the community attempts through Vishwakarma association to challenge the brahmanical ideology in the same language produced by the colonial–brahmanical discourse on history and knowledge production. Another section attempts to recreate asharippani in the new location and in the space–time. And yet another section leaves behind asharippani and relocates into other occupations, hoping that this will enable them to move higher in the hierarchical series of caste and knowledge. All of them recognize that as far these hierarchies exist, they will have to continue their resistance in various forms for a dignified life with self-respect.

Notes

1. The state of Keralam formally came into existence on 1 November 1956. After the formation of the state, even though regional differences were still significant, the social, economic, and political context of the Asharis in the earlier district of Malabar became comparable with those of the Asharis in the other regions of Keralam. Hence, the location of the analysis of this chapter moves from Malabar to Keralam and considers the Ashari activity within different regions in the state as a single process.

2. For example, the first formal activity of the Ezhava reform was the 'Ezhava Memorial', a memorandum submitted to the King of Thiruvithamkoor, demanding deserved share in government jobs and education. For an analysis of the early twentieth-century political formations and the role of communities in this process, see K. N. Yesudas, *The People's Revolt in Travancore: A Backward Caste Movement for Social Freedom* (Thiruvananthapuram: Kerala Historical Society, 1975).

3. J. Devika, 'Egalitarian Developmentalism, Communist Mobilization, and the Question of Caste in Kerala State, India', *Journal of Asian Studies* 69, no. 3 (August 2010): 799–820.

4. Satish Deshpande, 'Caste and Castelessness: Towards a Biography of the "General Category"', *Economic and Political Weekly* 48, no. 15 (April 2013): 32–39.

5. In the 1960s and 1970s, the NSS and the SNDP widened their network of schools and became leading groups in corporate management of the schools in the private sector. They significantly influenced the education policy of the government in this period, and the various political parties in the state,

including the Communist Party, attempted to create cordial relations with these community organizations for electoral gains. For a critical analysis of the role of community organizations in the education sector of Keralam, see Filippo Osella and Caroline Osella, *Social Mobility in Kerala: Modernity and Identity in Conflict* (London: Pluto Press, 2000).

6. A survey conducted by the Department of Small Industries in 1974 noted that between the period of 1960 and 1970, out of the total members of the artisanal castes under the age of twenty, less than 1 per cent appeared for the public exam at the tenth standard. See *Report of the Sample Survey on Artisanal Industries in Ten Districts of Kerala* (Thiruvananthapuram: Government Press, 1975): 31–32.

7. Interview with Shreedharan (12 May 2009).

8. Ramachandran Achari, 'Caste and Social Change in Keralam: A Study of Lower Castes in Malabar, 1947–1970', PhD dissertation, Calicut University, 1976, 43.

9. Achari, 'Caste and Social Change in Keralam', 56.

10. V. N. Menon, *Marunna Nadum Nagaravum* (Changing Village and City) (Kozhikode: Mathrubhumi, 1982), 49.

11. See B. A. Prakash, 'Gulf Migration and Its Economic Impact: The Kerala Experience', *Economic and Political Weekly* 33, no. 50 (December 1998): 3209–3213.

12. *Report of the Survey on Utilisation of Gulf Remittance in Kerala* (Trivandrum: Government Press, 1994), 13.

13. According to the survey conducted by the Department of Economics and Statistics in 1980, only 6 per cent of the total houses in Keralam used RC technology for roof. *Report of the Survey on Housing and Employment* (Trivandrum: Government Press, 1980), 68.

14. *The Survey Report on the Status of Housing in Kerala 1991*, Part 4 (Thiruvananthapuram: Government Press, 1992), 147.

15. The Kerala Municipal Corporations (Amendment) Act, 1970, passed by the Kerala Legislature, transferred a wide range of powers from the state government to the elected municipal administrative bodies. It also enhanced the scope of government control over construction works. Before the Act, one had to file an application before the local authorities to get permission for constructing a house. The 1970 amendment required that from then onwards, this application should be accompanied by drawings and estimates prepared by an approved civil engineer. This was one of the important moments when the engineers as the authority of architectural knowledge received a chance to directly enter the domain of house construction.

16. Eric Hobsbawm, 'Inventing Tradition', in *The Invention of Tradition*, ed. Eric Hobsbawm and Terence Ranger, 1–14 (Cambridge: Cambridge University Press, 1983), 2.

17. Most of these texts were already in circulation but only in very limited circles. In the 1990s, a number of local publishers started reprinting these works in

Malayalam, and most of them included introductions and interpretations by famous moothasaris. *Manushylaya Chandrika*, a Sanskrit text supposedly written by a Malayali Brahmin in the fifteenth or sixteenth century, was reprinted at least in five versions with five different interpretations during 1994–2002. See B. Raghavanachari (ed.), *Manushyalaya Chandrika* (Kodungalloor: Devi Books, 1994); K. V. Achuthan Achari (ed.), *Manushyalaya Chandrika* (Kottayam: D. C. Books, 1998); K. Neelakantan Ashari (ed.), *Maha Manushyalaya Chandrika* (Kodungalloor: Devi Books, 2000); Kanippayyoor Shankaran Nampoothirippad (ed.), *Manushyalaya Chandrika*, 12th edition (Kunnamkulam: Panjangam Book Stall, 2004).

18. See the Introduction.
19. H. Fazeli and A. Goodarzi, 'The Principles of Vastu as a Traditional Architectural Belief System from an Environmental Perspective', *WIT Transactions on Ecology and the Environment* 128 (2010): 97–108.
20. For an analysis of the pattern of Gulf migration from Keralam, see K. C. Zacharia, E. T. Mathew, and S. Irudaya Rajan, *Dynamics of Migration in Kerala: Dimensions, Differentials and Consequences* (Hyderabad: Orient Longman, 2003).
21. K. N. Harilal, 'Deskilling and Wage Differential in Construction Industry', *Economic and Political Weekly* 24, no. 24 (June 1989): 1347–1352.
22. For example, the survey conducted by R. Ramachandran in Palakkad district on the small manufacturing unit shows that by 1990, the number of carpentry workshop units in the rural areas increased by 23 per cent from that of the 1980s. He noted that almost 80 per cent of these were owned by Gulf-returned Asharis. *The Report of Survey on Small Manufacturing Units in Palakkad District* (Shornur: Saikatham Press, 1999), 27–29.
23. For a Marxist analysis of the effects of transformation of means of production in the artisanal practices in the early industrial societies, see Ronald Aminzade, *Class Politics and Early Industrial Capitalism* (Albany: State University of New York Press, 1981). For an anthropological study of means of production and its transformation in the industrial age, see Michael Brian Schiffer (ed.), *Anthropological Perspectives on Technology* (Arizona: The Amerind Foundation Inc., 2001).
24. In 1992, *Karmabhumi* published a table for conversion from the old system to the new system of measures, which showed that by then, Asharis had begun using the new units and tools of measurement along with the old ones. See 'Kai Kanakku Pattika (A Conversion Table for the Hand Measurements)', *Karmabhumi*, May 1992, 12. The interviews I conducted with the Asharis revealed that even now, the older generation of Asharis is reluctant to use measuring tapes with the measure of centimetre and inch. Even when Asharis use them, they translate them into the older measures in order to calculate the measures and designs.
25. See Chapter 2.

26. The early sociological scholarship beginning from Max Weber understood the process of industrialization as a rationalization process where the world is increasingly disenchanted and made human-centred. Following this scholarship, anthropologists and historians of technology mapped the disenchanting processes in the artisanal practices in the wake of mechanization and industrialization. For Weber's view on rationalization, see Stanislav Andreski, *Max Weber on Capitalism, Bureaucracy and Religion* (Oxford: Taylor & Francis, 2008). For a historical analyses of rationalization of artisanal production, see Steven M. Zdatny, *The Politics of Survival: Artisans in the Twentieth Century France* (Oxford: Oxford University Press, 1990); Robert Tarule, *The Artisans of Ipswich: Craftsmanship in Colonial New England* (Maryland: Johns Hopkins University Press, 2004). For a critique of rationalization approach from an anthropological perspective, see Deepak Mehta, *Work, Ritual, Biography: A Muslim Community in North India* (Delhi: Oxford University Press, 1997).

27. Aihwa Ong, *Spirits of Resistance and Capitalist Discipline: Factory Women in Malaysia* (Albany: State University of New York Press, 1987).

28. Susan George, *Religion and Technology in the 21st Century* (London: Information Science Publishing, 2006).

29. For example, Susan Hirsch in an early work gave the impression that craftsmen, when moved from the artisanal production practice to the factory system, in some way underwent a process of rationalization in their new workplace. The latest anthropological scholarship on factory practices notes that while the new tools and manufacturing systems had mechanized the human interaction with the tools, it would be wrong to consider this mechanization as a process of increased rationality. See Susan F. Hirsch, *Roots of the American Working Class: The Industrialisation of Craft in Newark* (Pennsylvania: University of Pennsylvania Press, 1978). For an anthropological criticism of the view of rationalization, see Pamela Smith, *The Body of the Artisan: Art and Experience in the Scientific Revolution* (Chicago: Chicago University Press, 2004).

30. C. Nadia Seremetakis (ed.), *The Senses Still: Perception and Memory as Material Culture in Modernity* (Chicago: University of Chicago Press, 1994); Kirsten Hastrup and Peter Hervik (eds.), *Social Experience and Anthropological Knowledge* (London: Routledge, 1994); and Paul Stoller, *The Taste of Ethnographic Things: Senses in Anthropology* (Pennsylvania: University of Pennsylvania Press, 1989).

31. Judith Okely, 'Vicarious and Sensory Knowledge of Chronology and Change: Ageing in Rural France', in *Social Experience and Anthropological Knowledge*, ed. Kirsten Hastrup and Peter Hervik (London: Routledge, 1994).

32. See Paul Feyerabend, *Against Method* (London: Verso, 1988); and Bruno Latour and Steve Woolgar, *Laboratory Life: Construction of Scientific Facts* (Princeton: Princeton University Press, 1986).

33. Interview with Ravindran (16 November 2009).

34. Interview with Ravindran (16 November 2009).

35. Interview with Rajan (23 January 23 2010).

36. See Harilal, 'Deskilling and Wage Differential in Construction Industry', 1347–1352.

37. For analyses of the transformation of artisanal practices based on the concept of deskilling or enskilling, see Harry Braverman, *Labor and Monopoly Capital: The Degradation of Work in the Twentieth Century* (New York: Monthly Review Press, 1974); Paul Thompson, *An Introduction to Debates on Labour Process* (London: Macmillan, 1989); and Harilal, 'Deskilling and Wage Differential in Construction Industry', 1347–1352.

38. V. Shanmukhan Achari, 'Yanthrayugavum Vishwakarmajarum (Machine Age and the Vishwakarmas)', *Karmabhumi*, no. 11, November 1992, 10–11, 11.

39. Interview with Divakaran (3 March 2010).

40. See the Introduction.

41. Each new government in the state, after being elected, appointed its own nominees to various public sector corporations and boards. In nominating these positions, the ruling political parties attempted to satisfy all the community organizations that supposedly helped them in the election. The Public Service Commission is an independent body appointed by the state government, which conducted all the selection processes of state government employees. The position in the commission is a prestigious post and the nomination of its member to this position shows the importance of the Kerala Vishwakarma Sabha in the political domain.

42. S. Madhava Menon, *The Vedic Tradition of India* (Madras: The Hindu Publishing Co., 1912); V. Neelakanta Sastri, *Brahmins and Indian Civilisation* (Madras: Saraswathi Printers, 1914); and K. Unni Moosathu, *Arsha Paramparyam* (The Arsha Tradition) (Thrissur: Mangalodayam Press, 1920).

43. P. Palpu, *Collected Articles of Dr. Palpu* (Trivandrum: Kairaly Press, 1934).

44. See Chapter 3.

45. A. B. Shivan, *Vishwakarmeeyam* (Kottayam: D. C. Books, 1999), 21.

46. Kidangur Raghavan Achari, 'Vedangalum Thachushasthravum (Vedas and the Architectural Science)', *Karmabhumi*, November 1998, 2–4.

47. P. Bhaskaranunni, *Keralam Irupatham Noottantinte Arambhathil* (Keralam in the Beginning of the Twentieth Century) (Thrissur: Kerala Sahitya Academy), 176.

48. The major Malayalam publisher D. C. Books published five books between 1998 and 2003 on Vastu and Vishwakarma, with interpretations by authors from the Vishwakarma community. Devi Books, Kodungalloor, published seven books affirming the Vishwakarma myth between 1994 and 2001. For example, see Raghavanachari (ed.), *Manushyalaya Chandrika*; Achari (ed.), *Manushyalaya Chandrika*; and Ashari (ed.), *Maha Manushyalaya Chandrika*. These books, while targeting a wider audience outside the Vishwakarma community, were part of the individual and organized attempts by the Vishwakarma community to popularize the origin story of the community.

49. V. Shanmukhan Achari, 'Vishwakarmajante Bhavi (The Future of Vishwakarmajan)', *Karmabhumi*, November 1989, 8.

50. See Chapter 1.

51. Many of the reform leaders from marginalized communities considered Brahmins as foreign invaders and imagined a golden period before this invasion, where their community practices were respected, and the society was more egalitarian. For example, Mahatma Jyotiba Phule in his works reinterpreted the brahmanical myth of Vishnu's ten incarnations as a story of Aryan invasion of India and argued that the society before Aryan domination was more egalitarian. See G. P. Deshpande (ed.), *Selected Writings of Jyotiba Phule* (New Delhi: LeftWord Books, 2002).

52. Scholars now map Sree Narayana Guru's meditations on knowledge in the phenomenological tradition, where the difference between the knower and knowledge is transcended in the process of knowing. Hence, for Guru, the practical work did not qualify even as an object of knowledge. For an exploration of Guru's deliberations on knowledge, see Filippo Osella and Caroline Osella, 'From Transience to Immanence: Conception, Life-cycle and Social Mobility in Kerala, South India', *Modern Asian Studies* 33, no. 4 (1999): 989–1020.

53. Ayyankali, unlike Sree Narayan Guru, did not attempt to create an abstract theory of knowledge. On the one hand, Ayyankali attempted to show the dominant castes the importance of agriculture labour by organizing a labour strike in 1903, demanding changes in the social attitude of the elite caste people. But at the same time, he encouraged the members of his community to join colonial educational institutions and move into occupations which were more respected and valued by the oppressive castes. For the details of Ayyankali's efforts on this regard, see M. Nisar and Meena Kandaswamy, *Ayyankali: Dalit Leader of Organic Protest* (Calicut: Other Books, 2007).

54. It is important to note that amidst all the claims of the universal nature of scientific knowledge, the nation has been considered as a genuine boundary of knowledge production. The nation's presence is not limited to the nationalistic organization of scientific institutions but is extended even to the epistemological characteristics. For an analysis of the relation between nation and science, see Patrick Catherine Jami Petitjean and Anne Marie Moulin, *Science and Empires: Historical Studies about Scientific Development and European Expansion* (Vienna: Springer, 1992).

55. Sree Karthika Peruman, 'Preface', in *Prajabodhanam* (Enlightening the Subjects) (Thrissur: Kainur Kandrenkavu, 1998).

56. Peruman, 'Preface', 1–3.

57. Peruman, 'Preface', 9–17.

58. Peruman, 'Preface', 117.

59. Shivan, 'Preface', in *Vishwakarmeeyam*.

60. Achari, 'Vedangalum Thachushasthravum'.

61. Interview with Shanmughan Achari (30 December 2009).

62. V. Rajan, a leader of the youth wing of the Kerala Vishwakarma Sabha, in an article pointed out that after a decade's work by the Sabha, several young members have absorbed Vishwakarma principles in their daily life both in the home and in the workplace. See V. Rajan, 'Yuvajanangalum Vishwakarma Sabhayum (The Youth and the Vishwakarma Sabha)', *Karmabhoomi*, December 2004, 3–4.

63. Christian missionaries, starting from the early nineteenth century, while condemning all the caste practices in India as idolatry, paganism, and superstition, specifically targeted the subaltern caste practices of witchcraft, magic, and other worship forms such as animal sacrifice. The dominant-caste reform movements attempted to divert the missionary criticism towards the subaltern caste practices to save Hindu religion by creating a civilized version of it. Later, in the twentieth century, in the wake of the strengthening of the revivalist forces in the name of the Hindu religion, the remaining oppressed caste gods and goddesses were absorbed into the 'great pantheons of Hindu gods'. For an analysis of the revivalist politics, see K. Jamanadas, 'Saffronization, Hinduisation or Brahminization?' *Counter Currents*, 1 December 2004, http://www.countercurrents.org/dalit-jamanadas011204.htm (accessed on 23 January 2010).

64. The reluctance among most Malayalis to engage in any kind of physical work has many genealogies, including the denigration of practical work in the colonial discourse. It would be interesting to observe how people negotiated the contradiction of the aforementioned idea and the increased financial difficulties, especially among the lower strata of the society. Gulf migration came as a blessing in this condition. The anonymity in the foreign space helped many migrants to shed the social stigma regarding physical work. See K. V. Joseph, *Keralites on the Move: A Historical Study of Migration from Kerala* (Ann Arbor, MI: University of Michigan Press, 2009).

65. According to the estimate of Kerala Vishwakarma Sabha in 2000, around 35 per cent of the community members have moved out of the traditional occupation and have entered into government or private sector jobs. See 'The Editorial', *Karmabhumi*, December 2000.

66. Translated by Bindu Menon.

Postscript
Towards an Artisanal Way of Practice of Knowing

This is a postscript and not a conclusion; it is a reflection on the contemporary politics of knowledge production in the background of the stories already told in the previous chapters. Further, this postscript is an impressionistic attempt to give the reader a feel of the fleeting images of knowing and doing, which are difficult to translate into a two-dimensional plane of the paper or the screen you read. The postscript starts in a familiar mode of academic discussion and slowly moves into a speculative mode: an expression of my hopes and dreams in the domain of knowledge production. I consider stepping towards an equitable society as the objective of educational practices and democracy as the basic condition for achieving this objective. These are the axioms from which I speculate some strategies for dismantling the colonial–brahmanical forms of knowledge production and to imagine certain democratic ways of knowing.

The challenges for creating a democratic system of practices of knowing are numerous. The first challenge is that of power–knowledge entanglement and its present manifestation in India as a hierarchical series of colonial–brahmanical knowledge. We have seen that power is not just an external enabling factor of knowledge production but also very much an intrinsic element of knowledge. Similarly, knowledge is not just something that can be used to gain power but also itself a form of power. The value and status assigned to knowledge has been empowering it, and this can be challenged only by bringing balancing forces in all the domains of application of power–knowledge. I explore the possibility of ethics, as privileged by Asharis in *asharippani*, working as a balancing force in the process of democratizing knowledge production. The Ashari ways of knowing as doing, as I tried to impress in the previous chapters, were certainly entangled with caste practices of Asharis, and hence, any kind of revival of traditional forms associated with these practices is problematic for a democratic system. However, as I argued in the Introduction, the power–knowledge entanglement has become 'problematic' only in a specific historical condition where knowledge became the measure of the status of a human in an unequal society. It may be impossible to untwine the power–knowledge entanglement; however, we may challenge the status of knowledge and hence make it less impactful. Here, we have to imagine the statuses of knowledge and power from a different perspective than that of the dominant discourses. In other words, in challenging the hierarchical series of colonial–brahmanical form of knowledge production, it is important not only to inquire into alternate forms of knowledge but also to reimagine the importance of knowledge itself. Towards this reimagination, the Ashari notion of knowing as doing could contribute in a significant manner.

The second challenge I am exploring is the role of higher education in reproducing new forms of the *jati* order by creating a minority of experts with tremendous authority and status and a large number of educated labourers who are subordinated in all aspects of decision-making. As I explained in the fourth chapter, as the dominant castes entered into the order of knowledge, they continued their domination in the modern institutions of knowledge production. In this postscript, I explore the nature of domination in practices of knowledge production in contemporary times. This is not a continuation of the traditional jati practices, but it carries the fundamental aspects of the jati order, such as the domination of the minority *savarna* jatis among the experts, both in number and in authority, and the over-representation of the oppressed castes among the labourers. I address this not just as an issue of representation but also as the problem of the authority given to the experts arising from the system. Although these new experts might defy some of the traditional rules of the jati order, such as practices of untouchability or even the practice of endogamous marriage (however, only to marry within the savarna castes), they still manage to hold together as savarnas and practise rules of exclusion and discrimination. They claim their superiority not through their capabilities in Sanskrit or 'Vedic knowledge' but mostly through English language and modern science, while still reproducing social and cultural inequalities by translating the jati practices into modern forms of rituals in public and private spheres, which continue to exclude people from the oppressed jatis and minority religious groups.

In exploring the role of higher education in reproducing the savarna domination, it is important to re-examine the assumed relation between education on the one hand and knowledge production and knowledge transfer on the other—that is, the question of whether the basic objective of education, as assumed in the contemporary education system, is knowledge transfer or knowledge production. In this situation, the Ashari understanding of learning enables us to explore this relation between education and knowledge production and transfer in alternate ways and to rethink the objectives of education.

The emphasis on doing in Ashari practices could be a provocation for this rethinking, as knowing is an effect or side effect of doing, and not a targeted outcome, in this conceptualization. Further, the emphasis on doing enables us to challenge the dichotomy between theory and practice and mental and manual labour. I underscore here that doing should not be reduced to practices of 'activity-oriented learning' or highlighting bodily activity as being in opposition to mental activity, as often conceived in the critique against rote-learning and textual learning.[1]

In the title of this postscript, I have named the ways of knowing as 'artisanal' for many reasons. First, the Ashari methods of knowing, as analysed in the earlier chapters, are largely applicable to other artisanal practices such as smithy, weaving, and pottery, and hence, these can be generalized as artisanal practices (of course, only after historically contextualizing them). Second, the Ashari methods, even after their incorporation into the order of knowledge as explained in Chapter 5, employ practices of art rather than the factory model of commodity production. The term 'artisan' in the contemporary sense thus signifies the complex practice of production of art using so-called 'traditional' and 'modern' technologies. The following discussion explores the possibilities of applying the artisanal ways of knowing in spaces of knowledge production and knowledge transfer such as universities.

Power, Force, and Knowledge Production

Power is the stored capacity that can be transformed into action when and where required. It can be acquired, stored, and transferred to the next generation. It signals more to a structural condition than its application as either a constructive or a destructive force. In Physics, power is the product of force and velocity. In other words, power appears or reveals itself as a product of force and rate of movement. At the same time, power is not destroyed when it is not in action; it remains as a possibility as potential energy. Potential energy, as defined in Physics, is a 'property of the system and not of an individual body or particle'.[2] For example, when a stone is raised above the earth, it has potential energy as being part of the system of the earth and its magnetic field. The stone accumulates this potential energy by the work done to raise it to the height against the gravitational force. If we conceal that history, we may think that it is natural for stones-at-heights to have potential energy and it is a property of the stone. Further, it could be considered as an individual 'capability' of the stone to move any object in its path when it falls down. The erasure of the genealogy of the accumulation of power enables the construction of certain natural truths and facts such as the notion that things-at-height naturally gained their power.

By definition, jati is an ascribed status, and hence, the power of jati is generally attained by birth. However, we saw in the previous chapters that, on the one hand, jati is determined at birth and, on the other, jati is also a training through which it is maintained and reproduced. In other words, while being a savarna person, especially a savarna man, is to have jati power, discriminating someone from a subaltern caste is the active enforcement of that power. This enforcement has gathered substantial attention and criticism and it was even made illegal by the Constitution of India. However, time and again, it has been proven that the illegality of caste-based discrimination has not prevented the savarnas from continuing their oppressive domination. One of the reasons may be that it is the 'enforcement' that is challenged and not the power. Even the Indian Constitution, which consciously intended to challenge caste power, made casteist practices (the enforcement) illegal; however, to claim to be in, or to belong to, a particular caste (to have the accumulated power) itself is not illegal. To reiterate, even when a savarna person distances himself or herself from any active discriminative practices, he or she will still be powerful and will have the potential for discrimination. One of the sources that produce this accumulation of power or potential is the field of knowledge production.

In the last two decades, Dalit and Muslim groups in various universities in India have organized intense struggles, naming the universities as the new 'Agraharas'. These struggles focused on the institutional discrimination of the subaltern groups in universities, and they were partially successful as they exposed the caste oppression in the supposedly caste-free modern spaces. I would like to extend the criticism raised in this struggle against the savarna domination at the representational and institutional levels to the domain of knowledge production. I argue that here the power that enables the enforcement of discrimination is the accumulated power in the form of disciplinary knowledge and pedagogic practices. It has now become clear that while the inclusion of students from the marginalized sections of society has challenged the domination of savarnas, it has not been able to challenge the methodologies of knowledge production. For example, the identification of the current form of historical scholarship as brahmanical is based on the content and perspective of these writings. It has been shown that these histories exclude the histories of Dalits, Adivasis, women, or other marginalized people, and even when they are included, it is written from a savarna man's perspective. Here again, criticism is typically focused on the enforcement of brahmanical power in history writing, whereas the root of this power lies in the methodologies of this form of knowledge production.

In the last three or four decades, scholars and activists have been successful in exposing the colonial–brahmanical nature of the subject matter in humanities, social sciences, and sciences. For example, historians of science have shown the influence of racist and colonialist conceptualizations of nature in Charles Darwin's theory of evolution.[3] Similarly, recently, biologists, inspired by queer and gender studies, have exposed the masculine perceptions regarding the nature of gender and sexuality of many species, including humans, beetles, penguins, and fish.[4] However, the gender of gravity, the race of the uncertainty principle, or the caste of general relativity theory are not enunciable in the current discourse of knowledge production, and neither am I suggesting that it will be in the future. The obvious reason for this is the assumption that the aspects of caste, gender, or race, which are attributes of human societies, are not part of the world of objects that are imagined as independent of the human knowledge about them. The very notion of gravity depends on universalization as method—the assumption that there exists a universal law applicable to all kinds of matter and energy in the universe. Hence, it is more correct to say that gravity is dependent on the idea of a universal law, rather than gravity is universal. Similarly, in our context, the influence of social power is not only on the subject matter of academic writing but also on the methodologies that construct universal truths.[5]

Universalism and objectivity are two aspects of methodological prescriptions that are achieved through erasure of the genealogy of 'primitive accumulation' of power. The local perspective of the European white men became universalized through colonial–racial–casteist accumulation, and by erasing this genealogy, a subjective practice was shown as objective. Chanda Prescod-Weinstein, a black feminist theoretical physicist, in her poetically written reflections on her life as a black woman scientist surrounded by white men, shows how subjective positions influence the observations and how certain observed data are considered relevant or irrelevant based on who observed it. She points out: 'A white person can never know what it's like to be Black from a first-person perspective. This perspective, the person's standpoint, affects what data they can personally sense.'[6] She insists that contribution from various standpoints will not only challenge the now-dominant colonial–white-supremacist methodologies but also necessarily enrich science and knowledge production in general. She mentions that her agenda in the initial years as a Black feminist scientist was that of inclusion: bringing more black women into the white-supremacist science, but soon, she recognized that it is a very limited project. Her dream has then shifted to respect for multiple perspectives within science and making scientific knowledge itself as one way among many other ways of understanding the world.

European colonialism—and its continuation in multiple forms in the present world—is able to universalize its local theories because it has universal power to do so. It has created institutions and daily practices that are required to reproduce the effect of universalism. It has the capacity to produce its own believers through these institutions and to make sure that a homogenized image is reflected, no matter which locality you are looking from. This is important because this power is often neglected, and universalization is sometimes understood as a capacity to abstract general laws from particulars, an ability which was considered lacking in people of colonies, especially among the artisans and others who engaged in 'practical' works. We have already seen that this was not true in the case of Asharis. Asharippani included located abstraction, a form of generalization which always returns to the particular and which extended only up to the boundaries where one could continuously participate in experiencing (see Chapter 1). Here, the experiencing is not considered an individual practice but a social practice of being in a multiverse, that is, being among other human beings, plants, animals, and objects. In short, the questioning of universalization did not originate from empiricism but from 'locatedness', which implies that knowing is limited by the boundaries of experiencing. However, science, with its claim as a provider of universalizable theories for technological practices— though this has been challenged within academia and outside—still dominates the monopoly of universal truths and at the same time rescues itself from any implication of these universal truths. Scientists claim the credit for discovering nuclear fission or fusion (an abstract theory) and transfer the responsibility to the politicians when it comes to the issue of the nuclear bomb (a particular instance of the theory). The absolute refusal to move from the abstracted universal truth to the particular is enabled by the accumulated power of science. This power is dependent not on whether an individual scientist recuses herself or himself from enforcing this power, but on the status of science as the single provider of truth.

In order to make science located, it is important to map the claims of objectivity as part of the scientific method. Asharis consider that the standpoint from which we approach the world determines the facts and truths one can construct from it. This history of approaching the world was an integral part of the story of asharippani; it cannot be erased and neither was there an attempt by Asharis to do so. Claims of objectivity are possible only through the erasure of this story. Scientists are not only trained to subjectively act on the material world but also to forget this part of the knowledge production to imagine themselves as objective. Analysing the practices in science, Karen Barad, a queer feminist theorist and theoretical scientist, explains that it is only by 'meeting the universe halfway' (the subjective part of social construction of facts) that scientists can produce facts; Barad calls this method 'agential realism'. In their explanation, the material objects and the discourse around these are equally agential and responsible for the facts constructed. Barad, exploring physicist Niels Bohr's observations, argued:

> Bohr proposed what is arguably understood as a proto-performative account of scientific practices. His early-twentieth-century epistemological investigations focused on issues of contemporary significance: (1) the connections between descriptive concepts and material apparatuses, (2) the inseparability of the 'objects of observation' and the 'agencies of observation', (3) the emergence and co-constitution of the objects of observation and the agencies of observation through particular material and conceptual epistemic practices, (4) the interdependence of material and conceptual constraints and exclusions, (5) the material conditions for *objective* knowledge, and (6) the reformulation of the notion of causality. (Emphasis added)[7]

The discursivity of the scientific fact, on the one hand, challenges the ideas of objective truth, but at the same time, it points out that the subjective elements are also discursive. The subjective element should be understood not as a random individual feeling but as part of a social experiencing and hence influenced by the social structures of power. The superiority of objectivity as a method is a nineteenth-century development, related to the colonial translation of 'power from distance' to 'knowledge from distance'. The question of objectivity became central in the context of samples (of leaves, flowers, rocks, and animals), or, more importantly, drawings of these samples arriving at Europe from colonies for the scrutiny of the 'trained eyes' of European scientists. The knowledge of the trees, animals, and humans at the distant colonies was needed in order to control and govern the colonies. The colonized were considered as not capable of producing this knowledge of themselves and it was the responsibility of the scientists in Europe to provide this knowledge for the government. On the one hand, the samples and drawings that arrived from colonies into a European library or laboratory were considered as truly representing the colonies. On the other hand, it was also generally known that these had been mediated by various interlocutors such as the colonial officers, travellers, or collectors and archivists who arranged or catalogued them in various libraries in the Metropole. The disparities in accounts, descriptions, and drawings—the subjective mediations—created heated debates among the scientists regarding the real nature of the object or the truth of the matter. It is in this context of knowledge from distance that 'distancing' as a method became dominant in scientific knowledge.[8] Standpoint theories in general and feminist standpoint theories in particular attempt to provincialize science practised as objective and universal, by locating it in its colonial foundations.

The crux of the feminist standpoint theory is anchored on two propositions. First, science is already a perspectival enterprise and therefore not universal; second is that multiple perspectives about the material world will not result in anarchy or despotism. Nokuthula Hlabangane in her analysis on colonization of knowledge systems in the African continent shows that 'while Western science has pushed for and assumed a universal status, it is, in fact, a provincial view of the world—a knowledge system that, like any other, vies for and underpins a particular perspective on the world'.[9] Nokuthula Hlabangane argues that universalism as method is ultimately an argument supporting the colonial invalidation of African ways of knowing. Linda Tuhiwai Smith, a Maori scholar and professor, in her now famous work *Decolonising Methodologies: Research and Indigenous People*, foregrounds the relation of the scientific methodological preferences such as objectivity and value-free knowledge with Western imperialism. She argues that these methodologies themselves are from a particular standpoint and not acceptable for indigenous research. She explains:

> The indigenous research agenda is broad in its scope and ambitious in its intent. There are some things which make this agenda very different from the research agenda of large scientific organizations or of various national science research programmes. There are other elements, however, which are similar to any research programme which connects research to the 'good' of society. The elements that are different can be found in key words such as healing, decolonization, spiritual, recovery. These terms seem at odds with the research terminology of Western science, much too politically interested rather than neutral and objective.[10]

According to Linda Smith, research and knowledge produced through research is a subset of the social and political movements, or, in other words, knowing is part of doing. There is, however, no claim that this methodology is applicable universally. The methods suggested such as healing and recovery are specific to the history of the indigenous community and to the colonial violence they experienced and not universally applicable outside that history. She underscores the point that the ethical considerations of indigenous peoples, which are based on the concept of social good, are different from the Western ideas of ethics based on individual rights. In this view, seeing the world from an indigenous perspective, or, in other words, epistemological relativism, is considered as a necessary part of decolonizing knowledge. Similarly, Natalie Alana Ashton, comparing feminist standpoint theory and perspectival realism as theorized by Ronald Giere,[11] shows that epistemological relativism is different from 'silly relativism', which might be seen as another expression of 'anything goes'. Thus, epistemological relativism is concerned with the nature of human knowledge rather than the nature of the material world.

Standpoint theories in science generally focus on the methodological and practical implications within science, where scientific methods are not considered as objective practice. When facts are considered as produced within a particular network and from a particular perspective, the implication is not just for the nature of scientific fact but for the human world itself. It is in this situation that ethics becomes an important factor in the evaluation of not just applied sciences but theoretical sciences as well. The question of ethics has been a serious concern for a long time in applied sciences such as biological research or in technological practices such as applied nuclear sciences or weapon technologies. However, knowledge as such was not brought under the scrutiny of ethics, and it is generally assumed that seeking knowledge irrespective of its method of production is in general desirable. In other words, although practices that were employed to produce knowledge may not be ethically correct, the final product is not considered stained by these unethical practices. Objectivity and distancing as methods were considered to be the agents of purification of knowledge, making it value-free and hence outside the purview of normative evaluations. By making the accumulated power visible, standpoint theories demand to bring knowledge under the critical examinations of ethical norms.

Prescod-Weinstein reminds us that if we avoid unethical practices, neither would it make scientific research reach a standstill nor will it create chaos in our living world. She narrates the story of the colonial appropriation of space (mountains) in Hawaii in order to mount telescopes, observations from which were crucial in producing our current understanding of the universe. She mentioned two kind of appropriations: the indigenous people of Hawaii were using the mountains for observation of the cosmos, and their knowledge was critical in establishing the telescopes by the colonialists after they colonized this place. She observes: 'In the end, I see the continuous use of unceded Hawaiian sacred spaces for Euro-American science without the permission of kānaka ōiwi as an example of using Indigenous knowledge to produce science without crediting indigenous knowledge.'[12] More importantly, she adds:

> Every time I think about it, I wonder how different things might be going on a global scale right now if scientists from the settler colonial states had always understood that the land and its ecosystems were part of the family. What if non-kanaka scientists had a scientific view that reflected this spiritual connection? Maybe we wouldn't be facing the catastrophe that is global warming.[13]

Prescod-Weinstein encourages us first to challenge or decolonize the practices of knowledge production and to situate knowledge within an ethical framework. For her, both the accumulated power through colonialism and the status of knowledge as an unchallenged measure of progress are problematic. The issue is not just institutional (that the elite men control most of the research institutions and universities) but epistemological as well, as observation and the reading of that observation already are from particular standpoints; in other words, observations are not just empirical but theoretical as well, as they are determined by the previous assumptions and presumptions. She notes:

> When we talk about decolonizing science (or anything, really), upending settler colonialism everywhere is central to that project. I cannot separate telling the truth about the history of Native Hawaiian astronomy from the fight to stop settler scientists from using the history of Native Hawaiian astronomy to excuse colonizing Hawaiian lands.[14]

In an ethical framework, questions such as 'What are the conditions in which knowledge production is not desirable?' or 'How do we perform or act in the world without depending on expert knowledge as the primary condition for acting?' would be enunciable. For example, if it is necessary to colonize and displace a marginal community or destroy the whole ecosystem of a particular place in order to research on subatomic particles, it could be decided that such a knowledge is not important (however great its imagined future contributions would be), until researchers find more acceptable methodologies. In such a situation, it would be also possible to limit the deployment of facts within a locality depending on the reach of experiencing that was required for constructing those facts. This would remove the burden on facts to be universal and they will be restricted within the experiencing community. The producers of knowledge would not transfer the responsibility of the implications of deploying the facts (both effects and side-effects) to the politicians but would share the responsibility and consequences of this responsibility. The experts will not just consult with the layman while keeping all the power in making decisions; both experts and all the individuals on whom the decisions would have an effect would equally participate in an informed way in the process of decision-making (like in a jury system). The attempt cannot be limited to decentralizing and redistributing political power; these need to be extended to power–knowledge as well.

Any attempt to decolonize knowledge requires us to distribute power democratically, such as assuring proper representation of marginalized communities and sections of the society in the institutions of knowledge production and decision-making bodies. But this will not neutralize the accumulated power of the disciplinary knowledges, which are central in producing and reproducing the hierarchies of knowledges. In representational democracy, without democracy in the methodology of knowledge production, the marginalized will be accommodated inside but in the slums of the knowledge-city in the name of merit. For example, there are very successful attempts to 'recover the voices of the subaltern' for History, and in this endeavour, oral narratives and memories have become valuable as forms of evidence. However, unless these narratives are converted into non-fictional writing, it will not attain institutional or legal status. By privileging writing over other forms of constructing the past (such as storytelling), and within writing by excluding all genres but prose, History already reinforces the accumulated power attained through primitive accumulation (which is mainly brahmanical and colonial extraction in India). We know that the subaltern communities, even before entering into the protocols of prose writing, have constructed their pasts according to their varied presents and there are sophisticated techniques of communicating this constructed past within a generation and to the next generations.[15] It is the compulsion that these pasts needed to be validated through the protocols of disciplinary History that make them marginalized in the domain of state-sanctioned knowledge of the past.

One of the major criticisms of pluralistic methodologies is regarding its affinity with relativism. The fear of relativism is based on the concern of not having a common ground for evaluation of both state policies and ethical judgments on how to live a life among others in the context of mutually incommensurable differences. It is a genuine concern if by methodological pluralism, we only mean 'let a hundred flowers bloom'. Standpoint theories as articulated by feminists take the responsibility not only of exposing the standpoints from where facts are made but also of comparing them for their effects for an equitable and sustainable society. It brings in ethical norms as the frame in which these (sometimes even incommensurable) facts can be laid out for comparison. Here, the effects of the procedures through which these facts are constructed are also under scrutiny, and ethics is the most important reference point for this scrutiny. In this evaluation of various methods, since knowledge is not the reference point of evaluation, the expert will not have the magic wand or some superpower, but they will share the table with all the stakeholders to make decisions democratically. The experts will have to oscillate continuously from the particular to the general and back to the particular as in asharippani, and knowledge will not be a conversation among experts. Once the questions of democracy and equality become the primary criteria of evaluation, they will not be considered as criteria that are outside the domain of knowledge production. This will incentivize us to think about methods that are suitable for evaluation criteria, and hence practices of knowing will internalize these normative values. In short, while standpoint perspectives do not answer the question of why democracy or equality should be preferred, these would provide pluralism and democracy without slipping into anarchy or ontological relativism.

Indian Context: From Brahmanical to Savarna Power–Knowledge

In the Indian context of untouchability, distancing as a method was very familiar for the dominant castes who entered into the colonial institutions of knowledge production. Their preference of various emerging colonial disciplines was directly related to the possibility of distancing and avoidance of physical closeness to polluted activities or objects. For example, in the initial decades of the nineteenth century, when individuals from savarna jatis began entering into the institutions of colonial knowledge production, theoretical science, law, literature, and mathematics were the preferred subjects over engineering, medicine, and any applied science.

This was reflected in the initial hesitance within the dominant castes, especially Brahmins, in their enrolling in engineering and medicine, both of which involve direct touch of either bodies of oppressed castes or objects that are considered untouchable. However, in the colonial context, it was clear that institutions of knowledge production would work as the gateway to the corridors of power and entering into the order of knowledge was a necessary prerequisite for entering into colonial modernity. As we saw in the case of Nampoothiris, the initial attempt to reject the colonial educational institutions soon transformed to attempts of creating a colonial–brahmanical modernity through activities such as translating *acharam*s in term of modern science. If it was impossible to translate some acharam into modern practice, it was reformed or even rejected. Earlier, if a Brahmin touched or even saw an untouchable at certain distance, he became polluted and had to undergo specific rituals to become purified again. This prevented Nampoothiris from enrolling in schools. However, this was soon reformed to the ritual of bathing after attending school and before entering home. This was possible because purity is translated in terms of hygiene, and bodily cleanliness and bathing are sufficient to remove pollution. The ritual of bathing has now become part of the knowledge of Nampoothiris regarding hygiene, health, and cleanliness. In the initial years of the modern medicine course in Calcutta Medical College, anatomy was not included for the fear of dominant-caste students not joining the course.

The history of vocational education in India in the colonial period is a clear example of the emergence of the colonial–brahmanical model of knowledge production. In the pre-colonial period, the artisanal caste groups in India controlled the technical knowledge and Brahmins were not part of these knowledge practices. The colonial discourse, especially after 1857, depicted education and public works as two important domains through which governance could be extended for shaping controllable and responsible subjects in the colony. The existing caste-based division of labour and labourers were an important factor that determined education policies. Instead of following a shop-based, apprentice-training model, which was the model for technical education in Britain at that time, the colonial government implemented classroom-based technical education, which would later become a three-tier hierarchical system of technical education institutions. Analysing the history of the modern engineering education in India, Ajantha Subramanian points out that 'the career of technical knowledge from the mid-nineteenth to the mid-twentieth century is one of shifts from guild to state, shopfloor to classroom, and lower to upper caste'.[16] The mathematization of technical knowledge and reformulation of technology as a theoretical knowledge separated from technical practices in this period also contributed to this transformation. In the new domain of technology, the colonialists considered reading and writing as the most important skill, and hence the savarna castes as the most suitable sociological group who could be trained as engineers. The colonial state also decided that artisans also needed to be taken out from the traditional models of training and put into separate institutions such as industrial training centres. General education was already pivoted around reading and writing and thus not appropriate for artisans or the general masses. As Subramanian pointed out, the emergence of the engineering college as the new form of a class-based, reading–writing-based technical training institution in colonial India in the mid-nineteenth century was a pointer towards the ways in which caste dominance would be translated, adapted into, and adopted by modern institutions in the next century and further.

The exploration of the history of the Indian Institute of Technology Madras by Ajantha Subramanian shows that after independence, the 'IIT culture' moved from Tamil Brahmin identification from the 1960s to the 1990s to a more savarna consolidation against the so-called reserved caste groups, especially after the implementation of the Mandal Commission Report in 1992.[17] The sociological grouping of savarnas against *avarnas* is also based on the mapping of mental and manual labour in the domain of knowledge production. The dominant castes were successful in carving out a space that involves only mental labour in the field of technology. The reservation policy entitled in the Constitution made this space polluted by giving the right to the avarnas to enter this sanctum sanctorum. What is important is that the opposition to this entry was never articulated in terms of caste but in the language of merit. Along with the institutional exclusion, from primary education to higher education, the training based on reading, writing, and memorizing, especially in mathematics, excluded artisanal ways of knowing as doing. A selection for engineering based on this particular form of mathematics is designed to exclude the subaltern groups who had neither the opportunity for training in this form nor the accumulated power to enforce their methods. Since this exclusion is also based on methodology, it was easy to present it in terms of merit. Speaking of jati in terms of merit enabled all the dominant castes to align as savarnas, which was otherwise impossible as these caste were also ordered in a hierarchy in the jati system. The savarna consolidation was also a sign of nationalization of caste, which was earlier fundamentally local. All these processes were neither without contradictions nor complete.

The exclusion of the marginalized communities based on the argument of merit cannot sustain itself without the help of persistent institutional marginalization. When individuals from the marginalized communities, crossing all the hurdles placed in the pretext of merit, reach the stage reserved for the 'meritorious' elite, the immediate reaction is to remove them through other measures. Professor M. Kunjaman's story is an appropriate example for this. Kunjaman who belongs to a marginalized community in Keralam completed his Master of Arts (MA) degree in Economics with first rank in the university and also completed his doctorate from a reputed research institution in Keralam. When he applied for a teaching position at the University of Kerala, he was ranked first by the interview committee. However, the university decided not to fill the position, citing that it was a post in the category that is called 'general merit', and as he was from the 'reserved category', he could not be appointed, even though he had proven his merit over other candidates, including those from the dominant castes. No wonder that he titled some of his chapters in his memoirs, *Ethir* (In Opposition), as 'I am a Pariah living in a hut at the outskirts of Higher Education', 'If a Dalit has to sit in the chair of Chief Minister, he has to be reborn as a bedbug', and so on.[18] The exclusionary practices in various universities in India, reflected in the institutional murders of several marginalized students such as Rohit Vemula, are a culmination of institutional and epistemological domination. The concluding section of this book summarizes some strategies to challenge this domination in the domain of knowledge production, through decolonization of the process of knowledge production.

Dreams about a Decolonized Future

The marginalized communities all over the world have attempted and are attempting to decolonize knowledge as part of their struggle for an equitable society. In this struggle, many communities were successful in varying degrees in entering and making their presence significant in the institutions of knowledge production. This representation has enabled marginalized communities to expose the elite biases of academic knowledge production and to include their voices in various disciplines of knowledge. Dalit and Muslim students' struggles in various central universities in India show that dominant castes have been opposing this representation using all forms of institutional power. From another side of the struggle, the power of academic disciplines as such has been challenged, for both their content and methodology, thus making interdisciplinarity a political question. The standpoint theories in science, including agential realism as theorized by Barad, the idea of intersectionality as initially theorized by Kimberle Crenshaw, Gopal Guru's conceptualization of theoretical Brahmins and empirical Shudras in social sciences in India, the writings on the Islamic contribution in science and mathematics, and the contribution of Amina Wadud, Lila Abu-Lughod, and others towards the scholarship on Islamic feminism, secularism, and religion, are all signs of these struggles from various spaces and standpoints across the world. In the discipline of History, the dominance of the elite has been challenged through shifting content such as incorporation of the subaltern voices and through methods such as oral history. However, the power of academic experts who are trained in modern educational institutions as the authentic bearers of knowledge is kept almost intact. For example, economists, political scientists, agricultural scientists, and engineers dominate over agriculture workers and farmers in deciding the policies of agriculture. These experts are considered to have deeper knowledge and broader understanding of farming compared to an actual cultivator. The agricultural worker supposedly has only practical experience, which is at the bottom of the hierarchy of knowledges, while expert knowledge is at the top.

In order to dismantle the hierarchical series of knowledge, it is important to break the power–knowledge entanglement by demystifying power and knowledge. The artisanal ways of knowing, which is knowing as doing, shows that knowledge in representational form is not a necessary factor in successfully navigating or manipulating the material world; knowing becomes part of this navigation as a side effect. Moreover, 'to know or not to know' is an ethical question and knowing is not always preferred. It also implies that the antonym of knowledge is not ignorance. Here, knowledge is not accumulated and only present at the time of doing, and knowing is not 'knowing of something' but an action such as swimming or walking. Learning is not a special activity but part of the production process in which the novice and the expert take part and work together. The chief carpenter not only organizes, designs, or supervizes the production process but also actively participates in the work.

In the current scenario, the objective of higher education is to create experts who are only capable of representational labour. In classrooms and laboratories, students are trained with models and representations. Most of the time, it is a training in reading and writing. The human capability to recognize and categorize the world through smelling, tasting, and touching is completely neglected in this form. Handwork is isolated into vocational or industrial training centres, where most of the students are from the marginalized groups because these vocations have the lowest social and economic status as both occupation and knowledge. Decolonizing the field of education requires challenging the domination of experts of reading and writing. If we adopt artisanal ways of knowing as a model for education, schools and colleges will not be mere isolated centres of learning but integrated to 'problem solving' (not to be mistaken for utilitarianism) in society. The field itself will be the classroom and the laboratory, and no one will be engaging or specializing in just reading and writing. There will be no field visits from which one returns and reflects on; every researcher will be living in the field and knowing through doing. No one will be paid for teaching activities that are only based on reading and writing. Farmers, machinists, doctors, and carpenters will be not just workers but teachers as well. In a complete interdisciplinary form of education, teaching farming will not only include learning breeding, sowing, ploughing, and harvesting, but also various aspects innately tied to farming, such as history, music, astronomy, and weather forecasting. Moreover, this interdisciplinarity would also include feeling, reasoning, and intuition, and all permutations and combinations of all five senses, as part of learning. Many readers might think that these are utopian concepts or dreams which are not practical at all. My answer is: yes, but to struggle is to dream of what is not practical now.

Notes

1. In most cases of activity-oriented learning, activity is a means for an end, which is learning the theories of a given discipline. In other words, activity is a pedagogic strategy rather than a form knowledge, and most often it is also assumed that the learning happens in the learners' mind. For an analysis of the concept of activity in the context of learning, see Jean Lave, 'Practice of Learning', in *Contemporary Theories of Learning*, ed. Knud Illeris, 200–208 (New York: Routledge, 2009).

2. *Encyclopaedia Britannica*, 'Potential Energy', 16 November 2021, https://www.britannica.com/science/potential-energy (accessed on 10 June 2020).

3. For a critical analysis of Charles Darwin's theory of evolution and its relation to European colonialism, see Tony Barta, 'Mr Darwin's Shooters: On Natural Selection and the Naturalizing of Genocide', *Patterns of Prejudice* 39, no. 2 (2005): 116–137, DOI: 10.1080/00313220500106170; Meena Radhakrishna, 'Of Apes and Ancestors: Evolutionary Science and Colonial Ethnography', *Indian Historical Review* 23, no. 1 (January 2006): 1–23.

4. See Catriona Mortimer-Sandilands and Bruce Erickson (eds.), *Queer Ecologies: Sex, Nature, Politics, Desire* (Bloomington: Indiana University Press, 2010); and J. Roughgarden, *Evolution's Rainbow: Diversity, Gender, and Sexuality in Nature and People* (Berkeley: University of California Press, 2013).

5. See W. J. Gonzalez, 'Methodological Universalism in Science and Its Limits: Imperialism versus Complexity', *Thinking about Provincialism in Thinking* 100 (2012): 155–175.

6. Chanda Prescod-Weinstein, *The Disordered Cosmos: A Journey into Dark Matter, Spacetime and Dreams Deferred* (New York: Bold Type Books, 2021), 154.

7. Karen Barad, *Meeting the Universe Halfway: Quantum Physics and the Entanglement of Matter and Meaning* (Durham: Duke University Press, 2017), 195.

8. For a history of the concept of objectivity in science, see Lorrain Daston and Peter Galison, *Objectivity* (New York: Zone Books, 2010).

9. Nokuthula Hlanbangane, 'The Underside of Modern Knowledge: An Epistemic Break from Western Knowledge', in *Decolonising the Human: Reflections from Africa on Difference and Oppression*, ed. Melissa Steyn and William Mpofu, 164–185 (Johannesburg: Wits University Press, 2001).

10. Linda Tuhiwai Smith, *Decolonizing Methodologies: Research and Indigenous Peoples* (New York: Zed Books, 2012), 122.

11. Natalie Alana Ashton, 'Scientific Perspectives, Feminist Standpoints, and Non-Silly Relativism', in *Knowledge from a Human Point of View*, ed. Ana-Maria Crețu and Michela Massimi, 71–86 (Cham: Springler, 2020).

12. Prescod-Weinstein, *The Disordered Cosmos*, 87.

13. Prescod-Weinstein, *The Disordered Cosmos*, 88.

14. Prescod-Weinstein, *The Disordered Cosmos*, 207.

15. For an analysis of alternative ways of engaging with the past by a subaltern community, see, Sanal Mohan, *Modernity of Slavery: Struggles against Caste Inequality in Colonial Kerala* (New Delhi: Oxford University Press, 2015).

16. Ajantha Subramanian, *The Caste of Merit: Engineering Education in India* (Cambridge, MA: Harvard University Press, 2019), 27.

17. Bhindeshwari Prasad Mandal, *Mandal Commission: Report of the Backword Classes Commission 1980*, vols. 1–2 (New Delhi: Govenment of India, 1980).

18. M. Kunjaman, *Ethir* (In Opposition) (Kottayam: D. C. Books, 2020).

Bibliography

Archives
Kerala State Regional Archives, Kozhikode

Malabar Collectorate Records.
Records of the Revenue Department, Malabar District.
Correspondences of Malabar Collector with Government of Madras.
Annual Reports of the Public Works Department, Malabar District.
Annual Reports of the Judicial Department, Malabar District.
Annual Reports of the Education Department, Malabar District.

Tamil Nadu State Archives, Chennai

Proceedings of the Public Works Department, Government of Madras (GoM).
Proceedings of the Board of Revenue, GoM.
Proceedings of the Industries Department, GoM.
Proceedings of the Education Department, GoM.
Proceedings of the Home Department, CRI, No 12–32B, 1887, GoM.
Proceedings of the Home Department 1909, GoM.
Proceedings of the Legislative Department, GoM.

National Archives of India, New Delhi

Proceedings of the Judicial Department, Government of India (GoI).
Proceedings of the Industries Department, GoI.
Proceedings of the Public Works Department, GoI.
Proceedings of the Education Department, GoI.
Proceedings of the Department of Industries and Commerce, GoI.

India Office Records, British Library, London

The Mackenzie Collection.
J. F. Heyer, Private Collection.
India Office, Public Works Department Files.

India Office, Surveyor's Office Records.
Council of India, Minutes and Memoranda.
Correspondence between India Office and Madras Government.

Reports

Basel Evangelical Mission Records, vol. 15, Mission Archives, Mangalore, 1899.
Census Report of India 1891, vol. 18, part 1.
Census of India 1911, vol. 12, Madras, part 2.
Census of India 1931, vol. 12, part 1.
Census of India 1951, vol. 11, part 2.
Census of India 1971, series 9: Kerala, part 5.
Census of India 1991, series 9: Kerala, part 4.
Education Reforms: A Report from the State of Madras (Madras: Government Press, 1952).
Report of the Malabar Tenancy Committee, 1915 (Madras: Government Press, 1917).
Report of the Committee on Weight and Measures, Government of India.
Report of Malabar Marriage Commission, Madras Legislative Records, 1891.
Report of the Sample Survey on Artisanal Industries in Ten Districts of Kerala, Industries Department (Thiruvananthapuram: Government Press, 1975).
Report of the Survey on Housing and Employment, Department of Economics and Statistics, (Trivandrum: Government Press, 1980).
Report of the Survey on Utilisation of Gulf Remittance in Kerala, Department of Economics and Statistics (Trivandrum: Government Press, 1994).
Report on Industrial Education, part 2, Education Department (Calcutta: Government Press, 1906).
Report on Land and Revenue of the Malabar District, Government of Madras, 1891–1910.
Report on Public Instruction, Madras Presidency (Madras, 1910).
The Nampoothiri Family Regulation Committee Report and Draft Regulation (Thrissur: Mangalodayam, 1925).
The Report of Survey on Small Manufacturing Units in Palakkad District (Shornur: Government Press, 1999).
The Report of the Industrial Survey of 1926, Madras Presidency (Madras: Government Press, 1928).
The Survey Report on the Status of Housing in Kerala 1991, Part 4 (Thiruvananthapuram: Government Press, 1992).

Books and Articles

Achari, Arumukhan. 1943. 'Asharimarum Acharangalum', *Vidyaposhini* 2, no. 6: 22–27.

Achari, B. Raghavan (ed.). 1994. *Manushyalaya Chandrika*. Kodungalloor: Devi Books.

Achari, Keshavan. 1993. *Prayogika Vastu Vidya* (Practical Architectural Knowledge). Kodungalloor: Jyothi Books.

Achari, Kidangur Raghavan. 1998. 'Vedangalum Thachushasthravum (Vedas and the Architectural Science)', *Karmabhumi*, November, 2–4.

Achari, K. V. Achuthan (ed.). 1998. *Manushyalaya Chandrika*. Kottayam: D. C. Books.

Achari, V. Shanmukhan. 1989. 'Viswakarmajante Bhavi (The Future of Vishwakarmajan)', *Karmabhumi*, no. 11, November, 7–9.

———. 1992. 'Yanthrayugavum Viswakarmajarum (Machine Age and the Vishwakarmas)', *Karmabhumi*, November, 10–11.

Afsaruddin, Asma (ed.). 1999. *Hermeneutics and Honor: Negotiating Female 'Public' Space in Islamic/ate Societies*. Cambridge, MA: Harvard University Press.

Agur, C. M. 1990 (1903). *Church History of Travancore*. New Delhi: Asian Educational Services.

Alvares, Claude. 1988. 'Science, Colonialism and Violence: A Luddite View'. In *Science, Hegemony and Violence: A Requiem for Modernity*, edited by Ashis Nandy. Oxford: Oxford University Press.

Ambedkar, B.R. *Dr. Babasaheb Ambedkar: Writings and Speeches*, vol. 17, part 2 (New Delhi: Government of India, 2014 [2003]).

———. 1949. *Who Were the Shudras?* Bombay: Thackers.

———. 2008. *The Untouchables*. Delhi: Sidhartha Books.

———. 2013. *Annihilation of Caste*. New Delhi: Samyak Prakashan.

Aminzade, Ronald. 1981. *Class Politics and Early Industrial Capitalism*. Albany: State University of New York Press.

Amma, N. Madhavi. 1949. 'Navothanathinu Shesham (After the Enlightenment)', *Mathrubhumi*, 20 October, 4.

Anderson, Benedict. 2006 (1983). *Imagined Communities: Reflection on the Origin and Spread of Nationalism*. London: Verso.

Anderson, Kay. 2007. *Race and the Crisis of Humanism*. London: Routledge.

Andreski, Stanislav. 2008. *Max Weber on Capitalism, Bureaucracy and Religion*. Oxford: Taylor & Francis.

Anujan, K. M. 1953. *Ormakalilute Oru Yathra*. Kozhikode: Jnyanavardhini.

Arbuthnot, W. 1901. *A Journey through Malabar Coast*. London: Trubner & Co.

Arunima, G. 1996. 'Multiple Meanings: Changing Concepts of Matrilineal Kinship in Nineteenth and Twentieth Century Malabar', *Indian Economic and Social History Review* 33, no. 3: 283–307.

———. 2003. *There Comes Papa: Colonialism and the Transformation of Matryliny in Kerala, Malabar, c. 1850–1940*. Hyderabad: Orient Longman.

Ashari, K. Neelakantan (ed.). 2000. *Maha Manushyalaya Chandrika*. Kodungalloor: Devi Books.

Ashton, Natalie Alana. 2020. 'Scientific Perspectives, Feminist Standpoints, and Non-Silly Relativism'. In *Knowledge from a Human Point of View*, edited by Ana-Maria Crețu and Michela Massimi, 71–86. Cham: Springler.

Ayya, Nagam. 1874. *The Travancore State Manual*. Thiruvananthapuram: Government Press.

Ayyar, Ullor S. Parameshwara. 1981. *Adi Shankaran*. Kottayam: National Book Trust.

Babu, I. V. 2001. *Keraleeya Navothanavum Nampoothirimarum* (The Enlightenment of Kerala and Nampoothiris). Kottayam: Sahithya Pravarthaka Sahakarana Sangham.

Baber, Zaheer. 1996. *The Science of Empire: Scientific Knowledge, Civilization and Colonial Rule in India*. Albany: State University of New York Press.

Balakrishnan, P. K. 1983. *Jati Vyavastayum Kerala Charithravum* (The Caste System and Kerala History). Kottayam: D. C. Books.

Bandopadhyay, Shekhar. 1997. *Caste, Protest and Identity in Colonial India: The Namasudras*. Richmond: Curzon Press.

Banerjee, Prathama. 2007. 'Caste and the Writing of History'. In *Dalit Assertion in Society, History and Literature*, edited by Imtias Ahmad and Shashi Bhushan Upadhyay, 214–238. New Delhi: Deshkal Publications.

Barad, Karen. 2017. *Meeting the Universe Halfway: Quantum Physics and the Entanglement of Matter and Meaning*. Durham: Duke University Press.

Barbosa, Duarte. 1866. *A Description of the Coasts of East Africa and Malabar*. London: Hakluyt Society.

Barta, Tony. 'Mr Darwin's Shooters: On Natural Selection and the Naturalizing of Genocide', *Patterns of Prejudice* 39, no. 2 (2005): 116–137. DOI: 10.1080/00313220500106170.

Bayly, Susan. 2001. *Caste, Society and Politics in India, from the Eighteenth Century to the Modern Age*. Cambridge: Cambridge University Press.

Berkeley, George. 2012. *A Treatise Concerning the Principles of Human Knowledge*. New York: Dover Publications.

Beteille, A. 1991. *Society and Politics in India: Essays in Comparative Perspective*. London: Athlone Press.

Bhaskaranunni, P. 1988. *Pathompatham Noottantile Keralam* (The Nineteenth Century Keralam). Thrissur: Kerala Sahithya Academy.

———. 2005. *Keralam Irupatham Noottantinte Arambhathil* (Keralam in the Beginning of the Twentieth Century). Thrissur: Kerala Sahitya Academy.

Bhattacharya, Sabyasachi (ed.). 2002. *Education and the Disprivileged: Nineteenth and Twentieth Century India*. New Delhi: Orient Blackswan.

Bhattathirippad, Krishnan. 1925. 'Nampoothiri Samudayam (Nampoothiri Community)', *Unni Nampoothiri* 10, no. 5: 21–23.

Bhattathiripad, M. R. 1936. 'Kal Noottantinullil (In a Quarter Century)', *Mathrubhumi*, 25 October, (Special Issue), 33–37.

Bhattathirippad, Narayanan. 1928. 'Sthree Vidyabhyasa Commissionte Report (The Report of the Women Education Commission)', *Unni Nampoothiri* 12, no. 4: 407–410.

Bhattathirippad, N. P. 1940. *Matangi Varatha Kalam* (The Time Which Will Never Return). Thrissur: Bharathi Printers.

Bhattathirippad, P. Anujan. 1913. *Puthiya Noottandu*. Kozhikode: Kalpadruma Publishers.

Bhattahiri, P. K. 1923. 'Nampoothirimarute Pouranikavum Naveenavumaya Vidyabhyasam (The Old and New Educational System of Nampoothiris)', *Unni Nampoothiri* 9, no. 3 (March): 310–314.

Bhattathirippad, P. N. 1923. *Ormakurippukal* (Memoirs). Kozhikode: P. K. Trust.

Bhattathirippad, V. Keshavan. 1909. 'Vidyabhyasavum Achara Samrakshanavum (Education and the Protection of Acharam)', *Kerala Pathrika*, no. 5 (May): 21–25.

Bhattathirippad, V. T. 1997. *Veetiyute Sampoorna Krithikal* (Complete Works of V. T.). Kottayam: D. C. Books.

Birdwood, George. 1884. *The Industrial Arts of India*. London: Chapman and Hall Ltd.

Boyd, Susan B. 1997. *Challenging the Public/Private Divide: Feminism, Law, and Public Policy*. Toronto: University of Toronto Press.

Braverman, Harry. 1974. *Labor and Monopoly Capital: The Degradation of Work in the Twentieth Century*. New York: Monthly Review Press.

Breton, David Le. 2017. *Sensing the World: An Anthropology of the Senses*. London: Routledge.

Buchanan, Francis. 1807. *A Journey from Madras through the Countries of Mysore, Canara and Malabar*. London: Cadell & Davies.

———. 1812. *A Report on the Native Customs of South India*. London: Abe Scot Publishing Company.

Carswell, Grace, and Geert De Neve. 2014. 'T-shirts and Tumblers: Caste, Dependency and Work under Neoliberalization in South India', *Contributions to Indian Sociology* 48, no. 1: 103–131.

Cartledge, Paul. 2002. *The Greeks: A Portrait of Self and Others*, 2nd edition. Oxford: Oxford University Press.

Chakravarti, Pulinbihari. 1975. *Origin and Development of the Samkhya System of Thought*. New Delhi: Oriental Books Reprint Corporation.

Chakyar, A. M. N. 2001. *Avasanathe Smartha Vicharam* (The Last Smarthavicharam), translated by K. K. Shankaran Nampoothiri. Thiruvananthapuram: Cultural Publication Division, Kerala Government.

Chandramohan, K. P. 2016. *Development Modernity in Kerala: Narayana Guru, SNDP Yogam and Social Reform*. Chennai: Tulika Books.

Chaplin, Joyce E. 1993. *Anxious Pursuits: Agricultural Innovation and Modernity in Lower South, 1730–1815*. Chapel Hill: University of North Carolina Press.

Chatterjee, Partha. 1993. *The Nation and Its Fragments: Colonial and Postcolonial Histories*. Princeton: Princeton University Press.

Chatterton, Alfred. 1901. *Industrial Education*. Madras: Government Press.

———. 1912. *Industrial Evolution in India*. Madras: The Hindu Office.

Chentharaseeri, T. H. P. 1981. *Poykayil Sree Kumara Guru Devan*. Thiruvananthapuram: Navaodayam Publishers.

———. 1991. *Ayyankali Nadathiya Swathanthrya Samarangal* (The Struggles for Independence Led by Ayyankali). Kozhikode: Mathrubhumi.

Cherukad, S. 1952. *Vidyalaya Chinthakal* (Thoughts on School). Kozhikode: Mathrubhumi.

Classen, Constance (ed.). 2014. *A Cultural History of the Senses in the Age of Empire*. London: Bloomsbury.

Cohn, Bernard S. 1965. 'Anthropological Notes on Dispute and Law in India', *American Anthropologist* (New Series) 67, no. 6: 82–122.

———. 1996. *Colonialism and Its Forms of Knowledge: The British in India*. Princeton Studies in Culture/Power/History. Princeton, NJ: Princeton University Press.

Daston, Lorraine, and Peter Galison. 2010. *Objectivity*. New York: Zone Books.

Derrida, Jacques. 1974. *Of Grammatology*, translated by Gayatri Chakravorty Spivak. Maryland: John Hopkins University Press.

Deshpande, Ashwini. 2000. 'Does Caste Still Define Disparity? A Look at Inequality in Kerala, India', *American Economic Review* 90, no. 2, Papers and Proceedings of the One Hundred Twelfth Annual Meeting of the American Economic Association (May): 322–325.

Deshpande, G. P. (ed.). 2002. *Selected Writings of Jyotiba Phule*. New Delhi: Leftword Books.

Deshpande, Satish. 2013. 'Caste and Castelessness: Towards a Biography of the "General Category"', *Economic and Political Weekly* 48, no. 15 (April): 32–39.

Devika, J. 2007. *En-Gendering Individuals: The Language of Re-forming in Early Twentieth Century Keralam*. Hyderabad: Orient Longman.

———. 2010. 'Egalitarian Developmentalism, Communist Mobilization, and the Question of Caste in Kerala State, India', *Journal of Asian Studies* 69, no. 3 (August): 799–820.

Dewey, John. 1997. *Experience and Education*. New York: Touchstone.

Dirks, Nicholas. 2003. *Caste of Mind: Colonialism and Making of Modern India*. New Delhi: Permanent Black.

Dubey, Amaresh, and Sonalde Desai. 2011. 'Caste in 21st Century India: Competing Narratives', *Economic and Political Weekly* 46, no. 11 (March): 40–49.

Dumont, Louis. 2009. *Homo Hierarchicus: The Caste System and Its Implications*. Complete revision. English edition. Delhi: Oxford University Press.

Elbow, Peter. 1993. 'The Uses of Binary Thinking', *Journal of Advanced Composition* 13, no. 1, Special Issue: Philosophy and Composition Theory (Winter): 51–78.

Elshtain, Jean Bethke. 1981. *Public Man, Private Woman: Woman in Social and Political Thought*. Princeton: Princeton University Press.

Fatnowna, Scott, and Harry Pickett. 2002. 'Indigenous Contemporary Knowledge Development through Research'. In *Indigenous Knowledge and the Integration of Knowledge Systems: Towards a Philosophy of Articulation*, edited by Catherine A. Odera Hoppers, 209–236. Claremont: New Africa Books.

Fazeli, H., and A. Goodarzi. 2010. 'The Principles of Vastu as a Traditional Architectural Belief System from an Environmental Perspective', *WIT Transactions on Ecology and the Environment* 128: 97–108.

Fernandes, Leela. 1997. 'Beyond Public Spaces and Private Spheres: Gender, Family and Working-Class Politics in India', *Feminist Theory* 23, no. 3 (Autumn): 525–547.

Feyerabend, Paul. 1988. *Against Method*. London: Verso.

LaFlesche, Francis. 1995. *The Osage and the Invisible World: Civilization of the American Indian*, vol. 21. Norman, OK: University of Oklahoma Press.

Foucault, Michel. 1980. *Power/Knowledge by Michel Foucault: Selected Interviews and Other Writings, 1972–1977*, edited by Colin Gordon. New York: Pantheon.

———. 1980. 'Two Lectures'. In *Power /Knowledge: Selected Interviews and other Writings, 1972–1977*, 78–108, edited by Colin Gordon. New York: Pantheon Books.

Fuller, C. J. 1976. *Nairs Today*. Cambridge: Cambridge University Press.

———. 1996. 'Introduction: Caste Today'. In *Caste Today*, edited by C. J. Fuller, 1–31. Delhi: Oxford University Press.

———. 2001. 'Orality, Literacy and Memorisation: Priestly Education in Contemporary South India', *Modern Asian Studies* 35, no. 1 (February): 1–31.

Fung, Edmund S. K. 2010. *Intellectual Formations of Chinese Modernity: Cultural and Political Thought in the Republican Era*. New York: Cambridge University Press.

Feynman, Richard. 1998. *The Meaning of It All*. Boston: Addison-Wesley.

Gandhi, M. K. 1977. *Hind Swaraj and Other Writings*. Cambridge: Cambridge University Press.

———. 1996. *Mahatma Gandhi: Selected Political Writings*. Indianapolis: Hackett Publishing Company.

George, Susan. 2006. *Religion and Technology in the 21st Century*. London: Information Science Publishing.

Ghurye, G. S. 1932. *Caste and Race in India*. London: Routledge.

Glassburn, Ashley. 2019. 'Settler Standpoints', *William and Mary Quarterly* 76, no. 3 (July): 399–406.

Gonzalez, W. J. 2012. 'Methodological Universalism in Science and Its Limits: Imperialism versus Complexity', *Thinking about Provincialism in Thinking* 100: 155–175.

Goody, Jack. 2002. 'The Anthropology of the Senses and Sensations', *La Ricerca Folklorica*, no. 45: 17–28.

Govi, K. M. 1998. *Adimudranam: Bharathathilum Malayalathilum* (The First Printing: In Bharatham and Malayalam). Thrissur: Kerala Sahithya Academy.

Gupta, Anima Sen. 1973. *Samkhya and Advaita Vedanta: A Comparative Study*. Calcutta: Sanskrit Pustak Bhandar.

Gupta, Dipankar, 1992. *Social Stratification*. Delhi: Oxford University Press.

———. 2000. *Interrogating Caste: Understanding Hierarchy and Difference in Indian Society*. New Delhi: Penguin.

Guru, Sree Narayana, and Muni Narayana Prasad. 2005. *Sree Narayana Guruvinte Sampoorna Krithikal* (The Collected Works of Sree Narayana Guru). Kottayam: DC Books.

Habib, Irfan. 1969. 'Potentialities of Capitalistic Development in the Economy of Mughal India', *Journal of Economic History* 29, no. 1: 32–78.

Harding, Sandra. 1986. *The Science Question in Feminism*. Ithaca: Cornell University Press.

Harilal, K. N. 1989. 'Deskilling and Wage Differential in Construction Industry', *Economic and Political Weekly* 24, no. 24 (June): 1347–1352.

Hastrup, Kirsten, and Peter Hervik (eds.). 1994. *Social Experience and Anthropological Knowledge*. London: Routledge.

Havell, E. B. 1883. *Report on the Native Industries in Madras Province*. Madras: Government Press.

———. 1902. *A Report on Madras School of Arts*. Madras: Government Press.

———. 1910. *The Basis for Artistic and Industrial Revival in India*. Madras: The Theosophist Office.

Heidegger, Martin. 1977. *The Question Concerning Technology, and Other Essays*. New York: Garland Publishing Inc.

Hirsch, Susan F. 1978. *Roots of the American Working Class: The Industrialization of Craft in Newark*. Pennsylvania: University of Pennsylvania Press.

Hlanbangane, Nokuthula. 2001. 'The Underside of Modern Knowledge: An Epistemic Break from Western Knowledge'. In *Decolonising the Human: Reflections from Africa on Difference and Oppression*, edited by Melissa Steyn and William Mpofu, 164–185. Johannesburg: Wits University Press.

Hobsbawm, Eric. 1983. 'Inventing Tradition'. In *The Invention of Tradition*, edited by Eric Hobsbawm and Terence Ranger, 1–14. Cambridge: Cambridge University Press.

Howes, David (ed.). 1991. *The Varieties of Sensory Experience: A Sourcebook in the Anthropology of the Senses*. Anthropological Horizons. Toronto: University of Toronto Press.

Howes, David, and Constance Classen. 2014. *Ways of Sensing: Understanding the Senses in Society*. New York: Routledge.

Hunter, W. (ed.). 1907. *Journal of Francis Buchanan, Mysore and Malabar 1821–22*. Madras: Government Press.

Ilayathu, K. Raman. 1931. 'Hindu Mathathinte Naveekaranavum Nampoothirimarum (The Reformation of the Hindu Religion and the Nampoothiris)', *Kerala Pathrika*, no. 5 (May): 34–39.

Inglis, Julian T. (ed.). 1993. *Traditional Ecological Knowledge: Concepts and Cases*. Ottawa: Canadian Museum of Nature.

Ingold, Tim. 2011. *Being Alive: Essays on Movement, Knowledge and Description*. New York: Routledge.

Innes, C. A., and F. B. Evans. 1905. *Malabar and Anjengu*. Madras: Addison & Co.

Iyer, L. A. Anantha Krishnan. 1934. *Castes of Cochin*. Kochi: Government Press.

Iyer, Parasurama.1926. 'Hindu Vishwasangalum Shasthravum', *Mangalodayam 6*, no. 5 (May): 81–90.

Iyer, Ramanatha. 1935. *Keralathinte Adicharithram* (The Ancient History of Kerala). Thrissur: Mangalodayam Publications.

Jeffrey, Robin. 1994. *The Decline of Nair Dominance: Society and Politics in Travancore, 1847–1908*. New Delhi: Manohar.

Jodhka, Surinder. 2015. *Caste in Contemporary India*. London: Routledge.

Jones, William. 1801. *The Works of Sir William Jones*. London: Robinson.

Joseph, K. V. 2009. *Keralites on the Move: A Historical Study of Migration from Kerala*. Ann Arbor, MI: University of Michigan Press.

Joseph, Tony. 2018. *Early Indians: The Story of Our Ancestors and Where We Came From*. New Delhi: Juggernaut.

Karmabhumi. 1992. 'Kai Kanakku Pattika (A Conversion Table for the Hand Measurements)', May, 12.

———. 2000. 'The Editorial', December.

Katz, C., and J. Monk. 1991. *Full Circles: Geographies of Women over the Life Course*. London and New York: Routledge.

K. N. 1922. 'Nampoothirimarute Naveena Vidyabhyasa Reethi (The Method of Modern Education of Nampoothiris)', *Unni Nampoothiri* 9, no. 12 (December): 194–204.

Kooiman, Dick. 1989. *Conversion and Social Equality in India: The London Missionary Society in South Travancore in the Nineteenth Century*. New Delhi: Manohar.

Kourany, Janet A. 2009. 'The Place of Standpoint Theory in Feminist Science Studies', *Hypatia* 24, no. 4 (Fall): 209–218.

Kunhikrishnan, V. V. 1993. *The Tenancy Legislation in Malabar, 1870 –1970: A Historical Analysis*. New Delhi: Northern Book Centre.

Kunjaman, M. 2020. *Ethir* (In Opposition). Kottayam: D. C. Books.

Kunjikuttan, Madampu. *Bhrashtu*. 1991. Kottayam: Sahithya Pravarthaka Sahakarana Sangham.

Kurup, V. N. 1934. 'Marunna Kudumba Kramangal (Changing Family Practices)', *Kerala Chandrika* 11: 34–37.

Lacourse, Michael G., Elizabeth L. R. Orr, Steven C. Cramer, and Michael J. Cohen. 2005. 'Brain Activation during Execution and Motor Imagery of Novel and Skilled Sequential Hand Movements', *NeuroImage* 27, no. 3: 505–519.

Laplantine, Francois. 2005. *The Life of the Senses: Introduction to a Model Anthropology*. London: Bloomsbury.

Larson, Gerald, and Ram Shankar Bhattacharya (eds.). 1987. *Encyclopaedia of Indian Philosophies*, vol. 4: *Samkhya, a Dualist Tradition in Indian Philosophy*. Princeton: Princeton University Press.

Latour, Bruno, and Steve Woolgar. 1986. *Laboratory Life: Construction of Scientific Facts*. Princeton: Princeton University Press.

———. 1993. *We Have Never Been Modern*. Cambridge, MA: Harvard University Press.

———. 2007. *Reassembling the Social: An Introduction to Actor-Network-Theory*. Oxford: Oxford University Press.

Lave, Jean. 2009. 'Practice of Learning'. In *Contemporary Theories of Learning*, edited by Knud Illeris, 200–208. New York: Routledge.

Lemercinier, Genevieve. 1984. *Religion and Ideology in Kerala*. New Delhi: D. K. Agencies.

Lévi-Strauss, Claude. 1975. *Tristes Tropiques*, translated by John Weightman and Doreen Weightman. New York: Penguin.

———. 2001. *Myth and Meaning*. London: Routledge.

Lindberg, David C. 2007. *The Beginnings of Western Science: The European Scientific Tradition in Philosophical, Religious and Institutional Context, Pre-history to A.D. 1450*. Chicago: University of Chicago Press.

Lloyd, G. E. R. 1987. *Polarity and Analogy: Two Types of Argumentation in Early Greek Thought*. Bristol: Bristol Classical Press.

Logan, William. 1887. *Malabar Manual*. Madras: Government Press.

Macpherson, Fiona (ed.). 2011. *The Senses: Classic and Contemporary Philosophical Perspectives*. Oxford: Oxford University.

Maggio, Rodolfo. 2014. 'The Anthropology of Story Telling and the Story Telling of Anthropology', *Journal of Comparative Research in Anthropology and Sociology* 5, no. 2 (Winter): 89–106.

Malafouris, Lambros. 2008. 'At the Potter's Wheel: An Argument for Material Agency'. In *Material Agency: Towards a Non-Anthropocentric Approach*, edited by Carl Knappett and Lambros Malafouris, 19–36. New York: Springer.

Malinowski, Bronislow. 1948. *Magic, Science and Religion and Other Essays*. Illinois: Free Press.

Malkin, Irad. 2004. 'Postcolonial Concepts and Ancient Greek Colonization', *Modern Language Quarterly* 65, no. 3: 341–364.

Mandal, Bhindeshwari Prasad. *Mandal Commission: Report of the Backword Classes Commission 1980*, vols. 1–2. New Delhi: Government of India.

Marks, Laura U. 2008. 'Thinking Multisensory Culture', *Paragraph* 31, no. 2: 123–137.

Marx, Karl. 1976. *Capital: A Critique of Political Economy*. London: Penguin Books.

Mateer, Samuel. 1991 (1870). *The Land of Charity: A Descriptive Account of Travancore and Its People*. New Delhi: Asian Educational Services.

McGowan, Abigail. 2009. *Crafting the Nation in Colonial India*. 1st edition. New York: Palgrave Macmillan.

McLuhan, Marshall. 1994. *Understanding Media: The Extensions of Man*. Cambridge, MA: MIT Press.

Mehta, Deepak. 1997. *Work, Ritual, Biography: A Muslim Community in North India*. Delhi: Oxford University Press.

Mencher, Joan P. 1996. 'Namboodiri Brahmins: An Analysis of a Traditional Elite in Kerala', *Journal of Asian and African Studies* 1, no. 3: 183–196.

Mencher, Joan P., and Helen Goldberg. 1967. 'Kinship and Marriage Regulations among the Namboodiri Brahmans of Kerala', *Man* 2, no. 1: 87–106.

Menon, A. Sridhara. 1967. *A Survey of Kerala History*. Kottayam: Sahithya Pravarthaka Sahakarana Sangham.

Menon, C. Raman. 1932. 'Chila Nyayangal (Some Justifications)', *Kerala Chandrilka* 32, no. 6: 43–49.

Menon, Dilip. 2007. *Caste, Nationalism and Communism in South India: Malabar 1900–1948*. Cambridge: Cambridge University Press.

Menon, M. Vasudeva. 1930. 'Visheshamaya Acharangal (Peculiar Customs)', *Vidyavinodini*, no. 1: 43–47.

Menon, Padmanabha. 1864. *The Travancore Manual*. Thiruvananthapuram: Government Press.

Menon, P. C. Kuttikrishna. 1957. *Pinnitta Pathakal* (The Treaded Paths). Thrissur: Vidya Vijayam Publishers.

Menon, P. Narayana. 1922. 'Khilafathum Congressum (The Khilafat and the Congress)', *Mathrubhumi*, 21 June.

Menon, S. Madhava. 1912. *The Vedic Tradition of India*. Madras: The Hindu Publishing Co.

Menon, V. K. 1954. *Smaranakal* (Memoirs). Ottappalam: Sudarshanam Publications.

Menon, V. N. 1982. *Marunna Nadum Nagaravum* (Changing Village and City). Kozhikode: Mathrubhumi.

Mill, James. 1840. *The History of British India*. London: James Madden and Co.

Mohan, Sanal. 2015. *Modernity of Slavery: Struggles against Caste Inequality in Colonial Kerala*. New Delhi: Oxford University Press.

Moosathu, K. Unni. 1920. *Arsha Paramparyam* (The Arsha Tradition). Thrissur: Mangalodayam Press.

Moosathu, K. Neelakantan. 1912. 'English Vidyabhyasa Bhramam (The Desire for English Education)', *Kerala Pathrika* 5, no. 8 (March): 20–23.

Moosathu, K. V. 1929. 'Acharavishengal (The Peculiarities of Customs)', *Vidyavinodini*, no. 12 (December): 34–38.

———. 1931. 'Hindukkalute Pracheena Vignyanam (The Ancient Knowledge of the Hindus)', *Arunodayam* 32, no. 5: 17–22.

———. 1963. *Kazhinja Kalangal* (The Bygone Days). Thrissur: Vidyavijayam Printers.

Moos, E. T. Divakaran. 1917. 'Achara Vicharam (Thoughts on Acharam)', *Malayala Manorama*, 19 June.

Mortimer-Sandilands, Catriona, and Bruce Erickson (eds.). 2010. *Queer Ecologies: Sex, Nature, Politics, Desire*. Bloomington: Indiana University Press.

M. R. K. C. 1924. 'Wireless Technology', *Unni Nampoothiri* 11, no. 10 (October): 130–134.

———. 1927. 'Prakrithi Virodham', *Unni Nampoothiri* 12, no. 2 (February): 124–128.

———. 1927. 'Hindu Mathavum Veda Jnyanavum (The Hindu Religion and the Vedic Knowledge)', *Unni Nampoothiri* 14, no. 5: 211–218.

Müller, Max. 1860. *A History of Ancient Sanskrit Literature*. London: Williams and Norgate.

Nair, A. V. Raghavan. 1922. 'Mathathinte Shasthreeyathvam (The Scientificity of Religion)', *Unni Nampoothiri* 10, no. 11: 69–79.

Nair, K. Madhavan. 1922. 'Malabar Lahalakku Shesham (After the Malabar Riots)', *Mathrubhumi*, 25 October.

Nair, Kuttppurathu Kesavan. 1925. 'Nattuvazhiyiloote (Through the Village Road)', *Kerala Nandini* 8, no. 2: 33–37.

Nair, P. N. 1932. 'Varnabhedavum Jathikalum (The Difference of Varna and Jatis)', *Mathrubhumi*, 21 June.

Nair, P. R. Gopinathan. 1976. 'Education and Socio-Economic Change in Kerala, 1793–1947', *Social Scientist* 4, no. 8 (March): 28–43.

Nampeeshan, K. N. 1930. 'Aharareethiyum Jathiyum (The Eating Habits and Jati)', *Arunodayam* 12, no. 2 (May): 28–34.

Nampoothiri, Elavoor Krishnan. 1927. 'Antharjanangalum Parishkaravum (The Antharjanams and Fashion)', *Unni Nampoothiri* 11, no. 7 (July): 89–96.

Nampoothiri, Kaplingad Narayanan. 1930. 'Adhyksha Prasangam (The Presidential Address)', *Bhasha Poshini* 20, no. 11 (November): 27–33.

Nampoothiri, K. P. 1916. 'The Report of the Annual Conference'. *Mangalodayam* 22, no. 11: 19–22.

Nampoothiri, K. P. K. 1972. *Madrasile Jeevitham*. Calicut: Mathrubhumi Publishers.

Nampoothiri, Krishnan. 1905. 'Nampoothirimarum Jati Dharmavum (Nampoothiris and Jati Responsibilities)', *Kerala Pathrika* 3, no. 12 (December): 3–5.

Nampoothiri, Krishnan K. 1924. 'Nampoothiri Yuvajan Sanghathinte Prvarthanodyesangal (The Objectives of the Nampoothiri Youth Wing)', *Unni Nampoothiri* 10, no. 11 (November): 26–31.

Nampoothiri, K. V. 1914. 'Nampoothirimarum Vidyabhyasavum (Nampoothiris and Education)', *Sahithya Chandrika* 1, no. 4 (April 1914): 30–35.

Nampoothiri, M. C. N. 1932. 'Rishimarum Vijnyanavum (The Sages and Knowledge)', *Yogkshemam*, no. 5, 13 May.

Nampoothiri, M. N. 1928. 'Keralavum Nampoothirimarum (Keralam and the Nampoothiris)', *Arunodayam* 10, no. 6 (June): 75–77.

Nampoothiri, M.V. 1926. 'Janmithavum Vidyabhyasavum (Landlordism and Education)', *Yogkshemam*, 23 March.

Nampoothiri, Narayanan. 1903. 'Acharavum Parishkaravum (Acharam and Reform)', *Yuvadeepthi* 2, no. 3: 27–35.

Nampoothiri, N. Damodaran. 1920. 'Vidyabhyasam: Ventathum Ventathathum (The Education: Desirable and Undesirable)', *Mangalodayam* 24, no. 6 (June): 88–93.

Nampoothiri, N. P. 1919. 'Nampoothiri Acharangalute Innathe Avastha (The Present Condition of Nampoothiri Acharams)', *Bhasha Poshini* 9, no. 8: 25–41.

Nampoothiri, Parameshwaran. 1911. 'Vinasha Kale (In the Period of Destruction)', *Prabhatham*, 23 March.

Nampoothiri, P. K. 1904. 'Janmi–Kutiyan Billum Achara Vyvasthakalum (The Janmi–Kutiyan Bill and the Order of Acharam)', *Malayala Manorama*, 12 October.

Nampoothiri, P. K. Raman. 1924. 'Pazhamakkarum Shasthravum (The Old and the Science)', *Vidya Vinodini* 3, no. 2 (March): 22–25, 23.

Nampoothirippad, A. K. T. K. M. Valiya Narayanan. 1925. 'The Presidential Address', *Unni Nampoothiri* 11, no. 12: 445–454.

Nampoothirippad, E. M. S. 1984 (1946). *Keralam Malayalikalute Mathrubhumi* (Keralam: The Motherland of Malayalis). Thiruvananthapuram: Chintha Publishers.

Nampoothirippad, Kanippayyoor Shankaran. 1926. 'Sthree Samajam (Women's Association)', *Unni Nampoothiri* 10, no. 2: 279–289.

———. 1964. *Ente Smaranakal* (My Memories). Kunnamkulam: Panchangam Pusthakasala.

——— (ed.). 2004. *Manushyalaya Chandrika*. 12th edition. Kunnamkulam: Panjangam Book Stall.

Nampoothirippad, Kuroor Unni. 1916. 'Nampoothiri Yuvajanangalude Katama (The Duty of Nampoothiri Youth)', *Mangalodayam* 22, no. 9: 30–34.

Nampoothirippad, Mozhikunnathu Brahmadathan. 2006. *Khilafat Smaranakal* (Memories of Khilafat). Kozhikode: Mathrubhumi Books.

Nampoothirippad, M. Raman. 1938. *Jatikalude Utbhavavam Charithravum* (The Origin and the History of Castes). Thalasseri: Kalpadrumam Publications.

Nampoothirippad, O. M. Vasudevan. 1933. 'Chathurvarnyam: Chila Charithra Vasthuthakal (The Four-Varna System: Some Historical Facts)', *Unni Nampoothiri* 17, no. 11 (November): 26–34.

Nampoothirippad, O. V. 1913. 'The Presidential Address', *Unni Nampoothiri* 2, no. 7 (March): 3–9.

Nampoothiri, V. R. 1937. *Hindu Mathathinte Charithram* (The History of the Hindu Religion). Thrissur: Vidyodayam Publications.

Natrajan, Balmurli. 2011. *The Culturalization of Caste in India: Identity and Inequality in a Multicultural Age*. New York: Routledge.

Nenminimangalam, Parvathi. 1932. 'Nampoothiri Billum Parvathi Nenminimangalavum (The Nampoothiri Bill and Parvathi Nenminimangalam)', *Manorama*, 10 March.

Nietzsche, Friedrich. 1996. *Untimely Meditations*. Cambridge: Cambridge University Press.

Nisar, M., and Meena Kandaswamy. 2007. *Ayyankali: Dalit Leader of Organic Protest*. Calicut: Other Books.

Nandy, Ashis. 1995. 'History's Forgotten Doubles', *History and Theory* 34, no. 2 (May): 44–66.

Oddie, G. A. 1979. *Social Protest in India: British Protestant Missionaries and Social Reforms*. Delhi: Manohar.

Okely, Judith. 1994. 'Vicarious and Sensory Knowledge of Chronology and Change: Ageing in Rural France'. In *Social Experience and Anthropological Knowledge*, edited by Kirsten Hastrup and Peter Hervik. London: Routledge.

Olson, Richard. 1990. *Science Deified and Science Defied: The Historical Significance of Science in Western Culture*. Berkeley and Los Angeles: University of California Press.

Ong, Aihwa. 1987. *Spirits of Resistance and Capitalist Discipline: Factory Women in Malaysia*. Albany: State University of New York Press.

Osella, Filippo, and Caroline Osella. 1999. 'From Transience to Immanence: Conception, Life-cycle and Social Mobility in Kerala, South India', *Modern Asian Studies* 33, no. 4: 989–1020.

———. 2000. *Social Mobility in Kerala: Modernity and Identity in Conflict*. London: Pluto Press.

Oyewumi, Oyeronke. 1997. *The Invention of Women: Making an African Sense of Western Gender Discourses*. Minneapolis: University of Minnesota Press.

Palpu, P. 1934. *Collected Articles of Dr. Palpu*. Trivandrum: Kairaly Press.

Pandian, M. S. S. 2007. *Brahmin and Non-Brahmin: Genealogies of Tamil Political Present*. New Delhi: Permanent Black.

Panikkar, K. N. 1977. 'Land Control, Ideology and Reform: A Study of the Changes in the Family Organization and Marriage Systems in Kerala', *Indian Historical Review* 4, no. 1: 30–46.

———. 1989. *Against Lord and State: Religion and Peasant Uprising in Malabar 1836–1921*. Delhi: Oxford University Press.

———. 1995. *Culture, Ideology, Hegemony: Intellectuals and Social Consciousness in Colonial India*. London: Anthem Press.

Parayil, Govindan (ed.). 2000. *Kerala: The Development Experience, Reflections on Sustainability and Replicability*. London: Zed Books.

Parpola, Marjatta, 2000. *Kerala Brahmins in Transition: A Study of a Namputiri Family*. Helsinki: Finnish Oriental Society.

Parry, Jonathan. 1985. 'The Brahmanical Tradition and the Technology of the Intellect'. In *Reason and Morality*, edited by Joanna Overing, 198–222. London: Tavistock.

Pateman, Carol. 1988. *The Sexual Contract*. Cambridge, UK: Polity Press.

Patton, Laurie (ed.). 1994. *Authority, Anxiety, and Canon: Essays in Vedic Interpretations*. Albany: State University of New York Press.

Peruman, Sree Karthika. 1998. 'Preface', *Prajabodhanam* (Enlightening the Subjects). Thrissur: Kainur Kandrenkavu.

Petitjean, Patrick Catherine Jami, and Anne Marie Moulin. 1992. *Science and Empires: Historical Studies about Scientific Development and European Expansion*. Vienna: Springer.

Pierotti, Raymond. 2011. *Indigenous Knowledge, Ecology, and Evolutionary Biology*. New York: Routledge.

Pillai, Elamkulam Kunjan. 1961. *Kerala Charithram* (The History of Keralam). Kottayam: National Book Stall.

Pisharody, N. K. 1927. 'Hindukkalaya Nammute Innathe Katama (The Responsibility of We Hindus Today)', *Vidya Vinodini* 9, no. 3 (October): 41–47.

Poesy, Darrell, and Kristina Plenderleith. 2011. *Indigenous Knowledge and Ethics: A Darrell Poesy Reader*. London: Routledge.

Polanyi, Michael. 1966. *The Tacit Dimension*. Chicago: Chicago University Press.

Pollock, Sheldon. 2006. *The Language of the Gods in the World of Men*. Berkeley: University of California Press.

Popper, Karl. 2002. *Conjectures and Refutations: Growth of Scientific Knowledge*. New York: Routledge.

Prakash, B. A. 1998. 'Gulf Migration and Its Economic Impact: The Kerala Experience', *Economic and Political Weekly* 33, no. 50 (December): 3209–3213.

Prakash, Gyan. 1992. 'Science "Gone Native" in Colonial India', *Representations* 40 (October): 153–178.

Prescod-Weinstein, Chanda. 2021. *The Disordered Cosmos: A Journey into Dark Matter, Spacetime and Dreams Deferred*. New York: Bold Type Books.

Radhakrishna, Meena. 2006. 'Of Apes and Ancestors: Evolutionary Science and Colonial Ethnography', *Indian Historical Review* 23, no. 1 (January): 1–23.

Raghaviah, J. 1990. *Basel Mission Industries in Malabar and South Canara (1834–1914): A Study of Its Social and Economic Impact*. Delhi: Gian Publishing House.

Raghavanachari, B. (ed.). 1994. *Manushyalaya Chandrika*. Kodungalloor: Devi Books.

Rajan, V. 2004. 'Yuvajanangalum Viswakarma Sabhayum (The Youth and the Vishwakarma Sabha)', *Karmabhoomi* 12, December, 3–4.

Raja, V. K. 1927. 'Acharangalum Shasthravum (The Acharams and Science)', *Mangalodayam* 11, no. 6 (June): 35–41.

Raj, Kapil. 2010. *Relocating Modern Science: Circulation and Construction of Knowledge in South Asia and Europe, 1650–1900*. London: Palgrave Macmillan.

Ramakrishnan, K. 1987. *Theevanti Malabaril: Oru Charithranweshanam* (Railway in Malabar: A Historical Inquiry). Shornoor: Kripa Publishers.

Raman, S. Subba. 1979. *History of Progress of Education in Madras State, 1875–1960*. Madras: Sakthi Publishers.

Rao, Anupama. 2005. *Gender and Caste*. Delhi: Kali for Women.

Ravindran, K. 1964. *A Study of Technical Education in Kerlam*, Industries Department, Government of Kerala. Thiruvanathapuram: Government Press.

Rege, Sharmila. 1996. *Caste and Gender: Violence against Women in India*. Florence: European University Institute.

———. 2006. *Writing Caste, Writing Gender: Reading Dalit Women's Testimonios*. New Delhi: Zuban.

Roughgarden, J. 2013. *Evolution's Rainbow: Diversity, Gender, and Sexuality in Nature and People*. Berkeley: University of California Press.

Roy, Tirthankar. 2008. 'The Guild in Modern South Asia', *International Review for Social History* 53, Supplement S16 (December): 95–120.

Saradamony, K. 1980. *Emergence of a Slave Caste Pulayas of Kerala*. Delhi: People's Publishing House.

Sarukkai, Sundar. 2012. 'Understanding Experience'. In *The Cracked Mirror: An Indian Debate on Experience and Theory*, edited by Gopal Guru and Sundar Sarukkai, 46–70. New Delhi: Oxford University Press.

Sastri, V. Neelakanta. 1914. *Brahmins and Indian Civilisation*. Madras: Saraswathi Printers.

Schiffer, Michael Brian (ed.). 2001. *Anthropological Perspectives on Technology*. Arizona: The Amerind Foundation Inc.

Schultz, Bart, and Georgios Varouxaki (eds.). 2005. *Utilitarianism and Empire*. Oxford: Lexington Books.

Scott, David. 1995. 'Colonial Governmentality', *Social Text* 43 (Autumn): 191–220.

Scott, James. 2009. *The Art of Not Being Governed: An Anarchic History of Upland Southeast Asia*. New Haven: Yale University Press.

Seremetakis, C. Nadia (ed.). 1994. *The Senses Still: Perception and Memory as Material Culture in Modernity*. Chicago: University of Chicago Press.

Sharma, Arvind. 1993. *The Experiential Dimension of Advaita Vedanta*. Delhi: Motilalal Banarasidass Publishers.

———. 2002. 'On Hindu, Hindustan, Hinduism and Hindutva', *Numan* 49, no. 1: 1–36.

Sharma, K. V. 1929. *Varna Vyvasthayum Shasthravum* (The Varna System and Science). Cochin: Pingala Printers.

Shivan, A. B. 1999. *Viswakarmeeyam*. Kottayam: D. C. Books.

Smith, Bardwell L. (ed.). 1976. *Religion and Social Conflict in South Asia*. Leiden: E. J. Brill.

Smith, Linda Tuhiwai. 2012. *Decolonizing Methodologies: Research and Indigenous Peoples*. New York: Zed Books.

Smith, Pamela. 2004. *The Body of the Artisan: Art and Experience in the Scientific Revolution*. Chicago: University of Chicago Press.

Srinivas, M. N. 1955. 'The Social System of a Mysore Village'. In *Village India*, edited by Mckinn Marriot, 1–35. Chicago: University of Chicago Press.

———. 1968. *Social Change in Modern India*. Berkeley: University of California Press.

Staal, Frits. 1990. *Rituals and Mantras: Rules without Meaning*. New York: Peter Lang Publishing.

Stoller, Paul. 1989. *The Taste of Ethnographic Things: Senses in Anthropology*. Pennsylvania: University of Pennsylvania Press.

Subramanian, Ajantha. 2019. *The Caste of Merit: Engineering Education in India*. Cambridge, MA: Harvard University Press.

Swain, Ashok. 1988. *Struggle against the State: Social Network and Protest Mobilization in India*. Burlington: Ashgate Publishing Company.

Tarule, Robert. 2004. *The Artisans of Ipswich: Craftsmanship in Colonial New England*. Maryland: Johns Hopkins University Press.

Temple, R. C. 1890. 'A Study of Modern Indian Architecture as Displayed in a British Cantonment'. *Journal of Indian Art* 15, no. 15: 57–61.

Tharakan, P. K. M. 1984. 'Socio-Economic Factors in Educational Development: Case of Nineteenth Century Travancore', *Economic and Political Weekly* 19, no. 45: 1930–1938.

Thirumulppad, T. N. 1929. 'Mathangalum Vijnyanavum (Religions and Knowledge)', *Mathrubhumi*, 23 September.

Thompson, Paul. 1989. *An Introduction to Debates on Labour Process*. London: Macmillan.

Thurston, Edgar. 1890. 'Notes on the Hindus of Madras', *Journal of Madras Museum* 2, no. 13: 20–27.

———. 1906. *Ethnographic Notes in Southern India*. Madras: Government Press.

———. 1909. *Castes and Tribes of Southern India*. Madras: Government Press.

Tilley, Helen. 2004. 'Ecologies of Complexity: Tropical Environments, African Trypanosomiasis, and the Science of Disease Control in British Colonial Africa, 1900–1940'. *Osiris* 19: 21–38.

Timalsina, Sthaneswar. 2009. *Consciousness in Indian Philosophy: The Advaita Doctrine of 'Awareness Only'*. New York: Routledge.

Travers, W. 1918. *A Journey through Malabar and Mysore*. Madras: Higginbotham and Co.

Variyar, K. P. Rama. 1963. *Pinnitta Vazhikaliloote* (Through the Treaded Paths). Kottakkal: Keraleeyam Press.

Variyar, P. Govinda. 1928. 'Marunna Nattinpuram (Changing Rural Area)', *Keralapathrika* 2, no. 4: 38–45.

Varma, V. Rajaraja. 1922. 'Nampoothirimarum Vedabhyasavum', *Unni Nampoothiri* 7, no. 11 (November): 6–10.

Varthema, Ludvico Di. 1863. *The Travels of Ludvico Di Varthema*. London: Hakluyt Society.

Venugopal, C. K. (ed.). 1997. *Natan Pattukalum Nattarivum*. Thrisur: Mudra Publishers.

Wang, Robin R. 2012. *Yinyang: The Way of Heaven and Earth in Chinese Thought and Culture*. New York: Cambridge University Press.

Wilson, H. H. 1865. *Essays: Analytical, Critical and Philological on Subject Connected with Sanskrit Language*. London: Trubner and Co.

Wing, Allan, Patrick Haggard, and Randall Flanagan. 1996. *Hand and Brain: The Neurophisiology and Psychology of Hand Movements*. California: Academic Press Inc.

Wylie, Alison. 2012. 'Feminist Philosophy of Science: Standpoint Matters', *Proceedings and Addresses of the American Philosophical Association* 86, no. 2 (November): 47–76.

Yesudas, K. N. 1975. *The People's Revolt in Travancore: A Backward Caste Movement for Social Freedom*. Thiruvananthapuram: Kerala Historical Society.

Zachariah, K. C., E. T. Mathew, and S. Irudaya Rajan. 2003. *Dynamics of Migration in Kerala: Dimensions, Differentials and Consequences*. Hyderabad: Orient Longman.

Zdatny, Steven M. 1990. *The Politics of Survival: Artisans in the Twentieth Century France*. Oxford: Oxford University Press.

Zelliot, E. 1992. *From Untouchable to Dalit: Essay on Ambedkar Movement*. Delhi: Manohar.

Index